Canada's Origins: Liberal, Tory, or Republican?

CANADA IS A TOOTHPICK ON THE DASHBOARD OF A PICKUP TRUCK. CANADA IS THE LONELINESS OF A LONG DISTANCE FOLK SINGER. CANADA IS A BROWN TROUT IN A FIELD OF MINT. CANADA IS A COLORFUL TREE. CANADA IS AUTUMN. CANADA IS AN AMERICAN DREAM. CANADA IS A FLOOR FILLED WITH PEANUT SHELLS IN A HOCKEY ARENA. CANADA IS A TABLE FILLED WITH BEER. CANADA IS A DEER STANDING IN A FIELD. CANADA IS A LAST CIGARETTE. CANADA IS SCRAP METAL. CANADA IS A PINE TREE – BURNING. CANADA IS A MINNOW IN A METAL BUCKET. CANADA IS A FOREIGN FILM. CANADA IS A FOREIGN FILM WITH SUBTITLES. CANADA IS A NEXT DOOR NEIGHBOR. CANADA IS A CROW ON A HIGHWAY.

CANADA'S ORIGINS
LIBERAL, TORY, OR REPUBLICAN?

with an introduction, concluding dialogue, and essays by
Janet Ajzenstat, Louis-Georges Harvey, Gad Horowitz,
Rainer Knopff, Colin D. Pearce, Peter J. Smith,
and Robert C. Vipond

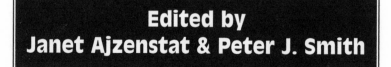

Edited by
Janet Ajzenstat & Peter J. Smith

Carleton University Press

Canadian Cataloguing in Publication Data

Main entry under title:
    Canada's origins: Liberal, Tory, or Republican?

(The Carleton library ; #184)
Includes bibliographical references.

ISBN 0-88629-274-3

    1. Canada—Politics and government—1967-
2. Liberalism—Canada. 3. Conservatism—Canada.
4. Republicanism—Canada. I. Ajzenstat, Janet, date-
II. Smith, Peter J., date- III. Series.

FC502.C35 1995   320.971   C95-900804-7
F1034.2.C35 1995

Cover art: *Canada Is* by Denis Tourbin, orginally commissioned
for *Canada : A Portrait* (Statistics Canada, 1992). Reproduced
with permission of the artist and Jonina Wood, editor of
Canada : A Portrait.
Cover and interior by Xpressive Designs, Ottawa.
Printed and bound in Canada.

Carleton University Press gratefully acknowledges the support
extended to its publishing programme by the Canada Council
and the financial assistance of the Ontario Arts Council. The
Press would also like to thank the Department of Canadian
Heritage, Government of Canada, and the Government of
Ontario through the Ministry of Culture, Tourism and
Recreation, for their assistance.

To my mother, Frances F. Smith,
my wife, Elizabeth Symthe, and my
son, Nathaniel

P. J. S.

To my husband, Samuel Ajzenstat

J. A.

CONTENTS

Acknowledgements
ix

PART I: CANADA'S ORIGINS IN NEW PERSPECTIVE
xi

Liberal-Republicanism:
The Revisionist Picture of Canada's Founding
Janet Ajzenstat and Peter J. Smith
1

PART II: THE TORY PARADIGM
19

Conservatism, Liberalism, and Socialism in Canada:
An Interpretation
Gad Horowitz
21

PART III: REPUBLICAN INFLUENCE
45

The Ideological Origins of Canadian Confederation
Peter J. Smith
47

The First Distinct Society:
French Canada, America, and the Constitution of 1791
Louis-Georges Harvey
79

Civic Humanism Versus Liberalism: Fitting the Loyalists In
Peter J. Smith
109

PART IV: LIBERAL ROOTS
137

Durham and Robinson: Political Faction and Moderation
Janet Ajzenstat
139

The Triumph of Liberalism in Canada:
Laurier on Representation and Party Government
Rainer Knopff
159

Egerton Ryerson's Canadian Liberalism
Colin D. Pearce
181

The Constitutionalism of Étienne Parent and Joseph Howe
Janet Ajzenstat
209

The Provincial Rights Movement: Tensions Between
Liberty and Community in Legal Liberalism
Robert C. Vipond
233

PART V: LOOKING AHEAD
263

Canada's Political Culture Today:
Liberal, Republican, or Third Wave?
Peter J. Smith and Janet Ajzenstat
265

Selected Bibliography
283

ACKNOWLEDGEMENTS

That this book builds on the work of others is very evident from the list of contributors and the selected bibliography. The editors gratefully acknowledge their debt to George Grant and S. F. Wise, two thinkers who supremely recognized the possibility and necessity of Canadian political thought. Peter J. Smith wishes also to thank Jill Vickers for her encouragement through the years. Janet Ajzenstat thanks Rainer Knopff for his example and insight.

The editors thank Dr. J. A. Johnson, Dean of the Faculty of Social Sciences, McMaster University, for a grant in aid of publication.

The editors are grateful to the Canadian Political Science Association, the Canadian Study of Parliament Group, the *Journal of Canadian Studies*, Prentice-Hall Canada, and the State University of New York Press, for permission to reprint the articles that appear in Parts II, III, and IV of this volume.

Janet Ajzenstat, "The Constitutionalism of Étienne Parent and Joseph Howe," and Louis-Georges Harvey, "The First Distinct Society: French Canada, America, and the Constitution of 1791," first appeared in *Canadian Constitutionalism 1791-1991*, edited by Janet Ajzenstat in 1992 for the Canadian Study of Parliament Group, in celebration of the bicentenary of the Constitutional Act of 1791.

Janet Ajzenstat, "Durham and Robinson: Political Faction and Moderation," was published in the *Journal of Canadian Studies* special issue on Lord Durham and his ideas (spring 1990).

Gad Horowitz, "Conservatism, Liberalism, and Socialism in Canada: An Interpretation," was first published in the *Canadian Journal of Economics and Political Science* (May 1966); the abbreviated version used in this volume appears in Hugh G. Thornburn, ed., *Party Politics in Canada*, 5th edition (Scarborough, ON: Prentice-Hall, 1985).

Rainer Knopff, "The Triumph of Liberalism in Canada: Laurier on Representation and Party Government," and Peter J. Smith, "Civic Humanism Versus Liberalism: Fitting the Loyalists In," were part of the special edition of the *Journal of Canadian Studies* on Canadian political thought, edited by Peter J. Smith and Janet Ajzenstat (summer 1991).

Colin D. Pearce, "Egerton Ryerson's Canadian Liberalism," was published in the *Canadian Journal of Political Science* (December 1988). Peter J. Smith, "The Ideological Origins of Canadian Confederation," appeared in the *Canadian Journal of Political Science* (March 1987).

Robert C. Vipond, "The Provincial Rights Movement: Tensions Between Liberty and Community in Legal Liberalism," is abbreviated from Chapter 5, "Provincial Autonomy and the Rule of Law," in *Liberty and Community: Canadian Federalism and the Failure of the Constitution* (Albany, NY: State University of New York, 1991).

CANADA IS A TOOTHPICK ON THE
DASHBOARD OF A PICKUP TRUCK.
CANADA IS THE LONELINESS OF
A LONG DISTANCE FOLK SINGER.
CANA UT IN

I

Canada's Origins in New Perspective

CHAPTER ONE

LIBERAL-REPUBLICANISM: THE REVISIONIST PICTURE OF CANADA'S FOUNDING

Janet Ajzenstat and Peter J. Smith

Twenty years ago it would have been a relatively straightforward matter to describe the formation of the Canadian political culture. The standard view argued that Lockean liberalism was the dominant influence in the nineteenth century, modified only by a strain of tory conservatism. The synthesis of liberalism, with its emphasis on equality, and tory notions of collectivity and the common good gave rise to socialism in its turn. In the late twentieth century the impact of the nineteenth-century ideologies could still be seen. Predominantly liberal, subject to occasional nostalgic fits of toryism, Canada was increasingly ready to welcome a socialist future.

This picture of Canada's origins now lies in pieces. A new intellectual outlook, grounded in new research, sees the configuration of political ideas and ideology in the nineteenth century in very different terms. The challenge to nineteenth-century liberalism arose from a republican ideology on the political left, rather than toryism on the right. The formative influence in Canada's past was not solely liberalism, or the combination of liberalism and tory conservatism, but a lively opposition between liberalism and a civic republican philosophy with a progressive agenda.

The new outlook derives from the work of historians, notably J. G. A. Pocock and Bernard Bailyn, who transformed our understanding of the political history of Britain and the United States with the argument that a civic republican ideology was central in those countries in the eighteenth and nineteenth centuries. Civic republicanism, as Pocock and Bailyn describe it, is a post-feudal ideology inspired by the works of classical historians, philosophers, and rhetoricians that emphasizes civic participation and the sense of community. Understanding the importance of republicanism in the political history of Britain and the United States, according to these scholars, calls in question the whiggish reading of modern history as the forward march of rights-based liberalism. Pocock in particular depicts republicanism as an ideology that is in competition with liberalism, valuing democracy and community in opposition to liberalism's emphasis on the individual and bias toward commerce and economic development. The suggestion is that not only in the nineteenth century but still today, the civic republican philosophy contains a powerful challenge to Lockean liberalism. When the searchlight of this new outlook is turned on Canadian political history it indeed finds little evidence of tory conservatism in Canada's past or in Canadian political culture today. Toryism is being read out of the ideological temple. What is revealed rather is that in this country, as in the United States, the definitive influence on political culture and political institutions was a contest between political radicals who advanced the republican philosophy, and liberal constitutionalists who clung to the tradition of John Locke.

Why this shift in intellectual outlook came about, and what it means for the study of Canada's political origins and for politics today, are the subjects of this book. The new outlook is important not only because it draws attention to neglected aspects of the historical record, in the process overturning cherished assumptions about the Canadian political identity, but also because it forces us to entertain hard questions about political prospects now before Canada. The promise of the new paradigm is that it will recover arguments, obscured by the interpretation of political history in terms of a tory-liberal-socialist progression, that can help us to think through central political issues of our time. It offers grounds for understanding such features of Canadian political life as the profound dissatisfaction with government and political leadership that has developed in recent decades. Few would deny that a "culture of mistrust" flourishes in the modern liberal democracies, and certainly in Canada.[1] Charles Taylor, for example, argues that Canadians feel a sense of "decline" in modern political life. According to Taylor, Canadians believe that something important is being lost even as our civilization "develops."[2] It is our contention that insight into the phenomenon of decline will be forthcoming if Canadians can discard entrenched misconceptions about Canadian political history, and bring into present discourse the nineteenth-century republican criticism of liberal modernity, and the liberal response to the republican challenge.

THE OLD PARADIGM IN NEW PERSPECTIVE

In the 1960s, Robin Winks perfectly captured the sense of what we are calling the old paradigm in Canadian historiography with his suggestion that Canadian historians can be divided into two camps, the "liberal" and the "laurentian."[3] In the liberal camp, according to Winks, are historians like Chester Martin and Aileen Dunham, who describe Canadian political history in terms of a movement toward greater political freedom. The great formative themes of Canadian history for the liberal historian are the campaign for responsible government in the first half of the nineteenth century, and the attempt to emancipate the Dominion from the conservative embrace of the British empire in later years. In the laurentian camp are those like Donald Creighton who single out as formative and admirable influences the Conservative party's vision of a society that is more law-abiding than the United States, and the Conservatives' attempts to strengthen the connection with Britain as a bulwark against continentalism.

In political science the debate turns on interpretations of the political thought of the United Empire Loyalists. Political scientists with a "laurentian" bent typically argue that the Loyalists were the bearers of a tory conservative strain of thought that modified and informed the prevailing liberalism of the period. Gad Horowitz's exposition is classic.[4] Horowitz has no sympathy for most aspects of conservatism, certainly none for conservatism's acceptance of rank and hierarchy. What he admires is toryism's supposedly "organic" view of society. He argues that tory conservatism inherited from the feudal era a sense of the common good that is superlatively absent in liberalism. The question for Horowitz is whether a

3

modicum of toryism's idea of the organic and communal has lived on in the Canadian political culture. He concludes that the existence of healthy socialist parties in Canada in the twentieth century can only be explained on the supposition that tory communalism survived in the Canadian mind, happily tempered over the years by a dose of liberal egalitarianism.

William Christian and Colin Campbell agree with Horowitz that the Loyalists and later British immigrants to Canada, while "by no means unalloyed Tories," were "sufficiently un-liberal to produce a different political culture," one that put a greater emphasis on constituted authority, order, and stability than on individualism.[5] Liberal individualism was bridled in Canada, and as a result the state was free to act on behalf of the entire community.[6] Christian and Campbell contend that the influence of the tory strain "contributed to the long-standing Canadian tendency to use the power of government to effect common goals or objectives; and moreover to use it with equanimity, and often with enthusiasm."[7] They differ from Horowitz in suggesting that the tory vision of community has much to recommend it; the socialist program is not Canada's sole option. But all in all Christian and Campbell conform very closely to the Hartz-Horowitz model. They conclude that "the tory belief in a society which places social order and collective or community values before individual rights is alive, if not exactly thriving, in the modern Conservative party."[8]

Kenneth McRae, and David Bell and Lorne Tepperman, in contrast, argue that the tory element in Canadian political culture is negligible.[9] They suggest that the Loyalists were not bearers of a strain of tory conservatism, but typical bourgeois liberals, like most citizens of the United States in the Revolutionary era. What the Loyalists brought to this country were liberal notions about the value of individual rights and self-government. From the beginning Canada was a thoroughly liberal polity, with John Locke as its spiritual head.[10]

The tendency of historians and political scientists in the "liberal" camp to suggest that toryism is not an element in the Canadian political culture is highly interesting from our perspective. But it must be noted that the "liberals" are as convinced as the "laurentians" that the key to understanding Canadian political culture lies in determining the relative influence of the liberal and conservative ideologies. McRae's argument for the dominance of liberalism and

Horowitz's claim for the centrality of a tory strain both depend on Louis Hartz's vision of political history as an inevitable progression from feudal conservatism, through Enlightenment liberalism, to modern socialism. McRae is suggesting that Canadian political history begins at the stage of liberalism; no tory strain is present. Horowitz argues that Canadian liberalism includes that crucial element of thought from the pre-liberal, pre-Enlightenment period. But at bottom both are attempting to depict the political arguments of the nineteenth century in this country in terms of the liberal-conservative polarity.

Thus it can be said that the question that occupied students of Canadian political culture to the exclusion of almost any other until very recently was whether Canada was shaped by a liberal ideology or by a combination of liberalism and conservatism. Did Canada acquire a definitively liberal and progressive stamp from the early waves of immigration? Did the struggles for responsible government and political independence express and confirm that liberal bent? Or is there in the Canadian past an appreciably conservative tendency of thought that contains within it the seeds of opposition to liberalism and modernity?

The flaws in the liberal-laurentian paradigm were there from its beginning, waiting for the scholars' attention. Even without an appreciation of the importance of civic republicanism in Canadian political history some of the old model's difficulties should have been evident. An obvious one is that it requires scholars to include under the aegis of tory conservatism two tendencies that are not easy to reconcile: a selfless sense of the common good, and a ruthless dedication to commerce and economic development. The disposition of governing élites in British North America and Canada to use the power of the state to effect common goals and objects, praised by Horowitz, and Christian and Campbell, as evidence of a tory sense of the common good, found expression in projects that would develop access to markets, foster trade, and all in all create a climate favourable to money-making.[11] The standard argument of the nineteenth-century radicals—surely one with considerable truth to it—held that colonial élites in the governing parties were self-seeking men, concerned primarily to enrich themselves, and their families and friends. We suggest that only the necessity of forcing all political ideas in nineteenth-century Canada into the strait-jacket of the liberal-conservative model has led historians and political scientists to transform these capitalist robber barons into benign tories with a feudal sense of responsibility for the good of the political community.[12]

In our view the most unfortunate consequence of Canadian infatuation with liberal-laurentianism is that political scientists and historians have been discouraged from exploring and evaluating the republicanism of the revolutionary radicals, the men like Mackenzie and Papineau who are Smith's subject in "Origins of Canadian Confederation" in this volume, as an independent and important influence in Canadian political history. Scholars have typically taken two approaches to the radicals. Those who argue that the radicals embraced an independent political philosophy tend to present them as an unimportant element in Canadian political history.[13] Those prepared to admit the radicals' importance attempt to assimilate their political ideas to mainstream liberalism. It is commonly argued, for example, that Mackenzie and Papineau were early advocates of the liberal democracy that came to characterize Canadian politics in the twentieth century. The constraints of the liberal-laurentian approach rule out the possibility that the revolutionary radicals were the bearers of a political philosophy profoundly critical of liberalism. Thus although Kenneth McRae comes to the conclusion that the tory strain was relatively unimportant in Canadian political history, he is not able to investigate the possibility that opposition to liberalism came from the political left. Insofar as historians and political scientists have looked for a critique of liberalism in nineteenth-century Canada's intellectual history, the presumption has been that it must be found in conservatism. It is remarkable that the very characteristics that Smith finds in the Canadian radicals and revolutionaries, the sense of community and the argument for citizen virtue, Horowitz and Christian ascribe to the tory conservatives and the Family Compact.

The second serious consequence of liberal-laurentianism is that it has led scholars to overlook or devalue the nineteenth-century liberal response to civic republicanism. Because the importance of the republican challenge is denied, the attempts of the liberal constitutionalists to combat it have had to be explained away. Vital elements in the political thought of men like John Beverley Robinson, Joseph Howe, and Étienne Parent, the subjects of Ajzenstat's articles in this volume, have been dismissed as a mere self-interested defence of party, property, and class. It is a fact that throughout the nineteenth century, the speeches and writings of the liberal constitutionalists in the Conservative and Liberal parties return constantly to the idea that "democracy" is a threat to be combatted by all legitimate means. The plain sense of these statements is that the liberals believed that the kind of democracy advocated by the civic republicans would endanger political liberty. But what is the danger? The great debate of Canada's formative years is about definitions of democracy, and about the tension between democracy as the radicals define it, and liberal rights and freedoms. What a pity that this tension has been almost completely obscured by historians and political scientists wearing the blinkers of the liberal-conservative paradigm. The usual pious accounts of the development of responsible government and colonial self-rule do not come close to doing the liberal argument justice.

One of the first challenges to the liberal-laurentian paradigm came with the publication of Gordon T. Stewart's *The Origins of Canadian Politics*.[14] Stewart breaks sharply with the Hartz-Horowitz approach, embracing the model of historical interpretation put forward by Bernard Bailyn. Like Bailyn, Pocock, John Murrin, and Gordon Wood, Stewart regards as the formative influence on eighteenth-century British and American political culture the debate between the defenders of classical republican values (the "country party") and the defenders of commerce, a strong monarchy, and a strong state (the "court party"). He concludes that whereas republican values triumphed in Revolutionary America, court values triumphed in nineteenth-century Canada. Indeed, he believes that the values of the court party were hegemonic in Canada. In sharp contrast to Smith, he argues that the reformers as well as the tories came under the sway of the court ideology.

Unlike Smith, then, Stewart finds no critique of liberalism, modernity, and commerce in the arguments of Canadian radicals. Although he develops his picture of Canadian political ideas with the aid of a model that gives full scope to the importance of civic republicanism in Britain and the United States, he is no more able than the "liberals" and "laurentians" of the old school of historiography to see that the British North American revolutionaries were the bearers of the republican philosophy that was an important influence in Canadian political history. It hardly needs to be added that Stewart also gives no account of the liberal response to republicanism.

7

REPUBLICANISM VERSUS LIBERALISM
IN CANADIAN HISTORY

The civic republican philosophy of the nineteenth-century Canadian radicals sets up in opposition to liberalism an argument for community and democratic participation that has its origins in the political philosophy of Jean-Jacques Rousseau and in the North American context is allied to Jeffersonian and Jacksonian conceptions of democracy. Envisaging a one-class society of small property owners, farmers, and independent craftsmen, civic republicanism supposes that those representing the community in institutions of government will articulate a sense of the common good and an idea of civic virtue to which all members of the polity adhere. As Louis-Georges Harvey argues in his article in this volume, civic republicanism supposes the cultivation of "a social context that favour[s] the preservation of virtue." Liberalism's toleration of selfish individualism and ambition is rejected, as is liberalism's embrace of commerce and technology. Republicanism, in Harvey's words, offers the "possibility of checking the growth of commerce and its attendant threat of political corruption." It encapsulates the dream of a society able to support citizens' aspirations to virtue by means of a collective definition of the good life.

In more concrete terms, the terms of first importance for the nineteenth-century radicals, civic republicanism promises to rescue government from the hands of the powerful and privileged. It scorns liberalism's mechanical system of political representation and voting, regarding it as a travesty of democratic participation. The argument is that although liberalism may allow citizens to put forward political claims, it virtually guarantees disappointment for most; very few people, especially those who are not members of the privileged classes, ever see their claims and demands mirrored in legislation. In contrast, civic republicanism's "context of virtue" ensures that citizens and leaders will see eye to eye so that people will almost always find their political wishes reflected in the decisions of their leaders. Republicanism's claim to foster democratic participation rests on this idea that citizens and leaders agree because they share that "context of virtue."

The radical's scorn for the nineteenth-century liberal constitution was enhanced by the fact that it was usually described at the time as a form of mixed or balanced government, comprising "monarchic," "aristocratic," and "democratic" elements. The monarchic element is the political executive or cabinet (Ministers of the Crown), the aristocratic branch is the upper legislative house, and the democratic branch is the lower house. The Canadian radicals argue that such a mixed constitution allows the privileged classes to overwhelm popular influence on government. In their eyes the mixed regime cannot be a formula for including the voice of the people in the institutions of government. It cements the dominance of the oligarchy. The fact that British North America lacked a landed aristocracy made the inclusion of "monarchic" and "aristocratic" elements the more absurd in the radical view.

Recapturing the republican perspective clears the way for a new appreciation of liberal political thought in Canadian history. How easy it has been for Canadians to feel superior to John Beverley Robinson, Sir John A. Macdonald, Joseph Howe, or Lord Durham, when they write about the importance of institutions to check "democracy," or describe popular leaders as "demagogues." Lacking an understanding of the republican vision, and the challenge it poses to liberal constitutionalism, it has been impossible to entertain the idea that a vital argument lies behind such statements.

What the nineteenth-century liberals feared in the republican argument for democracy was that it would promote what we today call democratic tyranny, or, in milder form, left-wing authoritarianism: one-party government. The notion that one communal way of life is to be preferred above all condones the suppression of political dissent and opposition. A regime that does not tolerate a variety of visions of the good life by definition militates against open and free debate about political issues. It is a formula for preferring in law one type of political leader, the type that adheres most closely to the definition of democratic, communal "virtue." The liberal argues that the great merit of the mixed constitution is exactly that it is designed to protect against just such oppression by one party or faction, whether democratic or oligarchic in origin.

The radicals regard as a fundamental argument against the mixed constitution that it appears to call for a landed aristocracy. Advocates of the liberal mixed constitution in the nineteenth century argue that although the system had originated historically with the "three estates" of English society before the Glorious Revolution, it no longer called for or depended on representation of social classes. It had become a system of checks and balances promoting

9

the alternation of political parties in office, the system of political "ins" and "outs" that today characterizes liberal democracies. Ajzenstat maintains that the mixed constitution of the eighteenth and nineteenth centuries is in essence the system of cabinet government that Canadians know today, and still operates to protect the aim dear to the proponents of mixed government in the nineteenth century, that no one political faction be able to claim permanent title to govern.

Although republicans charge that liberalism lacks the notion of the common good, liberals insist that the liberal constitution provides an adequate guarantee, indeed the only possible guarantee, that laws and policies will operate for the common good. Since a free society inevitably shelters a variety of religious, philosophical, and moral conceptions of the good life, it is only to be expected that proposals for legislation will become the object of vigorous criticism. But the liberal is reasonably confident that the give and take of political argument in a free polity will ensure the emergence of laws that promote the welfare of the citizenry.

Thus for civic republicanism the sense of community and the common good is the given, defining and constraining politics. For liberalism, politics is the given, promoting ever-changing notions of communal good.

THE GREAT DEBATE IN PRESENT FORM

It is sometimes said that the politics of British North America and Canada in the nineteenth century was primarily pragmatic, that the political figures of the time did not broach theoretical issues. Indeed, the idea that the Canadian historical record lacks philosophical depth is so well entrenched that even scholars who are deeply involved in describing the intellectual currents of Canadian history may subscribe to it. They insist on the paucity of political ideas and theory even while debating the influence of conservatism on Canadians' sense of community, the consequence of the Loyalist rejection of political revolution, or the impact of a liberal philosophy stemming from Locke. Self-deprecation is a style in Canadian historiography.

We argue that it is correct to see in the political debates of nineteenth-century Canada a reflection—a very sharp and interesting one—of a great debate between the advocates of community and the advocates of freedom that has characterized Europe and the Atlantic region from the period of the Enlightenment. It is time to reject the notion, so often reiterated in Canadian text books, and so well entrenched in Canadians' hearts, that the political thought of the modern era is marked by a conservative-liberal-socialist progression. Rather the political thought of the modern period moves between two poles, one reflecting the liberal philosophy of Enlightenment thinkers like John Locke and his successors, and the other the arguments of thinkers like Jean-Jacques Rousseau, who rejected the Enlightenment's central tenets.

What has captivated republican thinkers in Rousseau are the arguments suggesting that commerce and trade are contemptible, that it is morally repugnant to elevate the claims of the individual over the claims of the community, and that democracy in the true definition exists only where the sense of community is strong. We have already suggested that these ideas inform the thought of the British North American republicans. Our argument now is that Rousseau's critique of Lockean liberalism has remained a permanent element in the political culture and political thought of the West. Those who are dissatisfied with liberal democracy still today, whether they are merely searching for ways to accommodate collective rights and populist politics within the framework of the liberal constitution, or reject liberalism altogether in the name of a thoroughgoing collectivism, draw their ammunition from Rousseau.

Adherence to liberal-laurentianism has prevented Canadians from recapturing our particular contribution to this quarrel between the heirs of Locke and the heirs of Rousseau, and so hindered us from bringing the insights of our political history to bear on current political issues. The outlook we embrace in this book not only shines a light on facts that were previously relegated to the shadows. It provides us with a way to approach the central debate of our own time, the debate between liberal constitutionalism and the philosophy of communitarianism.[15]

It would never do to suggest that the present debate between liberals and communitarians simply recapitulates the quarrels of constitutionalists and republicans in Canadian history. The nineteenth-century arguments for freedom and community have undoubtedly undergone a sea change. To gain a full appreciation of them it is necessary to read them in the context of their period, exactly the task undertaken by the authors of the articles in this book. At the same time it is evident that the debate in our day picks up broad themes and arguments of the earlier period. Whether in the form of civic republicanism or communitarianism, the Rousseauian alternative remains the enduring challenge to the liberal perspective. It is easy to see the connection between nineteenth-century republicanism and today's communitarianism, because the historical debate left its mark on the Canadian political culture. Canadians still live with political institutions and ideas that received definitive shape in that period.

That republicanism and communitarianism share a core of ideas and are linked historically is argued by two seminal contributors to the liberal-communitarian debate, Charles Taylor and Michael Sandel. It is not their sympathy for the communitarian end of the spectrum that we wish to draw attention to here. It is the fact that Taylor and Sandel base their assessment of communitarianism on an argument that roots it in nineteenth-century republicanism.

Thus, Sandel argues that the republican ideology was dominant in the United States until the late nineteenth century; liberalism gained the upper hand only in the twentieth. "In the modern American welfare state," he says, "the liberal dimensions of our tradition have crowded out the republican dimensions, with adverse consequences for the democratic prospect and the legitimacy of the regime."[16] In similar fashion, Taylor argues that "The principal challenge to contemporary Western liberal societies like our own seems to concern their citizen republics."[17] His broad claim is that the "decline of politics" in Canada has been aggravated by the rise of a rights-based liberalism in the twentieth century that is undermining communitarian-republican elements in the Canadian political tradition.

REINTERPRETING CANADA'S POLITICAL ORIGINS

Among the many versions of the liberal-laurentianism, we have chosen to reprint in Part II Gad Horowitz's "Conservatism, Liberalism, and Socialism in Canada: An Interpretation." As H. D. Forbes has argued, Horowitz's article is the best-known and most influential argument about the origins of Canadian political culture. It is "one of the few things in the field that practically everyone has read and remembers."[18]

In Parts III and IV are the articles that present the evidence for the new interpretation of Canadian political history, the liberal-republican model.

The articles in Part III focus on the republican dimension. The publication of Peter J. Smith's "Origins of Canadian Confederation" in 1987 was the signal to the scholarly community in this country that liberal-laurentianism was being supplanted. It contains the exposition of J. G. A. Pocock and Bernard Bailyn that has informed our thesis in this Introduction. Smith's interpretation of Canadian political history suggests not only that civic republicanism was important historically in Canada, but that Canadian assumptions about the importance of the tory ideology in the British North American colonies and Canada after Confederation, and the Canadian habit of ignoring the republican influence, have blinded us to the important critique of liberalism embedded in civic republicanism. In Smith's view, republican arguments offer an unparalleled perspective from which to criticize Lockean liberalism, and more than this suggest how Canada today can develop a more democratic regime, open to citizen virtue.

The themes Smith advances in "Origins" are taken up by Louis-Georges Harvey in his contribution. Like Smith, Harvey rejects the liberal-conservative, feudal-capitalist dichotomy in Canadian historiography, arguing that it is "at best a dangerous oversimplification, at worst largely irrelevant." Pre-Confederation political discourse is better understood in the light of studies of the civic humanist, or civic republican, philosophy in Anglo-American political discourse. What interests Harvey especially is that civic republicanism informed the political statements of the Patriotes in Lower Canada. He builds a case to suggest that republicanism, drawn from the political culture of the United States in the early part of the nineteenth century, is a crucial component of the political thought of Quebec even today. He is in complete agreement with Smith that recapturing the republican argument enables a necessary reevaluation of liberalism.

As its title suggests, Smith's second article, "Civic Humanism Versus Liberalism: Fitting the Loyalists In," explores the role of Loyalist thought, that element so crucial for the old liberal-laurentian paradigm, in the context of the new outlook, and the new assessment of the importance of civic republicanism.

Part IV explores the liberal dimension of the new model. The argument in this case is that it is Lockean liberalism, rather than toryism or civic republicanism, that has been the dominant influence in Canadian political history. Taken together, the articles in this section offer a reasoned defence of liberalism, including a defence of the kind of political participation and sense of citizenship that is possible in the liberal regime.

In "Durham and Robinson: Political Faction and Moderation" Ajzenstat argues that Upper Canada's John Beverley Robinson, usually considered the very model of the feudal tory oligarch, fits the description of a classic Lockean liberal. She finds in Robinson's arguments a powerful defence of liberal right. In "The Triumph of Liberalism in Canada" Rainer Knopff explores the Lockean roots of Laurier's argument for party government. Laurier's task, as Knopff describes it, is exactly to persuade his ultramontane audience to abandon the idea that the best possible regime is one that encompasses a public definition of citizen virtue. Laurier's argument is that giving up the idea of communal virtue is the condition of liberal freedom and liberal opportunities for political participation. In "Egerton Ryerson's Canadian Liberalism" Colin Pearce argues that Ryerson (who, like Robinson, is usually dubbed a tory) must be regarded as a thinker in the Lockean tradition. What interests Pearce is the degree to which Ryerson manages to find a place in his liberal political ideology for religious belief, public spiritedness, and individual cultivation of moral virtues.

In her second article, "The Constitutionalism of Étienne Parent and Joseph Howe," Ajzenstat provides the evidence to suggest that liberal thinkers were acutely aware of the republican vision of democracy and community, and framed their defence of liberalism to counter it. It should be noted that Ajzenstat and Knopff present a picture of the political culture of Quebec that differs sharply from Harvey's. Whereas Harvey argues that republicanism was dominant in Quebec in the period before the Rebellions and has remained an important influence, Ajzenstat (on Parent) and Knopff (on Laurier) suggest that there was a strong tradition of liberal constitutionalism among French Canadians, and that in the end it was the liberal influence that proved more important.

Ajzenstat on Parent and Howe, and Vipond's chapter "The Provincial Rights Movement: Tensions Between Liberty and Community in Legal Liberalism," which concludes Part IV, tackle directly the question of liberalism in relation to civic republicanism. Ajzenstat suggests that republicanism went into eclipse after the Rebellion of 1837. Vipond explores the idea that it was revived in a fashion after 1867. He describes attempts by the liberal leaders of the provincial rights movement in the post-Confederation years to resurrect and define a sense of community and collective good, and to reconcile it with the liberal tradition of rights.

Robert Vipond's chapter offers the revealing suggestion that the notions of community and liberal freedom have rubbed up against each other throughout Canadian history.[19] In the conclusion to his chapter he summarizes Charles Taylor's argument for community, focusing especially on Taylor's suggestion that Canadian history teaches us to value the community-oriented good.[20] In Vipond's opinion, what Canadian political history teaches is not that community was dominant in our past, nor that it is the greater good. What we find in the historical record, he suggests, is that both the republican heritage and the liberal, both liberty and community, are inextricably interconnected and interdependent, while they remain at the same time always in tension.

It will be apparent to readers that there is no single set of opinions in this volume about the merits of liberalism as distinct from republicanism. Nor is there a single thesis about the relative importance of these two political philosophies in Canadian political history. The authors in Part III are inclined to believe that civic republicanism has played a large part in making Canada what it is today. They sympathize with republican objectives, and value the criticisms of liberalism implicit in the republican argument. The authors in Part IV regard liberalism as the crucial influence. It is apparent to them, moreover, that Canadians, both French- and English-speaking, have reason to be thankful today for this liberal heritage. On one level then *Canada's Origins* offers an exchange of views in the liberal-republican, liberal-communitarian, debate.

On a second level it offers grounds for a new interpretation of Canadian political history and political culture. From this perspective what is important about *Canada's Origins* is that it brings forward from the obscurity to which it has been assigned by liberal-laurentianism the political thought of Canada's nineteenth-century civic republicans, and the response of liberal thinkers to it. It argues that Canadian political institutions and the Canadian political culture were definitively shaped, in ways that are still of importance, by the nineteenth-century contest between liberals and republicans.

It is our hope that the book will give readers a sharper appreciation of both liberal constitutionalism and civic republicanism, and insight into historical and present-day dimensions of the contest between these poles of thought.

NOTES

1. The phrase is Jean Bethke Elshtain's. *Democracy on Trial*, The 1993 Massey Lecture Series (Toronto: Anansi, 1993).

2. Charles Taylor, *The Malaise of Modernity*, The 1991 Massey Lecture Series (Toronto: Anansi, 1991) 1.

3. Robin Winks, "Canadian Historians," in Robin Winks, ed., *The Historiography of the British Empire-Commonwealth* (Durham, NC: Duke University Press, 1966). Winks's term "laurentian" derives from Donald Creighton, *The Commercial Empire of the St. Lawrence 1760-1850* (Toronto: Ryerson, 1937).

4. Gad Horowitz, "Conservatism, Liberalism, and Socialism in Canada: An Interpretation," *Canadian Journal of Economics and Political Science* 32.2 (1966). An abbreviated version of this article is reprinted in Part I of this volume. It is reprinted in H. D. Forbes, ed., *Canadian Political Thought* (Toronto: Oxford University Press, 1985) 352-59. For a critical evaluation of Horowitz's influence see H. D. Forbes, "Hartz-Horowitz at Twenty: Nationalism, Toryism, and Socialism in Canada and the United States," *Canadian Journal of Political Science* 22.2 (1987).

5. William Christian and Colin Campbell, *Political Parties and Ideologies in Canada*, 2nd ed. (Toronto: McGraw-Hill Ryerson, 1983) 28.

6. As S. F. Wise argues, the endeavour to know the Canadian political way of life invariably prompts comparisons with the United States: "One learns little about the American polity from the Canadian idea of it, but much about Canadians." *God's Peculiar Peoples: Essays on Political Culture in Nineteenth-Century Canada*, ed. A. B. McKillop and Paul Romney (Ottawa: Carleton University Press, 1993) 147.

7. Christian and Campbell 28.

8. Christian and Campbell 8.

9. Kenneth McRae, "The Structure of Canadian History," in Louis Hartz, ed., *The Founding of New Societies* (New York: Harcourt, Brace and World, 1964). David Bell and Lorne Tepperman, *The Roots of Disunity: A Look at Canadian Political Culture* (Toronto: McClelland and Stewart, 1979).

10. Bell and Tepperman 30.
11. Many chapters in S. F. Wise, *God's Peculiar Peoples*, illuminate the character of the tory connection with commercial enterprise.
12. For a vivid depiction of the essential opposition between commerce and politics, see Jane Jacobs, *Systems of Survival: A Dialogue on the Moral Foundations of Commerce and Politics* (New York: Random House, 1992).
13. S. F. Wise argues that although "the fortunes of nineteenth-century radicalism have attracted the interest and sympathy of later historians, the Canadian radical tradition is so episodic in character that it may scarcely be said to have existed" (145).
14. Gordon T. Stewart, *The Origins of Canadian Politics: A Comparative Approach* (Vancouver: University of British Columbia Press, 1986).
15. Two books of note on the liberal-communitarian debate are Michael Sandel, ed., *Liberalism and Its Critics* (New York: New York University Press, 1984), and Shlmo Avineri and Avner De-Shalit, eds., *Communitarianism and Individualism* (Oxford: Oxford University Press, 1992).
16. Michael Sandel, "The Political Theory of the Procedural Republic," in Allan C. Hutchinson and Patrick Monahan, eds., *The Rule of Law, Ideal or Ideology?* (Toronto: Carswell, 1987).
17. Charles Taylor, "Alternative Futures: Legitimacy, Identity, and Alienation in Late Twentieth-Century Canada," in Alan C. Cairns and Cynthia Williams, eds., *Constitutionalism, Citizenship, and Society in Canada* (Toronto: University of Toronto Press, 1985) 206. This article is reprinted in Charles Taylor, *Reconciling the Solitudes: Essays on Canadian Federalism and Nationalism*, ed. Guy Laforest (Montreal: McGill-Queen's University Press, 1993).
18. "Hartz-Horowitz at Twenty" 287. Forbes observes that "Hartzian analysis" has flourished in Canada but languished in the United States. He was right when he wrote, but the picture is changed today. As the historians' case for civic republicanism comes to attention, it provokes interest in Hartz's older thesis.
19. Vipond's idea that the notions of community and liberal freedom have been evident throughout Canada's history is echoed in Leslie Armour's analysis of Canada's philosophical tradition in the late nineteenth and early twentieth centuries. In the ascendancy at the time in Canadian universities, according to Armour, was a form of Hegelian idealism that had transplanted the Scottish philosophy of Common Sense. Its main proponent was John Watson, a Scottish immigrant and professor at Queen's University. Watson directly addressed the issue of individualism versus community, combatting, as Armour argues, "what C. B. Macpherson has called the 'theory of possessive individualism.'" Watson's students, such as Adam Shortt and O. P. Skelton, emerged

from Queen's to join and shape the Canadian federal service in the twentieth century, the same federal service that later ushered in the welfare state. Given that contemporary communitarianism is depicted as having both Hegelian and Aristotelian antecedents, Watson's ideas and influence merit further study by Canadian political theorists. Leslie Armour, *The Idea of Canada and the Crisis of Community* (Ottawa: Steel Rail Educational Publishing, 1981).

20. Taylor, "Alternative Futures" 206.

II

The
Tory Paradigm

CHAPTER TWO

CONSERVATISM, LIBERALISM,
AND SOCIALISM IN CANADA:
AN INTERPRETATION

Gad Horowitz

THE HARTZIAN APPROACH

In the United States, organized socialism is dead; in Canada, socialism, though far from national power, is a significant political force. Why this striking difference in the fortunes of socialism in two very similar societies? It will be shown that the relative strength of socialism in Canada is related to the relative strength of toryism, and to the different position and character of liberalism in the two countries.

In North America, Canada is unique. Yet there is a tendency in Canadian historical and political studies to explain Canadian phenomena not by contrasting them with American phenomena but by identifying them as variations on a basic North American theme. I grant that Canada and the United States are similar, and that the similarities should be pointed out. But the pan-North American approach, since it searches out and concentrates on similarities, cannot help us to understand Canadian uniqueness. When this approach is applied to the study of English Canadian socialism, one discovers, first, that like the American variety it is weak, and, second, that it is weak for much the same reasons. These discoveries perhaps explain why Canadian socialism is weak in comparison to European socialism; they do not explain why Canadian socialism is so much stronger than American socialism.

The explanatory technique used in this study is that developed by Louis Hartz in *The Liberal Tradition in America*[1] and *The Foundation of New Societies*.[2] It is applied to Canada in a mildly pan-North American way by Kenneth McRae in "The Structure of Canadian History," a contribution to the latter book.

The Hartzian approach is to study the new societies founded by Europeans (the United States, English Canada, French Canada, Latin America, Dutch South Africa, Australia) as "fragments" thrown off from Europe. The key to the understanding of ideological development in a new society is its "point of departure" from Europe: the ideologies borne by the founders of the new society are not representative of the historic ideological spectrum of the mother country. The settlers represent only a fragment of that spectrum. The complete ideological spectrum ranges—in chronological order, and from right to left—from feudal or tory through liberal whig to liberal democrat to socialist. French Canada and Latin America are "feudal fragments": they were founded by bearers of the feudal or tory values of the organic, corporate, hierarchical community; their point of departure from Europe was before the liberal revolution. The United States, English Canada, and Dutch South Africa are "bourgeois fragments"; they were founded by bearers of liberal individualism who have left the tory end of the spectrum behind them.

The significance of the fragmentation process is that the new society, having been thrown off from Europe, "loses the stimulus to change that the whole provides."[3] The full ideological spectrum of Europe develops only out of the continued confrontation and interaction of its four elements; they are related to one another not just as enemies, but as parents and children. A new society that leaves part of the past behind it cannot develop the future ideologies that need the continued presence of the past in order to come into being. In escaping the past, the fragment escapes the future, for "the very seeds of the later ideas are contained in the parts of the old world that have been left behind."[4] The ideology of the founders is thus frozen, congealed at the point of origin.

Socialism is an ideology that combines the corporate-organic-collectivist ideas of toryism with the rationalist-egalitarian ideas of liberalism. Both the feudal and the bourgeois fragments escape socialism, but in different ways. A feudal fragment such as French Canada develops no whig (undemocratic) liberalism; therefore it does not develop the democratic liberalism that arises out of and as a reaction against whiggery; therefore it does not develop the socialism that arises out of and as a reaction against liberal democracy. The corporate-organic-collectivist component of socialism is present in the feudal fragment—it is part of the feudal ethos—but the radical-rationalist-egalitarian component of socialism is missing. It can be provided only by whiggery and liberal democracy, and these have not come into being.

In the bourgeois fragment, the situation is the reverse: the radical-rationalist-egalitarian component of socialism is present, but the corporate-organic-collectivist component is missing, because toryism has been left behind. In the bourgeois fragments, "Marx dies because there is no sense of class, no yearning for the corporate past."[5] The absence of socialism is related to the absence of toryism.

It is *because* socialists have a conception of society as more than an agglomeration of competing individuals, a conception close to the tory view of society as an organic community, that they find the liberal idea of equality (equality of opportunity) inadequate. Socialists disagree with liberals about the essential meaning of equality, because socialists have a tory conception of society.

In a liberal bourgeois society that has never known toryism, the demand for equality will express itself as left-wing or democratic liberalism as opposed to whiggery. The left will point out that all are not equal in the competitive pursuit of individual happiness. The government will be required to assure greater equality of opportunity—in the nineteenth century, by destroying monopolistic privileges; in the twentieth century, by providing a welfare "floor" so that no one will fall out of the race for success, and by regulating the economy so that the race can continue without periodic crises.

In a society that thinks of itself as a community of classes rather than an aggregation of individuals, the demand for equality will take a socialist form: for equality of condition rather than mere equality of opportunity; for co-operation rather than competition; for a community that does more than provide a context within which individuals can pursue happiness in a purely self-regarding way. At its most "extreme," socialism is a demand for the *abolition* of classes so that the good of the community can truly be realized. This is a demand that cannot be made by people who can hardly see class and community; the individual fills their eyes.

THE APPLICATION TO CANADA

It is a simple matter to apply the Hartzian approach to English Canada in a pan-North American way. English Canada can be viewed as a fragment of the American liberal society, lacking a feudal or tory heritage and therefore lacking the socialist ideology that grows out of it. Canadian domestic struggles, from this point of view, are a northern version of the American struggle between big-propertied liberals on the right and petit-bourgeois and working-class liberals on the left; the struggle goes on within a broad liberal consensus, and the voice of the tory or the socialist is not heard in the land. This pan-North American approach, with important qualifications, is adopted by Hartz and McRae in *The Founding of New Societies*. English Canada, like the United States, is a bourgeois fragment. No toryism in the past, therefore no socialism in the present.

But Hartz notes that the liberal society of English Canada has a "tory touch"; that it is "etched with a tory streak coming out of the American revolution."[6] Take as an example the central concern of this study, the differing weights of Canadian and American socialism. The CCF failed to become a major party in urban Canada, but it succeeded in becoming a significant minor party, a success denied to the American socialist.

The most important un-American characteristics of English Canada, all related to the presence of toryism, are (a) the presence of tory ideology in the founding of English Canada by the Loyalists, and its continuing influence on English Canadian political culture, (b) the persistent power of whiggery or right-wing liberalism in Canada (the Family Compacts) as contrasted with the rapid and easy victory of liberal democracy (Jefferson, Jackson) in the United States, (c) the ambivalent centrist character of left-wing liberalism in Canada as contrasted with the unambiguously leftist position of left-wing liberalism in the United States, (d) the presence of an influential and legitimate socialist movement in English Canada as contrasted with the illegitimacy and early death of American socialism, and (e) the failure of English Canadian liberalism to develop into the one true myth, the nationalist cult, and the parallel failure to exclude toryism and socialism as "un-Canadian," in other words, the legitimacy of ideological diversity in English Canada.

THE PRESENCE OF TORYISM AND ITS CONSEQUENCES

Many students have noted that English Canadian society has been powerfully shaped by tory values that are "alien" to the American mind. The latest of these is Seymour Martin Lipset, who stresses the relative strength in Canada of the tory values of "ascription" and "élitism" (the tendency to defer to authority), and the relative weakness of the liberal values of "achievement" and "egalitarianism."[7] He points to such well-known features of Canadian history as the absence of a lawless, individualistic-egalitarian American frontier, the preference for Britain rather than the United States as a social model, and, generally, the weaker emphasis on social equality, the greater acceptance by individuals of the facts of economic inequality, social stratification, and hierarchy, the belief in monarchy and the unity of the empire, greater stress on "law and order," revulsion against American populist excesses, different frontier experiences, and so on. One tory touch in English Canada is the far greater willingness of English Canadian political and business élites to use the power of the state for the purpose of developing and controlling the economy. Canada is not a feudal (tory) fragment but a bourgeois (liberal) fragment touched with toryism.

Let us put it this way: pre-revolutionary America was a liberal fragment with insignificant traces of toryism, extremely weak feudal survivals. But they were insignificant in the *American* setting; they were far overshadowed by the liberalism of that setting. The revolution did not have to struggle against them; it swept them away easily and painlessly, leaving no trace of them in the American memory. But these traces of toryism were expelled into a new setting, where they were no longer insignificant. In this *new* setting, where there was no pre-established overpowering liberalism to force them into insignificance, they played a large part in shaping a new political culture, significantly different from the American. As Nelson wrote in *The American Tory*, "the Tories' organic conservatism represented a current of thought that failed to reappear in America

25

after the revolution. A substantial part of the whole spectrum of European . . . philosophy seemed to slip outside the American perspective."[8] But it *reappeared* in Canada. Here the sway of liberalism has proved to be not total, but considerably mitigated by a tory presence initially and a socialist presence subsequently. In Canada, the Family Compacts were able to maintain ascendancy and delay the coming of democracy because of the tory touch "inherited in part from American Loyalism, which restrained egalitarian feeling in Canada."[9] The early power of whiggery serves to emphasize the importance of the tory touch in English Canada.

In the United States, the masses could not be swayed by the Federalist-Whig appeals to anti-egalitarian sentiments. In Canada, the masses *were* swayed by these appeals; the role of the Compacts was to save "the colonial masses from the spectre of republicanism and democracy."[10] What accounts for this is the tory presence in English Canadian political culture, the "greater acceptance of limitation, of hierarchical patterns."[11]

The next step in tracing the development of the English Canadian political culture must be to take account of the tremendous waves of British immigration that soon engulfed the original American Loyalist fragment. These British immigrants had undoubtedly been heavily infected with non-liberal ideas, and these ideas were undoubtedly in their heads as they settled in Canada. The political culture of a new nation is not necessarily fixed at the point of origin or departure; the founding of a new nation can go on for generations. If the later waves of immigration arrived before the point of congealment of the political culture, they must have participated actively in the process of culture formation.

Between 1815 and 1850 almost one million Britons emigrated to Canada. The population of English Canada doubled in twenty years and quadrupled in forty. The population of Ontario increased tenfold in the same period, from about 95,000 in 1814 to about 950,000 in 1851.[12] Is it not possible that the immigrants, while they were no doubt considerably liberalized by their new environment, also brought to it non-liberal ideas that entered into the political culture mix and that perhaps even reinforced the non-liberal elements present in the original fragment? If the million immigrants had come from the United States rather than Britain, would English Canada not be "significantly" different today?

The difficulty in applying the Hartzian approach to English

Canada is that although the point of departure is reasonably clear, it is difficult to put one's finger on the point of congealment. Perhaps it was the Loyalist period; perhaps it was close to the mid-century mark; there are grounds for arguing that it was in the more recent past. But the important point is this: no matter where the point of congealment is located in time, the tory streak is present before the solidification of the political culture, and it is *strong* enough to produce *significant* "imperfectionist" or non-liberal, un-American attributes of English Canadian society. My own opinion is that the point of congealment came later than the Loyalists.

The indeterminate location of the point of congealment makes it difficult to account in any precise way for the presence of socialism in the English Canadian political cultural mix, though the presence itself is indisputable. If the point of congealment came *before* the arrival of the first radical or socialist-minded immigrants, the presence of socialism must be ascribed primarily to the earlier presence of toryism. Since toryism is a significant part of the political culture, at least part of the leftist reaction against it will sooner or later be expressed in its own terms, that is, in terms of *class* interests and the good of the community as a corporate entity (socialism) rather than in terms of the individual and his or her vicissitudes in the competitive pursuit of happiness (liberalism). If the point of congealment is very early, socialism appears at a later point not primarily because it is imported by British immigrants, but because it is contained as a potential in the original political culture. The immigrants then find that they do not have to give it up—that it is not un-Canadian—because it "fits" to a certain extent with the tory ideas already present. If the point of congealment is very late, the presence of socialism must be explained as a result of *both* the presence of toryism and the introduction of socialism into the cultural mix before congealment. The immigrant retains his or her socialism not only because it "fits" but also because nothing really *has* to fit. Socialism is not un-Canadian partly because "Canadian" has not yet been defined.

Canadian liberals cannot be expected to wax enthusiastic about the non-liberal traits of their country. They are likely to condemn the tory touch as anachronistic, stifling, undemocratic, out of tune with the essentially American ("free," "classless") spirit of English Canada. They dismiss the socialist touch as an "old-fashioned" protest, no longer necessary (if it ever was) in the best (liberal) of all possible worlds in which the "end of ideology" has been achieved. The secret dream of the Canadian liberal is the removal of English Canada's "imperfections," in other words, the total assimilation of English Canada into the larger North American culture. But there is a flaw in this dream that might give pause even to the liberal. Hartz places special emphasis on one very unappetizing characteristic of the new societies, intolerance, that is strikingly absent in English Canada. Because the new societies other than Canada are unfamiliar with legitimate ideological diversity, they are unable to accept it and deal with it in a rational manner, either internally or on the level of international relations.

The European nation has an "identity which transcends any ideologist and a mechanism in which each plays only a part."[13] Neither the tory, nor the liberal, nor the socialist, has a monopoly of the expression of the "spirit" of the nation. But the new societies, the fragments, contain only one of the ideologies of Europe; they are one-myth cultures. In the new setting, freed from its historic enemies past and future, ideology transforms itself into nationalism. It claims to be a moral absolute, "the great spirit of a nation."[14] In the United States, liberalism becomes "Americanism"; a political philosophy becomes a civil religion, a nationalist cult. The American attachment to Locke is "absolutist and irrational."[15] Democratic capitalism is the American way of life; to oppose it is to be un-American.

To be an American is to be a bourgeois liberal. To be French Canadian is to be a pre-Enlightenment Catholic; to be an Australian is to be a prisoner of the radical myth of "mateship"; to be a Boer is to be a pre-Enlightenment bourgeois Calvinist. The fragments escape the need for philosophy, for thought-about values, because "where perspectives shrink to a single value, and that value becomes the universe, how can value itself be considered?"[16] The fragment demands solidarity. Ideologies that diverge from the national myth make no impact; they are not understood, and their proponents are not granted legitimacy. They are denounced as aliens, and treated as aliens, because they are aliens. The fragments cannot understand or deal with the fact that *all* people are *not* bourgeois Americans, or radical Australians, or Catholic French Canadians, or Calvinist South Africans. They cannot make peace with the loss of ideological certainty.

The specific weakness of the United States is its "inability to understand the appeal of socialism" to the Third World.[17] Because the United States has "buried" the memory of the organic medieval community "beneath new liberal absolutisms and nationalisms,"[18] it cannot understand that the appeal of socialism to nations with a predominantly non-liberal past (including French Canada) consists precisely in the promise of "continuing the corporate ethos in the very process" of modernization.[19] The American reacts with isolationism, messianism, and hysteria.

English Canada, because it is the most "imperfect" of the fragments, is not a one-myth culture. In English Canada ideological diversity has not been buried beneath an absolutist liberal nationalism. Here Locke is not the one true god; he must tolerate lesser tory and socialist deities at his side. The result is that English Canada does not direct an uncomprehending stare of intolerance at heterodoxy, either within its borders or beyond them. (What a "backlash" Parti-Pris or PSQ-type separatists would be getting if Quebec were in the United States!) In English Canada it has been possible to consider values without arousing the all-silencing cry of treason. Hartz observes that "if history had chosen English Canada for the American role" of directing the Western response to the world revolution, "the international scene would probably have witnessed less McCarthyite hysteria, less Wilsonian messianism."[20]

Americanizing liberals might consider that the Pearsonian rationality and calmness that Canada displays on the world stage— the "mediating" and "peace-keeping" role of which Canadians are so proud—is related to the un-American (tory and socialist) characteristics that they consider to be unnecessary imperfections in English Canadian wholeness. The tolerance of English Canadian domestic politics is also linked with the presence of these imperfections. If the price of Americanization is the surrender of legitimate ideological diversity, even the liberal might think twice before paying it.

Non-liberal British elements have entered into English Canadian society *together* with American liberal elements at the foundations. The fact is that Canada has been greatly influenced by both the United States and Britain. This is not to deny that liberalism is the dominant element in English Canadian political culture; it is to stress that it is not the sole element, that it is accompanied by vital and legitimate streams of toryism and socialism that have as close a relation to English Canada's "essence" or "foundations" as does liberalism. English Canada's "essence" is both liberal and non-liberal.

Neither the British nor the American elements can be explained away as "superstructural" excrescences.

UN-AMERICAN ASPECTS OF CANADIAN CONSERVATISM

So far, I have been discussing the presence of toryism in Canada without referring to the Conservative party. This party can be seen as a party of right-wing or business liberalism, but such an interpretation would be far from the whole truth; the Canadian Conservative party, like the British Conservative party and unlike the Republican party, is not monolithically liberal. If there is a touch of toryism in English Canada, its primary carrier has been the Conservative party. It would not be correct to say that toryism is *the* ideology of the party, or even that some Conservatives are tories. These statements would not be true even of the British Conservative party. The primary component of the ideology of business-oriented parties is liberalism; but there are powerful traces of the old pre-liberal outlook in the British Conservative party, and less powerful but still perceptible traces of it in the Canadian party. A Republican is always a liberal. A Conservative may be at one moment a liberal, at the next moment a tory, and is usually something of both.

If it is true that the Canadian Conservatives can be seen from some angles as right-wing liberals, it is also true that figures such as R. B. Bennett, Arthur Meighen, and George Drew cannot be understood simply as Canadian versions of William McKinley, Herbert Hoover, and Robert Taft. Canadian Conservatives have something British about them that American Republicans do not. It is not simply their emphasis on loyalty to the crown and to the British connections, but a touch of the authentic tory aura—traditionalism, élitism, the strong state, and so on. The Canadian Conservatives lack the American aura of rugged individualism. Theirs is not the characteristically American conservatism that conserves only *liberal* values.

It is possible to perceive in Canadian conservatism not only the elements of business liberalism and orthodox toryism, but also an element of "tory democracy"—the paternalistic concern for the "condition of the people" and the emphasis on the tory party as their champion—which, in Britain, was expressed by such figures as Disraeli and Lord Randolph Churchill. John A. Macdonald's approach to the emergent Canadian working class was in some respects similar to that of Disraeli. Later Conservatives acquired the image of arch reactionaries and arch enemies of the workers, but let us not forget that "Iron Heel" Bennett was also the Bennett of the Canadian New Deal.

The question arises: why is it that in Canada the *Conservative* leader proposes a New Deal? Why is it that the Canadian counterpart of Hoover apes *Roosevelt*? This phenomenon is usually interpreted as sheer historical accident, a product of Bennett's desperation and opportunism. But the answer may be that Bennett was not Hoover. Even in his "orthodox" days Bennett's views on the state's role in the economy were far from similar to Hoover's; Bennett's attitude was that of Canadian, not American, conservatism. Once this is recognized, it is possible to entertain the suggestion that Bennett's sudden radicalism, his sudden concern for the people, may not have been mere opportunism. It may have been a manifestation, a sudden activation under pressure, of a latent tory-democratic streak. Let it be noted also that the Depression produced two Conservative splinter parties, both with "radical" welfare state programs and both led by former subordinates of Bennett: H. H. Stevens's Reconstruction party and W. D. Herridge's New Democracy.

The Bennett New Deal is only the most extreme instance of what is usually considered to be an accident or an aberration—the occasional manifestation of "radicalism" or "leftism" by otherwise orthodox Conservative leaders in the face of opposition from their "followers" in the business community. Meighen, for example, was constantly embroiled with the "Montreal interests" who objected to his railway policies. On one occasion he received a note of congratulation from William Irvine: "The man who dares to offend the Montreal interests is the sort of man that the people are going to vote for."[21] This same Meighen expressed on certain occasions, particularly after his retirement, an antagonism to big government and creeping socialism that would have warmed the heart of Robert Taft; but he combined his business liberalism with gloomy musings about the evil of universal suffrage,[22] musings that Taft would have rejected as un-American. Meighen is far easier to understand from a British than from an American perspective, for he combined, in different proportions at different times, attitudes deriving from all three Conservative ideological streams: right-wing liberalism, orthodox toryism, and tory democracy.

31

The western or agrarian Conservatives of the contemporary period, John Diefenbaker and Alvin Hamilton, who are usually dismissed as "prairie radicals" of the American type, might represent not only anti-Bay Street agrarianism but also the same type of tory democracy as was expressed before their time by orthodox business-sponsored Conservatives such as Meighen and Bennett. The populism (anti-élitism) of Diefenbaker and Hamilton is a geniunely foreign element in Canadian conservatism, but their stress on the Tory party as champion of the people and their advocacy of welfare state policies are in the tory democratic tradition. Their attitudes toward the monarchy, the British connection, and the danger of American domination are entirely orthodox Conservative attitudes. Diefenbaker conservatism is therefore to be understood not simply as a western populist phenomenon, but as an odd *combination* of traditional Conservative views with attitudes absorbed from the western Progressive tradition.

Another aberration that may be worthy of investigation is the Canadian phenomenon of the red tory. At the simplest level, the red tory is a Conservative who prefers the CCF-NDP to the Liberals, or a socialist who prefers the Conservatives to the Liberals, without really knowing why. At a higher level, the red tory is a conscious ideological conservative with some "odd" socialist notions (W. L. Morton) or a conscious ideological socialist with some "odd" tory notions (Eugene Forsey). The very suggestion that such affinities might exist between Republicans and Socialists in the United States is ludicrous enough to make some kind of a point.

Red toryism is, of course, one of the results of the relation between toryism and socialism, which has already been elucidated. The tory and socialist minds have some crucial assumptions, orientations, and values in common, so that from certain angles they may appear not as enemies, but as two different expressions of the same basic ideological outlook. Thus, at the very highest level, the red tory is a philosopher who combines elements of socialism and toryism so thoroughly in a single integrated *Weltanschauung* that it is impossible to say that he or she is a proponent of either one as *against* the other. Such a red tory is George Grant, who has associations with both the Conservative party and the NDP and who has recently published a book that defends Diefenbaker, laments the death of "true" British conservatism in Canada, attacks the Liberals as individualists and Americanizers, and defines socialism as a variant of conservatism (each "protects the public good against private freedom").[23]

THE CHARACTER OF CANADIAN SOCIALISM

Canadian socialism is un-American in two distinct ways. It is un-American in the sense that it is a significant and legitimate political force in Canada, insignificant and alien in the United States. But Canadian socialism is also un-American in the sense that it does not speak the same language as American socialism. In Canada, socialism is British, non-Marxist, and worldly; in the United States it is German, Marxist, and otherworldly.

I have argued that the reasons the socialist ideas of British immigrants to Canada were not sloughed off are that they "fit" with a political culture that already contained non-liberal components, and probably also that they were introduced into the political culture mix before the point of congealment. Thus, socialism was not alien here. But it was not alien in yet another way: it was not borne by foreigners. The personnel and the ideology of the Canadian labour and socialist movements have been primarily British. Many of those who built these movements were British immigrants with past experience in the British labour movement; many others were Canadian-born children of such immigrants. And in British North America, Britons could not be treated as foreigners.

When socialism was brought to the United States, it found itself in an ideological environment in which it could not survive, because Lockean individualism had long since achieved the status of a national religion; the political culture had already congealed, and socialism did not fit. American socialism was alien not only in this ideological sense, but in the ethnic sense as well; it was borne by foreigners from Germany and other continental European countries. These foreigners sloughed off their socialist ideas not simply because such ideas did not "fit" ideologically, but because as foreigners they were going through a general process of Americanization; socialism was only one of many ethnically alien characteristics that had to be abandoned. The immigrant's ideological change was only one incident among many others in the general process of changing his or her entire way of life. According to David Saposs, "the factor that contributed most tellingly to the decline of the socialist movement was that its chief following, the immigrant workers, . . . had become Americanized."[24]

A British socialist immigrant to Canada had a far different experience. The British immigrant was not an "alien" in British North America. The English Canadian culture not only granted legitimacy to his or her political ideas and absorbed them into its wholeness; it absorbed the immigrant into the English Canadian community with relatively little strain, without demanding that he or she change a way of life before being granted full citizenship. He or she was acceptable to begin with, by virtue of being British. It is impossible to understand the differences between American and Canadian socialism without taking into account this immense difference between the ethnic contexts of socialism in the two countries.

The ethnic handicap of American socialism consisted not only in the fact that its personnel was heavily European. Equally important was the fact that it was a *brand* of socialism, Marxism, that found survival difficult not only in the United States but in all English-speaking countries. Marxism has not found the going easy in the United States; nor in Britain, Canada, Australia, or New Zealand. The socialism of the United States, the socialism of De Leon, Berger, Hillquit, and Debs, is predominantly Marxist and doctrinaire, because it is European. The socialism of English Canada, the socialism of Simpson, Woodsworth, and Coldwell, is predominantly Protestant, labourist, and Fabian, because it is British.

The CCF has not been without its otherworldly tendencies: there have been doctrinal disagreements, and the party has always had a left wing interested more in "socialist education" than in practical political work. But this left wing has been a constantly declining minority. The party has expelled individuals and small groups—mostly Communists and Trotskyites—but has never split. Its life has never been threatened by disagreement over doctrinal matters. It is no more preoccupied with theory than the British Labour party. It sees itself, and is seen by the public, not as a coterie of ideologists but as a party like the others, second to none in its avidity for office. If it has been attacked from the right for socialist "utopianism" and "impracticality," it has also been attacked from the right and the left for abandoning the "true" socialist faith in an unprincipled drive for power.

CANADIAN LIBERALISM: THE TRIUMPHANT CENTRE

Canadian Conservatives are not American Republicans; Canadian socialists are not American socialists; Canadian Liberals are not American liberal Democrats.

The un-American elements in English Canada's political culture are most evident in Canadian conservatism and socialism. But Canadian liberalism has a British colour too. The liberalism of Canada's Liberal party should not be identified with the liberalism of the American Democratic party. In many respects they stand in sharp contrast to one another.

The three components of the English Canadian political culture have not developed in isolation from one another; each has developed in interaction with the others. Our toryism and our socialism have been moderated by liberalism. But, by the same token, our liberalism has been rendered "impure," in American terms, through its contacts with toryism and socialism. If English Canadian liberalism is less individualistic, less ardently populistic-democratic, more inclined to state intervention in the economy and more tolerant of "feudal survivals" such as monarchy, this is due to the uninterrupted influence of toryism upon liberalism, an influence wielded in and through the conflict between the two. If English Canadian liberalism has tended since the Depression to merge at its leftist edge with the democratic socialism of the CCF-NDP, this is due to the influence that socialism has exerted upon liberalism, in and through the conflict between them. The key to understanding the Liberal party in Canada is to see it as a *centre* party with *influential* enemies on both right and left.

In English Canada, Liberal Reform, represented by King's Liberal party, has had to face the socialist challenge. Under socialist influence, it abandoned its early devotion to "the lofty principles of Gladstone, the sound economics of Adam Smith, and the glories of laissez-faire."[25] King's *Industry and Humanity* and the Liberal platform of 1919 mark the transition of English Canadian Liberalism from the old individualism to the new Liberal Reform.

King's Liberal Reform, since it had to answer attacks from the left as well as from the right, projected a notoriously ambivalent conservative-radical image:

Truly he will be remembered
Wherever men honour ingenuity
Ambiguity, inactivity and political longevity.

When he faced Bennett and Meighen, King was the radical warrior, the champion of the little people against the interests. When he turned to face Woodsworth and Coldwell, he was the cautious conservative, the protector of the *status quo*. He

... never let his on the one hand
Know what his on the other hand was doing.[26]

Hartz points out that the "pragmatism" of the New Deal enabled it to go further, to get more things done, than European Liberal Reform. "The freewheeling inventiveness typified by the TVA, the NRA, and WPA, the SEC"[27] was nowhere to be found in Europe. Defending itself against socialism, European Liberal Reform could not submerge questions of theory; it had to justify innovations on the basis of a revised liberal ideology; it had to stop short of socialism openly. The New Deal, since it was not threatened by socialism, could ignore theory; it "did not need to stop short of Marx openly"; hence it could accomplish more than European Liberal Reform.

King had to face the socialist challenge. He did so in the manner of European Liberal Reform. The similarity of socialism and Liberal Reform could be acknowledged; indeed it could be emphasized and used to attract the socialist vote. At the same time, King had to answer the arguments of socialism, and in doing so he had to spell out his liberalism. He had to stop short of socialism openly. Social reform, yes; extension of public ownership, yes; the welfare state, yes; increased state control of the economy, yes; but not too much. Not socialism. The result was that King, like the European liberals, could not go as far as Roosevelt. Like the European liberals, and unlike Roosevelt, he had to defend private property, he had to attack excessive reliance on the state, he had to criticize socialism as "impracticality" and "utopianism." "Half radical and half conservative—a tired man who could not make up his mind": is this not the living image of Mackenzie King?

"In America, instead of being a champion of property, Roosevelt became the big antagonist of it; his liberalism was blocked by his radicalism."[28] In Canada, since King had to worry not only about

Bennett and Meighen and Drew but also about Woodsworth and Coldwell and Douglas, he had to embark upon a defence of private property. *He* was no traitor to his class. Instead of becoming the antagonist of property he became its champion; his radicalism was blocked by his liberalism.

An emphasis on the solidarity of the nation as against divisive "class parties" of right and left was "of the very essence of the Reformist Liberal position in Europe." "Who," asks Hartz, "would think of Roosevelt as a philosopher of class solidarity?"[29] Yet that is precisely what Roosevelt would have been if he had had to respond to a socialist presence in the American political culture. And that is precisely what King was, in fact, in Canada. His party was "the party of national unity." One of the most repeated charges against the CCF was that it was a divisive "class party"; the purpose of the Liberal party, on the other hand, was to preserve the solidarity of the Canadian people, the solidarity of its classes as well as the solidarity of French and English.

The Liberal party has continued to speak the language of King: ambiguous and ambivalent, presenting first its radical face and then its conservative face, urging reform and warning against hasty ill-considered change, calling for increased state responsibility but stopping short of socialism, openly speaking for the common people but preaching the solidarity of classes.

In the United States, the liberal Democrats are on the left. There is no doubt about that. In Canada, the Liberals are a party of the centre, appearing at times leftist and at times rightist. As such, they are much closer to European, especially British, Liberal Reform than to the American New Deal type of liberalism.

In the United States, the liberal Democrats are the party of organized labour. The new men of power, the labour leaders, have arrived politically; their vehicle is the Democratic party. In English Canada, if the labour leaders have arrived politically they have done so in the CCF-NDP. They are nowhere to be found in the Liberal party. The rank and file, in the United States, are predominantly Democrats; in Canada at least a quarter are New Democrats, and the remainder show only a relatively slight, and by no means consistent, preference for the Liberals as against the Conservatives.

In the United States, left-wing "liberalism," as opposed to right-wing "liberalism," has always meant opposition to the domination of American life by big business, and has expressed itself in and through the Democratic party; the party of business is the Republican party. In Canada, business is close to both the Conservatives and the Liberals. The business community donates to the campaign funds of both and is represented in the leadership circles of both.

The Liberal party in Canada does not represent the opposition of society to domination by organized business. It claims to be based on no particular groups, but on *all*. It is not against any particular group; it is for *all*. The idea that there is any real conflict between groups is dismissed, and the very terms "right" and "left" are rejected. "The terms 'right' and 'left' belong to those who regard politics as a class struggle. . . . The Liberal view is that true political progress is marked by . . . the reconciliation of classes, and the promotion of the general interest above all particular interests."[30]

A party of the left can be distinguished from parties of the centre and right according to two interrelated criteria: its policy approach and its electoral support.

POLICY APPROACH

The policy approach of a left party is to introduce innovations on behalf of the lower strata. The Liberals, unlike the liberal Democrats, have not been a party of innovation. As a centre party they have allowed the CCF-NDP to introduce innovations; they have then waited for signs of substantial acceptance by all strata of the population and for signs of reassurance against possible electoral reprisals before actually proceeding to implement the innovations. Of course, by this time they are, strictly speaking, no longer innovations. The centre party recoils from the fight for controversial measures; it loves to implement a consensus. Roosevelt was the innovator *par excellence*. King, though he was in his own mind in favour of reform, stalled until public demand for innovation was so great and so clear that he could respond to it without antagonizing his business-sponsored right wing. He rationalized his caution into a theory of democratic leadership far different from Roosevelt's conception of the strong presidency:

Mackenzie King's conception of political leadership, which he often expressed, was that a leader should make his objectives clear, but that leadership was neither liberal nor democratic which tried to force new policies . . . on a public that did not consent to them.[31]

38

"He believed that nothing was so likely to set back a good cause as premature action."[32] This was the official Liberal explanation of King's failure to embark on any far-reaching program of reform until 1943. King himself undoubtedly believed that his caution was based at least in part on a "democratic" theory of leadership. But his diaries suggest that the reforms came when they did because CCF pressure became so threatening that it could no longer be ignored by King's right-wing colleagues—so threatening that King felt able to surrender to it without jeopardizing the unity of his party. The bare facts are these: in August 1943, the CCF became the official opposition in Ontario. In September 1943, the CCF overtook the Liberals in the Gallup poll (Canada: CCF 19 percent, Liberals 28 percent; Ontario: CCF 32 percent, Liberals 26 percent; the West: CCF 41 percent, Liberals 23 percent).[33] King's reaction is summed up in the following quotation from his diary:

In my heart, I am not sorry to see the mass of the people coming a little more into their own, but I do regret that it is not the Liberal party that is winning the position for them. . . . It can still be that our people will learn their lesson in time. What I fear is we will begin to have defections from our own ranks in the House to the CCF.[34]

Almost immediately after the release of the September Gallup poll, the Advisory Council of the National Liberal Federation, meeting at King's request, adopted 14 resolutions "constituting a programme of reform . . . of far reaching consequences."[35] King wrote in his diary, "I have succeeded in making declarations which will improve the lot of . . . farmers and working people. . . . I think I have cut the ground in large part from under the CCF."[36]

The Liberal slogan in the campaign of 1945 was "A New Social Order for Canada." The election of June 11 returned King to power with a drastically reduced majority. The CCF vote rose from 8.5 percent to 15.6 percent, and its representation in the Commons from 8 to 29. But King's swing to the left had defeated the CCF's bid for major party status. The CCF's success was much smaller than it had expected. The success was actually a defeat, a disappointing shock from which socialism in Canada has not yet recovered.

The Liberal-CCF relationship in 1943-45 is only the sharpest and clearest instance of the permanent interdependence forced upon each by the presence of the other, a relationship that one student describes as "antagonistic symbiosis." The Liberals depend on the CCF-NDP for innovations; the CCF-NDP depends upon the Liberals for implementation of the innovations. When the left is weak, as before and after World War II, the centre party moves right to deal with the Conservative challenge; when the left is strengthened, as during the war and after the formation of the NDP, the centre moves left to deal with the challenge.

In a conversation between King and Coldwell shortly before King's death, King expressed his regrets that Coldwell had not joined him. With Coldwell at his side, he would have been able to implement reforms that were close to his heart, reforms that had either been postponed until the end of the war or not introduced at all. He said the CCF had performed the valuable function of popularizing reforms so that he could introduce them when public opinion was ripe. Coldwell replied that it was impossible for him to join King, especially in view of the people who surrounded King.[37] There, in a nutshell, is the story of the relations between the Liberal party and the CCF-NDP. The Liberals, says King, are too conservative because the left has not joined them. The left has not joined them, replies Coldwell, because they are too conservative.

King wanted to show the people that he was "true to them." He was saddened that the CCF and not the Liberals were fighting the people's battles. But he could not move from dead centre until CCF power became so great that the necessity of moving was clear, not only to himself but to all realistic politicians. King's best self wanted to innovate; yet he saw the Liberal party not as a great innovating force but as the party that would implement reforms once they had been popularized by the CCF. Yet he wanted to absorb the CCF. The lot of the centrist politician is not a happy one.

The absence of Lockean "monotheism" strengthened socialism in Canada. Socialism was present in the political culture when liberalism began to concern itself with the problems of the industrial age; liberalism was therefore forced to react to the socialist challenge. In doing so, it was cast in the mould of European Liberal Reform (centre) parties—ambivalent, radical, and conservative, alternating attacks on the *status quo* with defence of the *status quo*. Socialism had sufficient strength in English Canada to force liberalism into the European rather than the American position, centre rather than left. King's liberalism was therefore not capable of reacting to the Depression in the Rooseveltian manner. As a result, socialist power grew.

Socialism was not powerless, so there was no New Deal. There was no New Deal, so socialism grew more powerful. Socialism grew more powerful, so King reacted with "A New Social Order for Canada." The centre and the left dance around one another, frustrating one another and living off the frustration; each is locked into the dance by the existence of the other.

I have been stressing the strength of Canadian socialism in order to make clear the differences between the Canadian and the American situations. Of course this does not mean that the differences between Canada and Europe can be ignored. Canadian socialism has been strong enough to challenge liberalism, to force liberalism to explain itself, and thus to evoke from it the same sort of centrist response as was evoked in Europe. But socialism in Canada has not been strong enough to match or overshadow liberalism. The CCF became a significant political force, but, except for the years 1942-45, it never knocked on the gates of national power.

In Europe, the working person could not be appeased by the concession of Liberal Reform. The centre was squeezed out of existence between its enemies on the right and on the left. In Canada, the centre party's concessions were sufficient to keep the lower strata from flocking en masse to the left. The concessions were not sufficient to *dispose* of the socialist threat, but they were sufficient to draw the socialists' sharpest teeth. In Canada the centre party emerged triumphant over its enemies on the right and on the left. Here, then, is another aspect of English Canada's uniqueness: it is the only society in which Liberal Reform faces the challenge of socialism *and* emerges victorious. The English Canadian fragment *is* bourgeois. The toryism and the socialism, though significant, *are* "touches."

ELECTORAL SUPPORT

There is a dearth of information about the influence of class on voting behaviour in Canada, but there are strong indications that the higher strata are more likely than the lower to vote Conservative, the lower strata are more likely than the higher to vote CCF-NDP, and both groups are about *equally* attracted to the Liberals. This would, of course, confirm the picture of Conservatives as the right, NDP as the left, and Liberals as the "classless" centre. This is in sharp contrast to the situation in the United States, where the lower strata prefer the Democrats, the higher prefer the Republicans, and there is no centre party.

Although this picture of the relation between class and voting is broadly true, it is also true that class voting in Canada is, generally speaking, overshadowed by regional and religious-ethnic voting. In some parts of Canada, Ontario for example, class voting is as high as in the United States or higher. Nevertheless, in Canada *considered as a whole* class voting is lower than in the United States; non-class motivations appear to be very strong.[38] Peter Regenstrief suggests that one factor accounting for this is the persistent cultivation by the Liberal party of its classless image, its "abhorrence of anything remotely associated with class politics,"[39] its refusal to appeal to any class *against* any other class.

What this points to again is the unique character of English Canada as the only society in which the centre triumphs over left and right. In Europe the classless appeal of Liberal Reform does not work; the centre is decimated by the defection of high-status adherents to the right and of low-status adherents to the left. In Canada, the classless appeal of King's centrism is the winning strategy, drawing lower-class support to the Liberals away from the left parties and higher-class support away from the right parties. This forces the left and right parties themselves to emulate (to a certain extent) the Liberals' classless strategy. The Conservatives transform themselves into Progressive Conservatives. The CCF transforms itself from a "farmer-labour" party into an NDP calling for the support of "all liberally minded Canadians." The Liberal refusal to appear as a class party forces both right and left to mitigate their class appeals and to become themselves, in a sense, centre parties.

Class voting in Canada may be lower than in the United States, not entirely because regional-religious-ethnic factors are "objectively" stronger here, but also because King liberalism, by resolutely avoiding class symbols, has *made* other symbols more important.

He blunted us.
We have no shape
Because he never took sides,
And no sides,
Because he never allowed them to take shape.[40]

NOTES

1. Louis Hartz, *The Liberal Tradition in America* (New York: Harcourt, Brace and World, 1955).
2. ———, *The Founding of New Societies* (New York: Harcourt, Brace and World, 1964).
3. Hartz, *New Societies* 3.
4. ———, *New Societies* 25.
5. ———, *New Societies* 7.
6. ———, *New Societies* 34.
7. Seymour Martin Lipset, *The First New Nation* (New York: Basic Books, 1963), esp. ch. 7.
8. William Nelson, *The American Tory* (Oxford: Clarendon Press, 1961) 189-90.
9. Hartz, *New Societies* 91.
10. ———, *New Societies* 243.
11. Lipset 251.
12. Hartz, *New Societies* 245.
13. ———, *New Societies* 15.
14. ———, *New Societies* 10.
15. ———, *Liberal Tradition* 11.
16. ———, *New Societies* 23.
17. ———, *New Societies* 119.
18. ———, *New Societies* 35.
19. ———, *New Societies* 119.
20. ———, *New Societies* 120.
21. Roger Graham, *Arthur Meighen*, 2 Volumes (Toronto: Clarke, Irwin, 1963), 2: 269.
22. Graham 3: 71-74.
23. George Grant, *Lament for a Nation* (Toronto: McClelland and Stewart, 1965) 71.
24. David Saposs, *Communism in American Unions* (New York: McGraw-Hill, 1959) 7.
25. Bruce Hutchison, *The Incredible Canadian* (Toronto: Longmans, Green and Co., 1952) 6.
26. F. R. Scott, "W.M.L.K.," *The Blasted Pine*, ed. F. R. Scott and A. J. M. Smith (Toronto: Macmillan, 1962) 28.
27. Hartz, *Liberal Tradition* 271.
28. ———, *Liberal Tradition* 267.
29. ———, *Liberal Tradition* 267.
30. J. W. Pickersgill, *The Liberal Party* (Toronto: McClelland and Stewart, 1962) 68.

31. Pickersgill, *Party* 26-27.
32. J. W. Pickersgill, *The Mackenzie King Record* (Toronto: University of Toronto Press, 1960) 10.
33. *The Globe and Mail* 29 September 1943.
34. Pickersgill, *Record* 571.
35. National Liberal Federation, *The Liberal Party* 53.
36. Pickersgill, *Record* 601.
37. M. J. Coldwell, personal interview, 28 March 1962.
38. R. Alford, *Party and Society* (Chicago: Rand McNally, 1963) ch. 9.
39. Peter Regenstrief, "Group Perceptions and the Vote," *Papers on the 1962 Election*, ed. John Meisel (Toronto, University of Toronto Press, 1964) 249.
40. Scott 27.

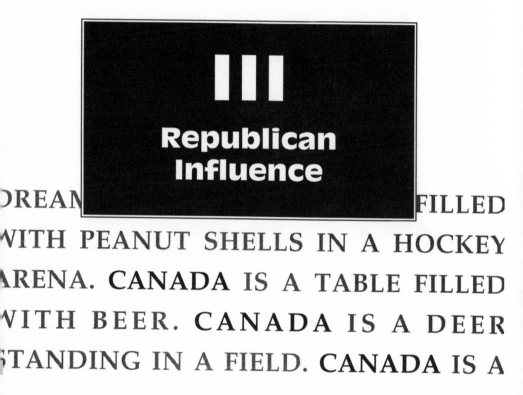

III

Republican Influence

DREAM FILLED WITH PEANUT SHELLS IN A HOCKEY ARENA. CANADA IS A TABLE FILLED WITH BEER. CANADA IS A DEER STANDING IN A FIELD. CANADA IS A

CHAPTER THREE

THE IDEOLOGICAL ORIGINS OF CANADIAN CONFEDERATION

Peter J. Smith

This article discusses the ideological origins of Canadian Confederation. It directly challenges a belief commonly held by Canadian political scientists and historians that Canadian Confederation was the product of a purely pragmatic exercise.[1] It will argue instead that the ideological origins of the Canadian federal state may be traced to the debate that characterized eighteenth- and nineteenth-century British, American, and French political culture, a debate between the defenders of classical republican values and the proponents of a rising commercial ideology formulated during the Enlightenment. The participants in this debate held clashing views of the state and its role in society. Only by understanding how this debate unfolded in nineteenth-century Canada can the particular configuration of the Canadian state that emerged triumphant in the 1860s be understood. Furthermore, an understanding of this debate also offers political scientists a broader context for interpreting long-held Canadian attitudes toward authority, the uses of political patronage, the public debt, capitalism, and the state and economic development.

This insight into the ideological origins of the Canadian state has only been made possible by the remarkable transformation that has occurred in the interpretation of seventeenth-, eighteenth-, and even nineteenth-century trans-Atlantic political thought. New scholarship on the Whig Revolution of 1688, the American Revolution of 1776, the Scottish Enlightenment, and the Jeffersonian era has, among other things, called into question the long-standing perception of John Locke as the fountainhead of eighteenth-century Anglo-American political culture. The list of contributors to this scholarly revisionism is impressive, the most notable being John Pocock.[2] As a result of these efforts, a richer and more complex assessment of the political and social thought of the period is now possible. Critical to this new understanding is an appreciation of the debate between, on the one hand, civic humanism, with its emphasis on civic virtue and classical citizenship (*homo politicus*), and, on the other, a commercial ideology with its emphasis on the economic (*homo mercator*).

One of the puzzling omissions of this intellectual renaissance is that while it has shed new light on the Anglo-American and even French political traditions, it has had little to say about Canada.[3] This is, indeed, curious, given that Canada received such an influx of immigrants from both the United States and Britain in the eighteenth and nineteenth centuries. Clearly, the revised perceptions of trans-Atlantic political thought provide valuable insights into not only Canadian political culture, but also the creation of Canadian political institutions, particularly federalism. I will argue that the debate between wealth and virtue, which reached its height in the writings of the Scottish Enlightenment, is critical to comprehending the clash between Reformer and tory in nineteenth-century Canada. I will begin by tracing the development of this debate in Britain, France, and America. Special consideration is given to the conflicting views of the state held by both sides in this debate. Next, the article examines the appearance of this debate in nineteenth century Canada, stressing the radically different perspectives Reformers and tories had of the state, particularly the idea of union, federal and legislative. Finally, this study shows how the tory conception of the state predominated in 1867.

THE DIALECTICS OF WEALTH AND VIRTUE

In historical terms the development of the civic humanist paradigm preceded the development of the commercial ideology, the latter responding to the former. Civic humanism had as its starting point the idea of virtue, which in turn was based on the ancient Greek and Roman notions of citizenship. Man, it was argued, was a political animal (*zoon politikon*) who fulfilled himself as a human being by participating in politics and by acting selflessly for the public good. Unfortunately, however, not everyone was fit for citizenship, since citizenship required a material base, preferably land, which gave individuals the personal independence and permanent stake in their country necessary to motivate them to act on its behalf. Citizenship, moreover, had a moral as well as material aspect, for if at any time those who should be devoting themselves to citizenship were led, for whatever reason, to place their personal private interests before public virtue, then according to the strict canons of civic humanism the political community would be threatened by corruption. Corruption was an active, destructive force that, if not checked, would erode the moral commitment of citizens to participate. The result would surely be a degeneration into despotic rule and the loss of political liberty.

This depiction of the ideal citizen, which had its roots in the ancient world, had been revived in the modern era by Machiavelli and James Harrington. The meaning assigned to corruption, for example, was Machiavellian, referring to those changes that might undermine the material base and the moral and institutional superstructure of the political community.

In eighteenth-century Britain elements opposed to the ruling whig oligarchy led by such figures as Lord Bolingbroke, John Trenchard, and Thomas Gordon, known otherwise as the Country party or Country opposition, saw corruption and decay near at hand.[4] One sure sign of corruption was the emergence of new forms of property, finance, and commerce, which in Country eyes injected luxury into society and brought certain decay. Greatly feared, therefore, was the financial and commercial revolution sweeping England. This had not only created a new class of moneyed men but also a vast expansion of state administration and public credit. Together they helped provide the places and pensions, the political patronage used to "entice" members of parliament into supporting the ministers of the Crown. Civic humanism, as it was incorporated into opposition thought, served as a powerful indictment against established or Court whiggism and its system of corruption, credit, and commerce. While in political terms the Country opposition accepted the notion of a parliamentary monarchy, it greatly feared the tendency of the Crown to centralize power and encroach on the independence of Parliament, and advocated instead some kind of separation of powers.

The most effective response to civic humanism may be found in the thought of the Scottish political economists. Although Scottish social theory provided an ideological justification for the whig regime, one must be careful not to reduce Scottish thought to only a debate between Court and Country. By Pocock's own admission his is a "tunnel history," the pursuit of a particular theme to its limits. Scottish thought was broader, and explored other dimensions and themes. In recent years scholars have re-examined Scottish social theory and put emphasis on yet another aspect—the importance of natural jurisprudence and the influence of Pufendorf and other natural law theorists on the Scots. These scholars, in turn, play down the centrality of the Scottish reply to civic humanism.[5]

Evidence abounds, however, of the importance of the Scottish encounter with civic humanism. In their response to civic humanism the Scots were intent on demonstrating how virtue and commerce could be reconciled. To do this it was necessary to transform the meaning of virtue by redefining it in a civil, not a civic, sense. That is, the accent on virtue was placed on the social—the economic, cultural, and moral—and not on the political and military.[6] Indeed, it can be argued that the Scots had but little choice to proceed along these lines, for with the Union with England in 1707, a union designed to stimulate Scotland's economic development, Scotsmen had sacrificed the institutional means by which civic virtue could be practised. As the writings of Nicholas Phillipson indicate, there arose in Edinburgh a form of Addisonian social culture, with clubs and societies devoted to improving economic efficiency, manners, learning, and letters. The civil virtues of politeness and enlightened taste replaced the civic humanist virtue of political participation.

The Scots, in brief, provided a sophisticated rebuttal to the charges made by opposition thinkers on the negative effects of wealth and luxury. Of all the Scots it was Hume who made the sharpest critique of opposition thought. Hume defended, for example, the system of commerce, wealth, luxury, and patronage that the civic humanists saw as such a threat. Commercial societies, he believed, were those societies most conducive to the creation of wealth and luxury, which he viewed in positive terms. Hume also criticized "men of severe morals [who] blame even the most innocent luxury and present it as the source of all the corruptions . . . incident to a civil government."[7] Furthermore, Hume favoured the Crown's use of patronage and influence to control Parliament, so necessary, he believed, to preserving the balance of Britain's mixed constitution. Another of Scotland's literati, Adam Smith, expressed similar views on the necessity for Crown "patronage" and "influence." Surveying the problems of the American colonies, Smith concluded that "the executive power has not the means to corrupt the colonial legislatures."[8]

What emerges, then, from the thought of the Scottish thinkers, in particular that of Hume and Smith, is the view of the state as important not so much as a means of political participation and fulfilment of political personality, but as a means of ensuring economic development. The state was charged with governing a complex market society, which while it enlarged men's faculties and encouraged politeness, simultaneously awakened ambitions, passions, and interests that were detrimental to the public good. The state therefore had to provide the framework of justice in which self-seeking individuals with their property and specialization were protected by law and authority. The purpose of government, after all, said Smith, was "to secure wealth and defend the rich from the poor."[9]

While Hume and Smith saw the relation between the state and economic development as complementary—the state protecting increasing wealth, increasing wealth providing revenue for a stronger state—they had differing opinions on a variety of issues. The most important of these was the critical issue of tolerating the public debt, which, along with the Bank of England, had underwritten the financial revolution that had so greatly altered the face of British political economy.[10] Hume, fearing that the public debt would lead to national bankruptcy, warned, "either the nation must destroy public credit or public credit must destroy the nation."[11] Adam Smith did not share Hume's dire pessimism on the public debt, although he did acknowledge that it might potentially grow too large and ruin the nation. To relieve the public debt Smith endorsed such financial instruments as the sinking fund, a special fund designed to eliminate the national debt. It was partially because the public debt was "contracted in the defence not of Great Britain alone, but of all the different provinces of the empire" that Smith advocated a union with

Ireland and America "to discharge the public debt."[12] Smith's idea that union might be used as a credit instrument to alleviate public debt and promote political stability parallels Canadian thinking, as I will indicate in the following section.

It should be stressed at this point that the debate over civic humanism was not merely an Anglo-American debate. It was a trans-Atlantic debate, keenly observed and commented on by the French, particularly Montesquieu, an object of admiration in Great Britain and the British colonies. In many ways *The Spirit of the Laws* reads as a synopsis of the debate over civic humanism, and he was acclaimed as an authority by all sides. It was in America, in particular, that the civic humanist paradigm, described by American scholars as the republican synthesis, was to be most pronounced, shaping not only the ideological justification for independence, but surviving throughout the Jeffersonian era and beyond in populist movements and in contemporary American political culture. In Bernard Bailyn's opinion, "the effective triggering convictions that lay behind the [American] Revolution were derived not from common Lockean generalities but from the specific fears and formulations of the radical publicists and opposition politicians of early eighteenth century England."[13] To many American colonists the English had become corrupt, and thereby lost the necessary qualities for freedom depicted in opposition thought. Americans, on the other hand, were certain that they were a virtuous people (in a civic sense), capable of sustaining a free society and a free government.

The social turmoil brought on in part by the Revolution and by America's increasing social heterogeneity undermined this optimism among revolutionary leaders. James Madison, for example, came to believe that Americans no longer fully possessed the moral qualities so necessary for a virtuous people and republic. Furthermore, America was too extensive and too diverse to form a single republican state. Madison, in his attempts to address the complex relation between representation, virtue, and extent of territory, is said to have relied heavily on David Hume's essay, "Idea of a Perfect Commonwealth."[14] Hume's idea of a perfect republic represented a means of avoiding the classical dilemma of choosing an appropriate form of government for a large territory. One did not have to choose between monarchy or the tumultous discord of small republics. In his essay Hume had argued,

In a large government, which is modelled with masterly skill, there is compass and room enough to refine the democracy, from the lower people, who may be admitted into the first elections or first concoction of the commonwealth, to the higher magistrates, who direct all the movements. At the same time the parts are so distant and remote, that it is very difficult, either by intrigue, prejudice or passion, to hurry them into any measures against the public interest.[15]

In the American case, what was being refined was civic virtue, which regrettably had become mixed with local bias and self-interest. The further one was removed from the people, that is, the more refined the choice of representative, the better the chance for distilled virtue, or the ability to act for the public good. The exclusion of citizens from direct participation in decision-making was, according to Madison, one of the strengths of the new republic created in Philadelphia. Its other great advantage, in Madison's opinion, was the institutionalization of factions and parties with their self-seeking passions, ambitions, and interests into "the necessary and ordinary operations of government."[16]

It is evident, then, that American Federalists were edging toward (but had not arrived at) the thought of Court whiggism. Alexander Hamilton went so far as to advocate the Court system of governing by influence, invoking Hume's name in its defence.[17] The advantages of an enlarged polity with enhanced political authority to restrain the passions and ambitions of men were now apparent. A strong central government with a powerful executive could govern a large territory and keep the states and people in check.

However much the federalism of Madison and Hamilton may have altered opposition thought, it did not signal its dénouement in America. In the 1790s Thomas Jefferson and the Republicans criticized Hamilton in much the same manner as the Country party had criticized Walpole and the whig regime seventy years previously. At the heart of the Republican differences with Washington's government were Hamilton's policies, which included a vision of America as a great centralized commercial and military empire bound together by public credit, British investment, a healthy system of public finance including a national bank, a standing army, and a powerful executive.[18] The Republican disdain for commercial capitalism and urban life became a fundamental component of the American political tradition, and was best personified in the antipathy of Thomas Jefferson toward David Hume. What Hume extolled,

Jefferson denounced. While the English may have once been a wise and virtuous people,

Commerce and a corrupt government have rotted them to the core. Every generous, nay, every just sentiment, is absorbed in the thirst for gold. I speak of their cities, which we may certainly pronounce to be ripe for despotism, and fitted for no other government. Whether the leaven of the agricultural body is sufficient to regenerate the residuary mass, and maintain it as a sound state, under any reformation of government, may well be doubted.[19]

The above discussion, I would argue, clearly indicates the extent to which the debate over civic humanism, with its emphasis on the dialectic of wealth and virtue, provides a new alternative for the study not only of eighteenth-century British and French political culture, but also of the turbulence of the revolutionary era in America and the rise of Jeffersonian democracy. Furthermore, there is ample evidence to indicate that this debate continued into nineteenth-century America, Britain, France, and Canada as well. Admittedly it does not tell the entire story, for it was to be complemented by admixtures of other belief systems, for example, those of the Dissenting religions, Cobbett radicalism, Chartism, Utilitarianism, Socialism, and Cobdenism. Yet throughout the nineteenth century the concept of corruption, with all its moral connotations, was used to attack the established order.[20] As Robert Kelley notes, in England, Canada, and America,

Tories and Republicans, as Liberal-Democrats saw the matter, ruled not simply through aristocratic elites, but through skillful use of corruption. From Jefferson's day to Cleveland few issues so obsessed the Liberal-Democratic mind as this one. . . . In nineteenth century Canadian and American politics, Liberal-Democratics were convinced that corruption was the principal danger that faced democracy and responsible government. [Alexander] McKenzie and Cleveland both believed it was the enemy's chief means for deforming the government and debasing the morals of the people at large.[21]

LAND AND COMMERCE: THE CANADIAN DEBATE

It is evident, then, that in the nineteenth century, fear of corruption was still widespread, its presence fed by centralization and growing executive power. Those opposed to corruption, like their predecessors in the eighteenth century, emphasized the importance of virtue, independence, political participation, decentralization of political power (in the United States and Canada at least), and the primacy of the petty producer. Furthermore, it was realized that capitalism, particularly commercial and financial capitalism, would lead to the destruction of the participatory society and toward a society and state based on privilege, influence, and centralized political power.

In Canada, the quarrel between agrarian and commercial interests had its origins in the early years of the nineteenth century. According to Donald Creighton, "the most important feature of the new age was ... the growing antipathy between the merchants and the small rural proprietors." Commenting upon the situation in Upper Canada, Creighton notes that "this quarrel conformed in general to a type of political conflict which was repeated regularly throughout the history of the Thirteen Colonies and the United States."[22]

Reformist Perspectives on State and Society

This antipathy between agrarian and commercial interests was particularly marked in Upper and Lower Canada, and centred around a bitter battle over patronage, tories believing the government possessed too little, Reformers believing it had too much. The struggle over patronage in both provinces was critical, representing, as it had in eighteenth-century England, the battle to control the civil list and public expenditure. Reformers like William Lyon Mackenzie perceived the Crown's influence as a threat to legislative independence. He asserted that "the power of the Crown had increased, is increasing and ought to be diminished."[23] Mackenzie's statement, however, was not original. He had taken it from John Dunning, an eighteenth-century British parliamentarian and supporter of the Country program, who had used the same words in support of a motion he brought before the House of Commons in April 1780.[24] Mackenzie and other members of the Upper Canadian Assembly proceeded to claim in their Seventh Report on Grievances that "the almost unlimited extent of the patronage of the Crown, or rather of the Colonial Minister for the time being and his advisers here, together with the abuse of patronage are the chief causes of colonial discontent."[25]

In Lower Canada Papineau expressed similar sentiments, charging in 1831 that the provincial administration was corrupt "in its head and in all its members" and that the "hirelings" who administered it were "too corrupt to be reformed and too rotten and too gangrenous to be healed."[26] The Ninety-two Resolutions of 1834 were to make a similar point. Crown influence, though, was just one aspect of a societal system of influence and corruption that was threatening the independence of the petit-bourgeoisie. Commercial and financial capitalism with its banks and credit system was every bit as threatening. A Reformist newspaper, *The Constitution* of Toronto, advised farmers to look upon the Bank of Upper Canada as their enemy, maintaining that "this abominable engine of the state has been the curse of Canada. It has controlled our elections, corrupted our representatives, depreciated our currency, obliged even Governors and Colonial ministers to bow to its mandates."[27]

Against the tory system of centralized élite control and influence Reformers posed democracy. Democracy, to Reformers, did not simply refer to a system of government, it referred to a type of society as well. What was being argued, in Aristotelian terms, was that the social constitution of a country, its material base, very much limited the institutions that could be erected upon it. Papineau, for example, argued that the social base of Canada was democratic, and he dreamed of a one-class democracy of small property owners. In 1836 he proclaimed in the House, "The Ministers have wished to put into action and into force aristocratic principles in the Canadas[,] whose social constitution is essentially democratic, where everyone is born and dies a democrat; because everyone is a property owner; because everyone has small properties."[28]

Democracy, moreover, required special qualities of a people. If virtuous, one political pamphlet claimed, the people "would keep the reins of government in their hands until corruption and intrigue wrested them out." Being a system based upon virtue, democracy was the "only form of government . . . in accordance with every feeling of an honest heart, and the happiness and prosperity of any country. Let education be encouraged, and a strict guard placed against corruption; and then democracy will be as lasting as the world."[29]

The people, in the opinion of Reformers, French and English, represented the petty producers of Canada, particularly the farmer. One letter to the *Upper Canadian Agriculturalist and Canadian Journal* went further than most when it claimed farmers are the *first class*, in the noblest and best sense. The Merchants, Mechanics, Priests, Lawyers, Artists, Literati, etc., etc., are all non-producers—mere hangers-on, dependents of the husbandman. He can do without them, they cannot live without him. If you wish to see genuine virtue, true patriotism, unostentatious benevolence, sterling honesty and practical piety, go among the cultivators of the soil. Look not for these rarities in the crowded city; they will not vegetate in the tainted atmosphere that surrounds the haunts of busy, plotting rivalry, priestly intrigue, scheming political selfishness, loyal trickery, and reckless commercial gambling. Even in a country as young as Canada, with a changing, heterogeneous population, the truth of this contrast becomes every day plainer to the view. The sturdy yeoman are the true conservatives of society. They are the substratum—the foundation of the social fabric—and if that be defective, the whole building will tumble in ruins. It has been so in all past time, in all countries, it is so in ours.[30]

Because farmers formed the "substratum" of society, it was argued that political institutions, like other social institutions, had to reflect this fact. Government, like the farmer, had to be simple, honest, independent, virtuous, and close to the people. A one-class democracy of property owners demanded a more democratic government. The House of Assembly, for example, had to be independent and the principal forum of decision-making, not the executive or legislative council. What was needed was responsible government conducting public affairs with the advice of officers possessing the confidence of the people's representatives in Parliament. Government also had to be cheaper, efficient, debt-free, and responsive to local concerns. Inevitably comparisons were made with state governments in the United States, which seemed to possess these features. However, only when the House of Assembly controlled public expenditures and taxation could the goal of cheap, simple government be realized.

The efforts of Reformers to construct a society and state harmonizing with their vision were dealt a severe blow by the failure of the 1837 Rebellion, which severed the links between the more radical Reform leaders (who were either exiled, imprisoned, or hanged) and their rural base. In the decade that followed, a much more moderate urban Reform leadership emerged, with Robert Baldwin, Francis Hincks, and Louis Hippolyte Lafontaine becoming the primary spokesmen for responsible government. Linked intimately to the emerging notion of responsible government was the very old quarrel over patronage.[31] Baldwin and Lafontaine demanded, and eventually received, the power to control dismissals and make appointments so necessary to open the system to their supporters and build a political base. The result in Canada, as in the United States, was the introduction of the spoils system into the civil service. In the decades that followed, patronage became the "guiding principle" of civil service appointments, with scant regard for efficiency and merit. It is, indeed, highly ironic that in Canada, as in the United States under Andrew Jackson, the "democratizing" of appointments through the spoils system did not have the salutary effect that early Reformers thought it would. Offices became the rewards of party loyalty, and political patronage and corruption became entrenched more strongly than ever before.

The old Reform hostility to patronage and corruption was by no means extinguished, however. In Upper Canada in the late 1840s, the Clear Grits, reasserting the more radical agrarian element of Reformism, emerged to challenge what they perceived as the bland, moderate élitism of Baldwin. The Clear Grits were unabashed in their admiration for the American political system. As one of their supporters, the Toronto *Examiner*, put it, "must we abjure a republican simplicity and assume the paraphernalia ... of an aristocratical government?"[32]

While the Clear Grits became a significant political force in Upper Canadian politics, the established Reform party, now led by George Brown and an alliance of rural and urban forces dominated by Toronto business interests, rejected their platform, which had planks calling for election of officials throughout government, including the governor, the legislative council, and "public functionaries of every grade."[33] Despite Brown's close business connections, his paper, the *Globe*, peppered its pages with the traditional language of Reform. The *Globe* spoke frequently of the "intelligent and incorruptible yeomanry" of Upper Canada, and never tired of attacking the corruption of the cities, the Grand Trunk, and the bureaucracy.[34]

In Lower Canada the radical elements of the Reform movement never revived to the extent they did in Upper Canada. Unlike Robert Baldwin, who abandoned politics under the pressure of growing radicalism, Lafontaine, aided by his adept dispensation of patronage, managed to turn back the challenge posed by the Rouge party. Lafontaine grew steadily more conservative, strengthened by his alliance with the increasingly Ultramontane Catholic Church, which had replaced the professional petit-bourgeoisie as leader of the habitants.

The habitants, the social base of early French-Canadian Reformism, became disillusioned by the Rebellion's defeat and gradually slipped into a value system that, while retaining much of its agrarian republican symbolism, became both politically and economically conservative, retreating from politics as well as commerce. This value system was combined with messianism and antistatism and is best reflected in the popular literature of the period. Novels were filled with the image of the land and the Catholic Church as sources of the economic and cultural salvation of French Canadians. The most popular was Antoine Gérin-Lajoie's *Jean Rivard*, which was widely read in French Canada in both the nineteenth and twentieth centuries. Originally printed in 1862, it enjoyed ten printings, seven alone between 1913 and 1958.[35] Gérin-Lajoie's values are captured succinctly in an abstract taken from his diary of 1849:

I have returned to my project of going to live in the country as soon as possible. Oh, if only I were a farmer! He does not become rich by beggaring others, as lawyers, doctors, and merchants sometimes do. He draws his wealth from the earth: his is the state most natural to man. Farmers form the least egotistical and most virtuous class of the population. But this class has need of educated men who can serve its interests. The educated farmer has all the leisure necessary to do good; he can serve as a guide to his neighbours, counsel the ignorant, sustain the weak, and defend him against the rapacity of the speculator. The enlightened and virtuous farmer is to my mind the best type of man.[36]

As is clearly evident, the power of the republican idea, its disdain for commercial and city life, and its praise of agrarian pursuits, are central themes in Gérin-Lajoie's work. In *Jean Rivard* the parish, in essence, becomes a mini-republic possessing the virtuous life missing in the city. The plight of the unemployed professional and the salesman looking for jobs in business is contrasted with the rosy well-being of the farmer. Writes one of the central characters from the city to the hero:

If you knew my friend, how much anxiety and poverty are hidden sometimes under a fashionable topcoat. One thing is certain, in the agricultural classes, with all their frugality, simplicity and apparent deprivation, there is a thousand times more happiness and I might say real wealth than in the homes of the majority of our city dwellers with their borrowed luxury and deceitful life.[37]

There is little in this to differentiate it from other portrayals of the rural republican ideal sketched so far. What is distinctive, however, is a rejection of the political process and a willingness to accede to the hierarchy and authority of the Catholic Church. For example, in the novel, the hero, Jean Rivard, becomes a member of parliament. Not long after, he becomes disillusioned with this level of government. He finds that political parties dominate the process and nothing can be accomplished by voting as an independent. He decides to withdraw from the partisanship and turbulence of politics and return to the peace, harmony, and isolation of his parish-cum-republic headed by the local priest.

In many ways *Jean Rivard* reflects the political culture of Quebec in the nineteenth and twentieth centuries. Ralph Heintz-man argues that the traditional political culture of Quebec, from 1840 to 1960, was shaped by the "dialectic of patronage." The pre-occupation of the political system with patronage and the spoils system, Heintzman claims, prompted two simultaneous but con-tradictory tendencies in the French-Canadian mind, devotion to, yet suspicion of, the political process, and attempts to insulate "government" from "politics."[38]

Canadian Tories and the Need for Strong Government

If Reformers, particularly those of the pre-Rebellion era, displayed an aversion to centralized political power, patronage, and commerce, tories perceived matters differently. Patronage, for example, was not only a necessary check upon democracy, but a means of enhanc-ing executive power and political stability. It was also the key to controlling public expenditures and economic development. This desire to check democracy and strengthen the executive was evi-dent in the very creation of Upper and Lower Canada in 1791. Lord Grenville, British secretary of state at the time, felt the American colonial governments had become unbalanced in part because of

weak executive authority. He believed that the defects of "the constitution and administration of executive Government . . . had,
unquestionably, a powerful operation, in producing the defection of
the colonies." One of the more glaring defects of executive government in the American colonies, one that had to be corrected in
Canada, was the lack of influence of the colonial governors. While
in the mother country the Sovereign could obtain political support
by the means of "honours, and emoluments," in the colonies the
case was different: the "rewards of the Crown were few" and "conferred little distinction." This would be a difficult problem to remedy, Grenville observed, in a government "yet in its infancy," but
without due weight and influence government itself would be
diminished and its duties poorly performed.[39]

Throughout the first half of the nineteenth century there
were persistent calls to strengthen the executive, as a counterweight
to democratic assemblies. In Lower Canada, tories felt the problem was particularly pressing. David Chisholme, for example, wrote
in 1829 that French Canadians, acting in a spirit of "licentiousness,
faction and envy," were threatening to swallow up all branches of
government. The executive was particularly enfeebled, for "Neither the King nor government holds any patronage in the provinces,
which can create attachment and influence sufficient to counteract
the restless arrogating spirit, which in popular assemblies, when
left to itself, will never brook an authority that checks and inter-
feres with its own."[40] Earlier, Camillus (John Henry) had made
essentially the same point. Part of the problem, though, lay in the
fact that too many appointments were made in England:

In Canada the Executive Government has no influence in the Commons, and
very little out of it. The PATRONAGE, limited and comparatively insignificant
as it is, does not rest exclusively with the king's representative. Many appointments to offices in Canada are made in England; and if made injudiciously
without regard to individual merit and local circumstances, have a direct
tendency to diminish the influence of the Governor; on whom every office
ought to feel his dependence, and with whom he ought to cooperate.[41]

In Upper Canada, tories had much the same attitude to patronage.
And in Nova Scotia, Attorney-General Richard Uniacke expressed
these sentiments:

So many petty states as now exist in the colonies, having the power of legislation ill defined and as badly executed, govern'd by persons whose small salaries and emoluments are inadequate to support the dignity of the kings [sic] representatives or to uphold the authority of the mother country, together with the dependence of most of the officers of Government on the Colonial assemblies, diminishes the authority of the British Government and places those who should support it in a state of dependence.[42]

It is obvious, then, that by the third decade of the nineteenth century Canadian tories were tired of petty provincial politics, with their factious encroaching assemblies that thwarted their dreams of economic development. They wanted an alternative, a state they could control, one capable of providing political stability, promoting economic development, and serving as an outlet for the ambitions of public men.

Uniacke suggested that political union, either legislative or federal, might be the answer.[43] Many tories agreed, and frequently proposed legislative and federal union. These proposals were hardly novel, resting as they did on premises similar to ones advanced earlier by the Loyalists. William Smith, later Chief Justice of Quebec, and Jonathan Sewell, a Massachusetts Loyalist, for example, believed that a centralized federal union of the American colonies would have prevented the American Revolution by providing a counterweight to the colonial legislatures and by enlarging the opportunities (the offices) open to colonial politicians. "Like Adam Smith," writes W. H. Nelson, "they wanted to tame the Americans by increasing their responsibility."[44] Nelson's insight is instructive, for Smith's thoughts on union parallel those of Loyalists and Canadian tories. Because this is the case they merit detailed consideration.

Adam Smith and Imperial Union

Smith's plan for imperial union possessed two necessary ingredients for an expanded commercial state: first, a strong executive and political stability, underwritten by the availability of offices, the prizes of ambition necessary to mute the spirit of faction and party, and second, healthy public credit provided by an enlarged tax base, which also promoted political stability.

In brief, Smith's arguments went as follows: Men desire to participate in the management of government largely because of the importance it gives them. The stability and durability of free government rest on the power that leading men, "the natural aristoc-racy of every country," have to defend this importance. In Smith's opinion, the "whole play of domestic faction and ambition" in the American colonies stemmed from the attacks leading men made on one another's importance and in the defence of their own. They were most tenacious in defence of the power of local assemblies. Smith claimed that

almost every individual of the governing party in America fills . . . a station superior, not only to what he had ever filled before, but to what he had ever expected to fill; and unless some new object of ambition is presented either to him or to his leaders, if he has the ordinary spirit of a man, he will die in defence of that station.

That new object of ambition, Smith suggested, should be represen-tation in the Parliament of Great Britain. Instead of quarrelling over the small local prizes of colonial faction, "they might then hope, from the presumption which men naturally have in their own ability and good fortune, to draw some of the great prizes which sometimes come from the wheel of the great state lottery of British politics."[45]

Union would mean that the most ambitious men would be attracted to the mother Parliament. The combination of distance and skillful management of Parliament would mean that the fac-tionalism of the colonies would subside. Smith believed that in all great countries under one uniform government factionalism pre-vailed less in remote provinces than it did in the centre of the empire. In Smith's opinion, "the distance of those provinces from the capi-tal, from the principal seat of the great scramble of faction and ambi-tion, makes them enter less into the views of any of the contending parties and renders them more indifferent and impartial spectators of the conduct of all." "The spirit of party," he noted, "prevails less in Scotland than in England."

The influx of American representatives to the centre could be managed and the balance of the constitution preserved only if the American colonies were taxed. Through American taxation, "the number of people to be managed would increase exactly in propor-tion to the means of managing them; and the means of managing, to the number of people to be managed."[46] Smith also saw union as an instrument of public credit, which would alleviate Britain's massive public debt and thereby strengthen the faith lenders had in government's ability to pay. The authority of government would thus be enhanced. Union and American taxation, then, were vital not only to the stability of the colonies but also to government at home.

Tory Proposals for Union in the Pre-Confederation Era

In the nineteenth century the extent to which Canadian tories continued to think along these lines is evident in their pre-Confederation proposals for union, legislative and federal. Three themes emerge from these plans for union: the need to strengthen the position of the Crown in the British North American provinces, the need for outlets of ambition, and the importance of economic development.

Most tory proposals for union in the pre-Confederation era had as their starting point the need to strengthen executive power, a need stemming from the ever-present threat of democratic excess. It was expected that as the powers of the Crown increased, the influence of democratic and factious provincial legislatures would be reduced. This, at least, was the opinion of Justice Sewell of Quebec, who, in his first call for federal union in 1807, lamented the fact that "the Crown has but little influence in the democratic branches of [the]˙provincial legislatures."[47] In Sewell's mind the legislatures were factious and petty, and failed to take into account the interests of the province as a whole. His proposal not unexpectedly called for a considerable reduction in the powers of the local legislatures. J. B. Robinson, attorney general of Upper Canada, with the works of Justice Sewell before him, reflected similar concerns. Provincial legislatures were too factious and democratic; the executive branch was too often at their mercy and its independence and strength too insecure. Robinson proposed a highly centralized federal union of the provinces.[48] Bishop John Strachan repeated Robinson's diagnosis of the ills of the provinces in his observations in 1824 on the bill for uniting Upper and Lower Canada. The "influence of the Executive is trifling," he said, and the politics of the provinces "too agitated by local concerns and popular views."[49] Rather than accept a legislative union, Strachan and Robinson formulated a joint proposal for a federal union of the provinces.[50]

Similar themes were to be repeated in the following decades. In the 1850s and 1860s, P. S. Hamilton of Nova Scotia, in his calls for first legislative and later federal union, expressed concern over the lack of a strong executive in the provinces. In 1864 Hamilton argued that a major cause of political instability in the colonies was the frequent change of governors general. "We require," he said, a "permanent executive at home." Hamilton's political science told him that governments without permanent executives—republics— were short-lived, and the recurring changes of governors general meant "our political institutions are essentially republican." Hamilton's first proposal called for a legislative union of all the provinces, led by a hereditary viceroy. Such a union, he believed, would be able to transcend the pettiness, partyism, and factionalism endemic to colonial legislatures. It would also ensure British ascendancy, a desire also expressed in the proposals of Sewell, Robinson, Strachan, and Lord Durham. "One great object to be obtained by the Union," Hamilton said, "is a complete breaking down of all local prejudices, and a fusion of races, throughout the provinces."[51]

Of all the themes entertained by the writers just considered none is more ubiquitous than what to do with ambitious men. Most tory advocates of union believed that the dissensions and discontents of colonial politics would be vastly ameliorated by a union of the provinces that would provide worthier offices and outlets for the ambitious few. These offices would serve as a safety valve for colonial discontent and would attract men of greater talent to political office. Once their importance was recognized, and elevated positions provided, it was argued, political passions would cool within the larger union, men would become more responsible, and discontent and factionalism would virtually cease. This argument, I would point out, conforms with the lessons of eighteenth- and nineteenth-century political science, which taught that the territorial size of a state and the strength of executive authority were linked to political stability.

J. B. Robinson, for instance, argued that political union "would elevate the colonies" and "put an end to all danger and inconvenience from petty factions and local discontent."[52] These sentiments were frequently repeated. Uniacke argued that by means of a federal union able men would find opportunities for their abilities, thus ending petty intrigues.[53] Lord Durham differed little from Canadian tories on this subject. Like Adam Smith, Durham was troubled by the problem of what to do with the ambitious few who had caused so much trouble in Upper and Lower Canada. Like Smith, he came to the conclusion that they could only be restrained by allowing them to assume higher offices and participate in decision-making:

As long as personal ambition is inherent in human nature, and as long as the morality of every free and civilized community encourages its aspirations, it is one great business of a wise Government to provide for its legitimate development. . . . We must remove from these colonies the cause to which the sagacity of Adam Smith traced the alienation of the Provinces which now form the United States: We must provide some scope for what he calls "the importance" of the leading men in the Colony beyond what he forcibly terms the present "petty prizes of the paltry raffle of colonial faction."[54]

For Durham, either a general legislative union or a federal union of the provinces would have provided the necessary scope for the ambitious few.

Later proposals for federal and legislative union were to make similar arguments. The debates of the British American League in 1849, for example, emphasized the importance of federal union as an outlet for ambition. J. W. Johnston, in 1854, continued to press the same point. He argued that the provinces were too small, too poor, too backward for the British constitutional system to work properly. Only by a larger union, in this case a legislative union, could "an enlarged and more wholesome public opinion, a wider range for talent, and more extended scope for the aspirations of ambition, . . . be found."[55] Finally, one finds that P. S. Hamilton made much the same argument. Hamilton felt that personal ambitions were being thwarted in British America, the result of which was "a strong feeling of discontent among the more intellectual and better educated classes, and the splitting up of the whole community into small, but violent political factions." A union of the colonies would remove the causes of discontent and smother the factious spirit of the colonists. The ambitions of the few satisfied, "the old, narrow, partizan spirit would readily die out . . . and politicians . . . would move with a higher and nobler aim."[56]

There were other arguments for political union, of course, besides those of political stability. In particular, the problems of economic development and public debt also compelled Tories to issue calls for union. Throughout the nineteenth century they had demonstrated little fear of mounting a large public debt to finance public works. Bishop Strachan, for example, had taken David Hume directly to task for his gloomy prognostications on the public debt, arguing that they simply had not come to pass. Wrote Strachan, "Mr. Hume, in the first edition of his essays, asserted that we could not maintain our credit when our debt reached 100 millions, but he lived to see double this sum, and prudently expunged this passage in the future editions of his works observing that it was impossible to conjecture how far we might extend our credit, or what amount the debt might be raised." In Strachan's opinion a national debt meant expensive government. This, in turn, meant high taxes. But "enormous taxes [were] the natural consequences of the greatness of our wealth." Furthermore, argued Strachan, "the existence of a national debt may be perfectly consistent with the interest and prosperity of the Country, and it is only when the borrowing system has been abused, that it has become alarming."[57] The state, in brief, was seen as a credit instrument necessary for the economic development and prosperity of the country.

The fall of John Strachan and the Family Compact with its excesses does not mean there was a disjuncture between their belief system and that of later tories. On the contrary, claims S. F. Wise, there is an "essential continuity of Upper Canadian with subsequent provincial history."[58] Indeed, it is the argument here that in its essentials the nineteenth-century tory view of the state remained much the same. From Strachan to the Confederation period, for example, tories left no doubt that in a reorganized political union, the state, with its stronger credit position, would play a more active role in the financing and building of necessary public works. In 1854, P. S. Hamilton called for a legislative union on the basis that "political isolation hinders the provinces from carrying out any great work [for instance, railways] in which they are interested in common, and requires their joint efforts."[59] The economic motivation underlying these plans for union has been underscored in the research of economic historians. The necessity for capital expenditures by the state was not only responsible for the act of union, argues Harold Innis, it was also responsible for Confederation and its "expenditures on railways."[60]

Given the attitudes of Canadian tories it is not difficult to understand why both French Canadian and English Canadian Reformers displayed such an aversion to tory calls for union, legislative and federal. Until the 1850s, the only French Canadian proposals for a federal union came from Étienne Parent, a Reform leader. Parent's perspective on federalism was distinctly different from that of the tories, emphasizing as it did local autonomy.[61] Parent viewed federalism not as a means of economic advancement, but as a means of preserving the French Canadian nation. This was to be a common refrain of later French Canadian discussions of federalism: would the federal state possess adequate powers to protect the interests of the "nation canadienne"? Whereas the English commercial class tended to view federal union as an economic venture and as a means of underwriting the cost of economic development, French Canadians came to view it as a means of protecting their cultural identity. Parent was merely the first to see it in this light.[62]

Similarly, it is not difficult to understand why English Canadian Reformers were reluctant to accept the tory idea of federal union. Not until George Brown gave it his blessing in the late 1850s did Reformers give it active consideration. Proposals for federations were advanced by Mackenzie and Robert Gourlay in the 1820s, but they were so sketchy and incomplete that it is very difficult to comment on them.[63] It appears that Mackenzie saw federalism as a step toward greater control over local concerns, the post office, bankruptcy laws, or the poor laws, for example. Unfortunately for Mackenzie, his view of the state was not reflected in the federal scheme that emerged in 1867.

CANADIAN TORYISM AND CANADIAN CONFEDERATION

What finally did emerge in 1867 very much represents a fulfilment of the historical tory desire for a strong united commercial state. Just how the founding of Canadian Confederation was expressive of tory values may be illustrated by briefly indicating the extent to which the central themes of previous plans for unions reappear in the 1860s. These include the need to provide an outlet for political ambition, the importance of political stability, and the role of the state in underwriting economic development.

Canadian Confederation: The Prize of Ambition

Peter Waite has indicated that the question of ambition was a pervasive one on the eve of Confederation. The first chapter of *The Life and*

Times of Confederation is essentially concerned with the theme of ambition, although its ideological significance is not recognized by Waite, who (mistakenly, I would argue) views Confederation as a "practical" and non-theoretical exercise. Waite argues that by 1860

there was one characteristic common to all the provinces, especially Nova Scotia, and one which is not easy to describe: it might be called restlessness. There was a pervasive feeling that colonial ambitions had reached a dead end. The bars of these Provincial cages were clearly too confining for Nova Scotia; and this same feeling was reflected in the growth of territorial ambitions in Canada West. The little worlds of Halifax, Charlottetown, Fredericton, Quebec, perhaps even of St. John's were becoming cramped for some of the politicians who made their careers there.[64]

Colonial politicians, in essence, were tiring of their "provincial cages." They wanted something more, they wanted greater respect from other nations and to be elevated in the eyes of the mother country.

Such sentiments were expressed by John A. Macdonald at Charlottetown in September 1864: "For twenty long years I have been dragging myself through the dreary waste of Colonial politics. I thought there was no end, nothing worthy of ambition but now I see something which is worthy of all I have suffered."[65] Similar statements were to be made *ad nauseam* throughout the Confederation Debates. D'Arcy McGee, for example, emphasized the new importance Confederation would give the colonies: "We have given . . . to every man . . . a topic upon which he can fitly exercise his powers, no longer gnawing at a file and wasting his abilities in the poor effort of advancing the ends of some paltry faction or party."[66] It is evident from the above that McGee, like Macdonald, thought federation a worthy object of ambition for public men and an escape from the narrowness and pettiness of provincial life.

The Need for Strong Central Government

Ambition, then, led to the desire for a larger stage for the colonists, an empire and nation of their own. A critical question at the time was how would this nation be institutionally expressed? In the tradition established by Loyalism and Canadian toryism, the Fathers of Confederation were concerned with extricating themselves from what they perceived to be the pettiness and perpetual deadlock of provincial politics. Only a state with strong central controlling power could bring the desired political stability. The American Revolution and Civil War had proved that. Macdonald was of the opinion that the American states had always acted as distinct and sovereign bodies with little in common. The inevitable result was civil war. "We must," he said,

reverse this process by strengthening the General Government and conferring on the Provincial bodies only such powers as may be required for local purposes. All sectional prejudices and interests can be legislated for by local legislatures. Thus we shall have a strong and lasting government under which we can work out constitutional liberty as opposed to democracy, and be able to protect the minority by having a powerful central government.[67]

A careful reading of Macdonald's comments confirms that he linked democracy with locality and political instability. Only a strong central government could bring stability, counteract democracy, and ensure constitutional liberty. In particular it was agreed that the executive had to be strengthened to provide the central authority so desperately needed. Again American experience was to serve as a guide. The great defect of American government, claimed G.-É. Cartier, "was the absence of some respectable executive element. . . . Such a system could not produce an executive head who would command respect."[68]

To ensure a strong central government and executive the general government was granted all the powers, mechanisms of control, and patronage that it needed to establish its supremacy within Confederation. From now on all the important "prizes" in the raffle of Canadian politics would be in the hands of the central government. None of this was lost upon the opponents of Confederation. A. A. Dorion, for example, came to this conclusion concerning the political beliefs of Cartier and Macdonald:

They think the hands of the Crown should be strengthened and the influence of the people, if possible, diminished—and this Constitution is a specimen of their handiwork, with a Governor-General appointed by the Crown; with local governors . . . appointed by the Crown; with [the] legislative council . . . in the General Legislature . . . nominated by the Crown.

According to Dorion it was public knowledge that the potential promise of these positions and others was "one of the reasons assigned for the great unanimity which prevailed in the [Quebec] Conference" of 1864.[69]

Canadian Confederation and Economic Development

While Canadian Confederation was definitely believed to be the answer to the pettiness and political instability plaguing the provinces, it was also seen as the solution to the economic problems they faced, particularly the massive public debt contracted for the creation of a transportation infrastructure. The burden of public debt eventually prompted the British to support the idea of Confederation. Donald Creighton claims this support "might be interpreted as an effort to assist in the creation of a great holding company in which could be amalgamated all those divided and vulnerable North American interests whose protection was a burden to the British state and whose financial weakness was a grievance of British capital."[70] In brief, Confederation was to be a credit instrument that would provide the resources necessary for the economic development of the British North American colonies.

This, at least, was the opinion of Alexander Galt. Galt believed union would provide a means of solving the problems of public debt and improving public credit. It was clear, in Galt's opinion, that "the credit of each and all the provinces [would be] greatly advanced by a union of their resources," thus removing "those apprehensions which have latterly affected the public credit of this country."[71] Besides the pressure the mounting public debt put on politicians there was another important economic problem confronting the British North American provinces, the impending abrogation of the Reciprocity Treaty with the United States. The Reciprocity Treaty had opened American markets to Canadian products and with its threatened loss Canadians had to find alternative markets that would ensure prosperity. No longer could they rely on Britain, where they had lost protected markets in the 1840s and 1850s. They had to rely on one another.

These concerns are also reflected in Alexander Galt's speech during the Confederation Debates. Union, he said, would mean that the tariffs that had impeded the free flow of goods between the provinces would be removed, thereby "opening up . . . the markets of the provinces to the different industries of each."[72] There is little in all of this to distinguish Galt from Adam Smith. Smith, as noted earlier, had argued for a union between Britain and its colonies for very similar reasons. In Smith's opinion a union, in this case an imperial union, would have alleviated the public debt, strengthened public credit and government, and also provided for free trade. Many others in the debates echoed Galt's arguments, particularly those concerning public debt.

CONCLUSION

The government that emerged conformed very closely to the image of union held by generations of tory politicians. In many ways it could be said that John A. Macdonald obtained most of what Alexander Hamilton wanted in 1787. This included a strong central government that not only would possess the political offices that would mute political discontent and provide political stability, but would, at the same time, vastly enhance public credit and provide the capital to underwrite commercial expansion across a continent. The localist attachments in Canadian political culture, particularly in French Canada and among English Canadian Reformers, would have to be satisfied with the greatly inferior provincial governments they were given.

Canadian Confederation, then, was not without ideological underpinning. In nineteenth-century Canada, there were two constitutional philosophies at work, both acting in the tradition of the eighteenth-century debate between wealth and virtue, land and commerce. In the case of Canada the commercial ideology of Canadian tories was to predominate politically in 1867. Nevertheless, the political ideology of agrarian democracy was not to be extinguished in Canada. It was to emerge as powerful as ever on the prairies in the twentieth century, giving sustenance to radical movements of both the left and the right.

NOTES

* Earlier versions of this article were presented in 1985 at the Tenth Anniversary Conference of the British Association for Canadian Studies in Edinburgh, Scotland, and at the annual meeting of the Canadian Political Science Association,

Montreal. I am grateful to David V. J. Bell for his comments and suggestions at the CPSA meeting, and also for the comments of Elizabeth Smythe.

1. This is a common refrain of Canadian political scientists and historians. Edwin Black, for example, argues that "Confederation was born in pragmatism without the attendance of a readily definable philosophic rationale" (E. R. Black, *Divided Loyalties: Canadian Concepts of Federalism* [Montreal: McGill-Queen's University Press, 1975] 4). Peter Waite states that Confederation had a "fundamentally empirical character" about it and was essentially a practical exercise (*The Life and Times of Confederation 1864-1867: Politics, Newspapers, and the Union of British North America* [Toronto: University of Toronto Press, 1962] 25). Donald Smiley writes that "Unlike Americans . . . in the eighteenth century . . . Canadians have never experienced the kind of decisive break with their political past which would have impelled them to debate and resolve fundamental political questions" (*Canada in Question: Federalism in the Eighties*, 3rd ed. [Toronto: McGraw-Hill Ryerson, 1980] 285). Finally, J. K. Johnson makes the following observation on one of the leading Fathers of Confederation: "John A. Macdonald's political 'ideas' or 'beliefs' have been subjected to more learned scrutiny than those of almost any other Canadian leader, a fact which is more than a little surprising, considering that the scholarly consensus has been that he was not a man of ideas at all." Johnson also maintains that "it is true he was essentially pragmatic, even opportunistic by nature. He did not disguise his pragmatism with political rhetoric; he positively boasted of it." The image of "John A." was that of "the plain, no-nonsense practical man of good sense" (J. K. Johnson, "John A. Macdonald," in J. M. S. Careless, ed., *The Pre-Confederation Premiers: Ontario Government Leaders, 1841-1867* [Toronto: University of Toronto Press, 1980] 223-24). One of the few political scientists to take Macdonald seriously as a man of ideas is Rod Preece ("The Political Wisdom of Sir John A. Macdonald," *CJPS* 17 [1984]: 459-86).

2. Some of the more prominent contributors include: John Dunn, "The Politics of Locke in England and America in the Eighteenth Century," in John W. Yolton, ed., *John Locke: Problems and Perspectives* (Cambridge: Cambridge University Press, 1969); Bernard Bailyn, *The Ideological Origins of the American Revolution* (Cambridge, MA: Belknap Press, 1969); Gordon S. Wood, *The Creation of the American Republic 1776-1787* (Chapel Hill: University of North Carolina Press, 1969); H. T. Dickinson, *Liberty and Property: Political Ideology in Eighteenth-Century Britain* (London: Weidenfeld and Nicolson, 1977); Reed Browning, *Political and Constitutional Ideas of the Court Whigs* (Baton Rouge: Louisiana State University Press, 1982); Lance Banning, *The Jeffersonian Persuasion* (Ithaca: Cornell University Press, 1978); Duncan Forbes, *Hume's*

Philosophical Politics (Cambridge: Cambridge University Press, 1978); J. G. A. Pocock, *The Machiavellian Moment* (Princeton: Princeton University Press, 1975). My debt to Pocock's work is obvious in the first part of this article.

3. The work of Janet Ajzenstat is one exception. See, for example, her "Modern Mixed Government: A Liberal Defence of Inequality," *CJPS* 18 (1985): 119-35.

4. The Country opposition, however, was hardly a homogeneous group. Dickinson provides a succinct overview of their internal divisions, which centred around religious matters and the question of who should enjoy active political power (163-80).

5. For a good overview on how these approaches have been applied to Scottish social thought see J. G. A. Pocock, "Cambridge Paradigms and Scotch Philosophers: A Study of the Relations Between the Civic Humanist and the Civil Jurisprudential Interpretation of Eighteenth Century Social Thought," in Istvan Hont and Michael Ignatieff, eds., *Wealth and Virtue: The Shaping of Political Economy in the Scottish Enlightenment* (Cambridge: Cambridge University Press, 1983) 235-53.

6. This is particularly the view of Nicholas Phillipson, "Adam Smith as Civic Moralist," Hont and Ignatieff 179-203, and "The Scottish Enlightenment," in R. Porter and M. Teich, eds., *The Enlightenment in National Context* (Cambridge: Cambridge University Press, 1981) 19-40.

7. David Hume, "Of Refinement in the Arts," *Essays Moral, Political and Literary*, ed. T. H. Green and T. H. Grose (London: Longmans, Green and Co., 1875) 300.

8. Adam Smith, *The Wealth of Nations*, ed. E. Canaan (New York: Random House, 1937) bk. 14, chap. 7, 551.

9. ———, *Lectures on Justice, Police, and Arms*, ed. Edwin Canaan (Oxford: Clarendon Press, 1896), as quoted in Anand C. Chitnis, *The Scottish Enlightenment* (London: Croom Helm, 1976) 104.

10. Smith also had a more integrated and historical understanding of the relationship between the economic and the political than did Hume, believing as he did in the four stages theory of development—hunting, pastoral, agriculture, and commerce. Smith was also less optimistic than Hume about the beneficial effects of commercial society. For a good overview of the intellectual differences, see John Robertson, "Scottish Political Economy Beyond the Civic Tradition: Government and Economic Development in The Wealth of Nations," *History of Political Thought* 4 (1983): 451-82.

11. David Hume, "Of Civil Liberty," *Essays* 162-63.

12. Smith, *Wealth of Nations* bk. 5, chap. 3, 896, 897.

13. B. Bailyn, *The Origins of American Politics* (New York: Random House, 1972) 56-58.

14. For more on Hume's influence see Douglas Adair, "That Politics May Be Reduced to a Science: David Hume, James Madison and the Tenth Federalist," *Huntington Library Quarterly* 30 (1956-57): 343-60.

15. David Hume, "Idea of a Perfect Commonwealth," *Essays* 497.

16. James Madison, *The Federalist Papers*, no. 10, introd. Clinton Rossiter (New York: Mentor Books, 1961) 79. On this point see Adair, "That Politics May Be Reduced to a Science," and James Moore, "Hume's Political Science and the Classical Republican Tradition," *CJPS* 10 (1977): 809-39.

17. See Max Farrand, ed., *The Records of the Federal Convention of 1787* (New Haven: Yale University Press, 1966) 1: 296, 376, 381.

18. For more on this point see Banning, *The Jeffersonian Persuasion*, and Gerald Stourzh, *Alexander Hamilton and the Idea of Republican Government* (Stanford: Stanford University Press, 1970).

19. Thomas Jefferson, "Letter to Ogilvie, 1811," in Saul K. Padover, *Thomas Jefferson on Democracy* (New York: Mentor Books, 1939) 136.

20. Of all of the above, Cobbett radicalism was sharpest in its attack upon corruption. See H. T. Dickinson, *British Radicalism and the French Revolution 1789-1815* (Oxford: Basil Blackwell, 1985) 70, 71. One of Cobbett's greatest admirers was Robert Gourlay, a radical leader in Upper Canada during the 1820s, whose views, according to his biographer, were close to "an almost forgotten party called the Country Party which opposed court corruption" (Lois Dorroch Milani, *Robert Gourlay, Gadfly* [Thornbury, Ontario: Ampersand Press, 1971] 26).

21. Robert Kelley, *The Transatlantic Persuasion: The Liberal-Democratic Mind in the Age of Gladstone* (New York: Knopf, 1969) 409.

22. Donald Creighton, *The Empire of the St. Lawrence* (Toronto: Macmillan, 1972) 45.

23. *The Seventh Report from the Select Committee of the House of Assembly of Upper Canada on Grievances* (Toronto: M. Reynolds, 1832) iii.

24. See Dickinson, *Liberty and Authority* 208. I am grateful to James Moore for bringing this to my attention.

25. *The Seventh Report.*

26. L. J. Papineau, *Address to the Electors of the West Ward of Montreal* (Montreal: Fabre, Perrault and Co., 1831) 1.

27. Toronto *Constitution* 14 June 1837.

28. L. J. Papineau, *La Minerve* 17 March 1836 as quoted in F. Ouellet, *Lower Canada 1791-1840* (Toronto: McClelland and Stewart, 1980) 218.

29. Robert Davis, *The Canadian Farmer's Travels in the United States* (Buffalo: Steel's Press, 1837) 97.

30. Reprinted in Trevor H. Lavere and Richard A. Jarrell, eds., *A Curious Field-Book: Science and Society in Canadian History* (Toronto: Oxford University Press, 1974) 160, 161.

31. For the relationship between patronage and responsible government see Susan Mann Trofimenkoff, *The Dream of Nation* (Toronto: Macmillan, 1982) 86-87.

32. *The Examiner* 19 September 1849, as quoted in J. M. S. Careless, *The Union of the Canadas* (Toronto: McClelland and Stewart, 1967) 167.

33. Careless, *Union* 167.

34. Frank Underhill, "Some Aspects of Upper Canadian Radical Opinion in the Decade Before Confederation," in Ramsay Cook, ed., *Upper Canadian Politics in the 1850s, Canadian Historical Readings* (Toronto: University of Toronto Press, 1967) 2.

35. See the introduction by Vida Bruce to Antoine Gérin-Lajoie's *Jean Rivard* (Toronto: McClelland and Stewart, 1977).

36. Antoine Gérin-Lajoie, as quoted in Marcel Rioux, "The Development of Ideologies in Quebec," in Richard Schultz, Orest M. Kruhlak, and John C. Terry, eds., *The Canadian Political Process*, 3rd ed. (Toronto: Holt, Rinehart and Winston, 1979) 101.

37. Gérin-Lajoie, *Jean Rivard* 65.

38. Ralph Heintzman, "The Political Culture of Quebec, 1840-1960," *CJPS* 16 (1983): 3-59.

39. Quoted in Adam Shortt and Arthur G. Doughty, *Documents Relating to the Constitutional History of Canada*, pt. 2 (Ottawa: J. de L. Taché, King's Printer, 1918) 984.

40. David Chisholme, *The Lower-Canada Watchman* (Kingston: James Macfarlane, 1829) 305. Chisholme (1776?-1842) was born in Scotland and emigrated to Canada in 1822, where he worked as a journalist and editor for the Montreal *Gazette*. He was also a close friend of Lord Dalhousie.

41. Camillus (John Henry), *An Enquiry into the Evils of General Suffrage* (Montreal: Nahum Mower, 1820), as reprinted in John Hare and Jean-Pierre Wallot, eds., *Confrontations* (Trois-Rivières: Boréal Express, 1970) 100. The emphasis is Henry's. John Henry (1776-1820) was probably born in Ireland, moving to the United States at the turn of the century and then to Canada, where he became connected with the North West Company.

42. "Uniacke's Memorandum to Windham, 1806," *Canadian Historical Review* 17 (1936): 35.

43. For more on the two plans of union see B. C. U. Cuthbertson, "The Old Attorney General, Richard John Uniacke, 1735-1830," M.A. thesis, University of New Brunswick, 1970.

44. W. H. Nelson, "The Last Hopes of the American Loyalists," *Canadian Historical Review* 32 (1951): 23.

45. Adam Smith, "Essays on the Colonies," in Sir George Cornwell Lewis, ed., *Governance of Dependencies* (London: M. Walter Dunne, 1901) 76, 77, 78. Most of Smith's essay in replicated in *Wealth of Nations*.

46. *Wealth of Nations* bk. 5, chap. 3, 898; bk. 4. chap. 7, 551. If Donald Winch is correct there are parallels not only with Loyalists and tories but with Madison's thoughts on federal union. See his *Adam Smith's Politics: An Essay in Historiographic Revision* (Cambridge: Cambridge University Press, 1978) 161-62.

47. Jonathan Sewell, Jr., "Memoir on the Means of Promoting the Joint Interests, 1807," in J. B. Robinson, *Plan for a General Legislative Union of the British Provinces in North America* (London: W. Clowes, 1822) 7. Justice Sewell of Quebec was the son of Jonathan Sewell, Sr., of Massachusetts.

48. J. B. Robinson, *Letter to the Right Hon. Earl Bathurst* (London: William Clowes, 1825) 31.

49. John Strachan, "Observations on a Bill for Uniting the Legislative Councils and Assemblies" (London, 1824), in J. L. H. Henderson, *John Strachan: Documents and Opinions* (Toronto: McClelland and Stewart, 1969) 157.

50. John Strachan (and J. B. Robinson), "Observations of the Policy of a General Union of all the British Provinces of North America" (London: William Clowes, 1824), in Henderson, *John Strachan* 68.

51. P. S. Hamilton, *Union of the Colonies of British North America, Being Three Papers Upon This Subject* (Montreal: John Lovell, 1864) 10, 58.

52. J. B. Robinson, *Plan for a General Legislative Union* 40.

53. Cuthbertson, "The Old Attorney General" 224.

54. *Lord Durham's Report*, ed. Gerald M. Craig (Toronto: McClelland and Stewart, 1963) 162.

55. "J. W. Johnston," in Edward Manning Saunders, *Three Premiers of Nova Scotia* (Toronto: William Brigges, 1909) 255.

56. P.S. Hamilton, "Observations upon a Union of the Colonies, 1854-1855," in *Union of the Colonies* 18.

57. John Strachan, *A Discourse on the Character of King George Addressed to the Inhabitants of British America* (Montreal: Nahum Mower, 1810) 29, 30, 50.

58. S. F. Wise, "Upper Canada and the Conservative Tradition," in Edith G. Firth, ed., *Profiles of a Province* (Toronto: Ontario Historical Society, 1967) 21. See also R. Whitaker, "Images of the State in Canada," in Leo Panitch, ed., *The Canadian State* (Toronto: University of Toronto Press, 1977) 28-71.

59. Hamilton, "Observations upon a Union" 20.

60. Harold Innis, *The Fur Trade in Canada* (Toronto: University of Toronto Press, 1973) 396.

61. See Louis Nourry, "L'idée de fédération chez Étienne Parent, 1831-1852," *Revue d'Histoire de l'Amérique Française* 26 (1973): 533-57.

62. See A. L. Silver, *The French-Canadian Idea of Confederation* (Toronto: University of Toronto Press, 1982).

63. W. L. Mackenzie, "Letter to John Neilson, December 7, 1829," in Margaret Fairly, ed., *The Selected Writings of William Lyon Mackenzie* (Toronto: Oxford University Press, 1960); Robert Gourlay, "To the Honourable the Commons of Upper Canada Met in Assembly, December 24, 1825," Public Archives of Canada. Co. O. 42 Vol. 380.

64. Waite, *The Life and Times of Confederation* 93-94.

65. Quoted by Whelan, "Union of the British Provinces," in Waite, *The Life and Times of Confederation* 80.

66. D'Arcy McGee, *Parliamentary Debates on the Subject of the Confederation of the British North American Provinces* (Quebec: Hunter and Rose and Co., 1865) 128.

67. Joseph Pope, ed., *Confederation: Being a Series of Hitherto Unpublished Documents Bearing On the British North America Act* (Toronto: Carswell, 1895) 55. Minutes and notes of discussion of the Quebec Conference were kept by Hewitt Bernard.

68. *Confederation Debates* 62.

69. *Confederation Debates* 255, 256.

70. D. G. Creighton, *British North America at Confederation : A Study Prepared for the Royal Commission on Dominion-Provincial Relations* (Ottawa: Queen's Printer, 1963) 9.

71. *Confederation Debates* 64.

72. *Confederation Debates* 64.

CHAPTER FOUR

THE FIRST DISTINCT SOCIETY:
FRENCH CANADA, AMERICA, AND
THE CONSTITUTION OF 1791

Louis-Georges Harvey

Since its inception, Canadian constitutionalism has struggled with the definitions of collective identity that came into conflict with its individualistic and libertarian foundations. In the case of the Constitutional Act it was the constitution's inability to accommodate the aspirations of French Canadian politicians that led to its ignominious and violent demise in Lower Canada. Still, the inherent limitations of a colonial constitution never intended to confer local autonomy do not solely explain its rejection in Lower Canada. For even had the constitution been amended by the mystical formula of responsible government, the *Patriotes* would have rejected it. As Papineau pointed out in 1836, an executive council could never be responsible, because ministers would inevitably be "bribed or tampered with."[1] Simply put, by the 1830s French Canadian political discourse was dominated by idioms that ran contrary to the evolution of British parliamentary democracy. Indeed, the dominant view in French Canada at the time of the Rebellions was that constitutionalism had been utterly corrupted in Britain, a society itself in marked decline.

To understand the political language of the past we have to understand its structures. One of the key assumptions of a contextualist approach to the evolution of political discourse is that it assumes that historical actors knew precisely of what they spoke, that they and their audiences shared an understanding of the meaning of key words and concepts, and that, surprisingly, they did not need to have read in the future in order to give their discourse significance. To avoid anachronism, we must suspend the tendency to assume that political texts are transparent; that is, we must begin from the assumption that the meaning of political terms is not constant over time.[2]

Putting political discourse in its proper context, creating a true history of meaning in the political sense, has not been a dominant theme in Canadian historiography. The historiography dealing with Lower Canada reveals on the contrary a long tradition of present-minded debate on the relationship between "liberalism" (usually undefined) and "nationalism" (usually over-emphasized). The obvious contemporary references in the work of these historians has led one recent commentator to refer to one school's interpretation as "cité libriste."[3] The anachronistic nature of this debate can be demonstrated in the tendency of historians on the one hand to chastise the *Patriotes* for not having been mid-nineteenth-century English liberals, which of course they could not have been, and, on the other, to make them perhaps the most advanced political and economic thinkers on the planet at the time, espousing an "entrepreneurial spirit," to quote one commentary from the entrepreneurial eighties.[4]

Like so much in Canadian history, the origins of this debate might be traced back to our dear Lord Durham, who, as Ajzenstat has so rightly argued, deserves a central place in our historical consciousness. Durham's critique of French Canada was based on the fact that it did not correspond to his vision of a dynamic and progressive society. Moreover, Durham enshrined the notion of the superficiality of French Canadian liberalism, writing that the *Patriotes* "used their democratic arms for conservative purposes, rather than those of a liberal and enlightened movement."[5] While Durham's assimilation prescription has been reviled by generations of historians, this aspect of his interpretation of French Canadian political discourse and behaviour has been taken up, and admittedly simplified, in the work of historians down to the present day. As brilliantly perceptive as Durham was, it is good to remember that he too was a product of his time and his culture; and at the risk of sounding heretical, we might also speculate that he too might have missed the essential meaning of French Canadian political discourse, because it was so radically different from his own.

I am maintaining that the liberal-conservative, traditional-modern, and feudal-capitalist dichotomy posited in much of the historiography as the central element of conflict within the period is at best a dangerous oversimplification, at worse largely irrelevant. A few suggestive recent studies support such a contention. Consider, for example, the simple question of the definition of liberalism in French Canadian political discourse. Few historians have been explicit about what they meant by the term. André Vachet, however, has forcefully challenged the notion of a coherent French Canadian liberalism for the whole of the nineteenth century precisely by attempting a more accurate definition.[6] While we might disagree with his analysis of the 1850s, surely Vachet's argument that French Canadian discourse before 1837 was not liberal, because it rejected the notion of possessive individualism, is supported implicitly by most of the historiography. More recently, a highly suggestive article by Peter Smith argues that pre-Confederation political discourse might be more appropriately analyzed in the light of studies on civic humanism in Anglo-American discourse. Smith maintains that the dialectic of wealth and virtue was the central component of that discourse and bemoans the fact that this potentially rewarding avenue of research has not been explored by Canadian intellectual historians.[7] Here I find myself in complete agreement with Smith, at least where French Canadian political discourse before 1837 is concerned, having arrived separately at the same conclusion.

The argument here then is that the first distinct society, that defined by the *Patriotes*, was constructed in the language of civic humanism. Additionally, I contend that this language was given meaning by an extremely powerful and positive image of the United States that emerged in French Canada between 1815 and 1837. Following the Anglo-American lead, the *Patriotes* sought to preserve an agricultural society that they saw as a means of protecting the population's political virtue from corruption by an alliance of commerce and political power. In this they represented one strand of a civic humanist or classical republican tradition that found fertile ground and took firm root in the New World.

In *The Machiavellian Moment*, Pocock traced the development and redeployment in a number of different historical contexts of a pattern of political discourse associated with classical theories of power and corruption. Pocock argues that a particular view of the basis of political power and the cyclical nature of historical development in political entities, which he identifies as civic humanism, was first developed in Florentine Italy, revived and used in political analysis in seventeenth-century England, re-emerged in the opposition literature of mid-eighteenth-century England, and finally was transferred to America, where it helped shape the political discourse of American revolutionaries.[8]

The "Machiavellian moment" was, then, first, the point where Florentine writers attempted to come to terms with the historical development of their republic. These writers were themselves influenced by certain patterns "in the temporal consciousness of medieval and early modern Europeans [that] led to the presentation of the republic and the citizen's participation in it, as constituting a problem in historical self-understanding."[9] Pocock presents their dilemma as one that constituted a "historically real" problem, one that brought forth an explicit definition of the difficulties that republics faced in attempting "to remain morally and politically stable in a stream of irrational events conceived as essentially destructive of all systems of secular stability."[10] In defining this problem Machiavelli and his contemporaries developed a particular language, or idiom, within which certain terms acquired a great deal of importance. At the root of this pattern of discourse was the assumption that the instability of republics grew out of a confrontation between the "virtue" of their citizenry, the essential requirement for political stability, and the threat to that virtue posed by "fortune" and the inevitable "corruption" it brought with it.

The "Machiavellian moment," writes Pocock, also "had a continuing history, in the sense that secular political self-consciousness continued to pose problems in historical self-awareness, which forms part of the journey of Western thought from the medieval Christian to the modern historical mode."[11] Here he is arguing that the language of Florentine thinkers, the idioms and modes of argument they used, "left an important paradigmatic legacy." Pocock finds the language of Florentine Italy restated in the Anglo-American thought

of the seventeenth and eighteenth centuries, with the same emphasis on "virtue" and "corruption."

To be sure, he readily admits that this language underwent a
transformation in its adaptation to each new circumstance, and that
in Anglo-American discourse it existed alongside a "constitutionalist" mode of political discourse; but the language of civic humanism proved well suited to dealing with the political contexts of these
differing periods and was adapted by new historical actors to fit the
contexts of their political situations. Thus, in seventeenth-century
England, writers such as James Harrington meshed the language of
civic humanism with the English "common law understanding of
the importance of freehold property," and thus made property "the
basis of political personality." In the same way, Harrington moved
away from a purely moral definition of corruption to one that
stressed the disjuncture between the distribution of property and
the distribution of power within the state.[12]

Once integrated into English political culture, civic humanism became a form of discourse available for use in later situations.
In the eighteenth century, opposition politicians came to see corruption in the concentration of power in the hands of a few ministers. What is more, they argued that land ownership accounted for
the political virtue of the English citizenry. Thus, the discourse of
English opposition groups came to be dominated by references to
the corruption of the "Court party" and by dire warnings of the
threat posed to liberty by the machinations of moneyed interests
connected with the King's ministers. This form of discourse, argues
Pocock, was transferred in the second half of the century to the
American colonies. Against the background of the deepening imperial crisis, colonists came to see the threat to their liberty as growing
out of the same corruption of moneyed interests. Because the colonial economy was primarily agricultural, and because colonial society was in large part made up of landholders, the pattern of discourse that was derived from civic humanism allowed colonial
leaders to define their society as politically virtuous, and contrast it
to the increasingly corrupt political system of the mother country.[13]

In establishing the presence of civic humanism in Anglo-
American political discourse, Pocock challenged historical interpretation that stressed the rise of liberalism as the principal component of that discourse from Locke forward. Rather he argues that a
liberal, or modern, political theory of property was in conflict with

a more ancient understanding of the role of property in "determining the relations of personality to government."[14] The persistence of this "agrarian ideal" also shifted the focus of Anglo-American political theory toward a consideration of the struggle between "virtue and corruption" within society itself. "From 1688 to 1776 (and after)," writes Pocock, "the central question in Anglophone political theory was not whether a ruler might be resisted for misconduct, but whether a regime founded on patronage, public debt, and professionalization of the armed forces did not corrupt both governors and governed; and corruption was a problem in virtue, not in right, which could never be solved by asserting the right of resistance. Political thought therefore moves decisively, though never irrevocably, out of the law centred paradigm and into the paradigm of virtue and corruption."[15]

Although their studies were not predicated on an explicitly contextualist theory, Bernard Bailyn and Gordon Wood made much the same point in their examinations of early American thought. Analyzing the political discourse of their periods, they found that the civic humanist paradigm was not only operative, but dominant in the discourse of the revolutionary generation. Indeed, American intellectual historians have traced the continuing history of civic humanist and classical forms through the political debates between Republicans and Federalists down to those that opposed Jacksonian Democrats and their whig critics in the 1830s and 1840s. Lance Banning, for instance, found that the ideology of Jeffersonian Republicans was laden with the language of eighteenth-century English opposition groups and that this language formed the core of the debates over Hamilton's economic program, the American debate over the French Revolution, and the Republican reaction to the Alien and Sedition Acts. Robert Remini and Daniel Walker Howe found the same idioms present in the discourse of the Jacksonian period, shaping the political culture of both the Democrats and whigs.[16] It is useful to note that the Jeffersonians and the Jacksonians were both contemporaries and neighbours of the *Parti canadien* and the *Parti patriote*, and that American politics were widely reported in Lower Canada.[17]

By the late eighteenth and early nineteenth centuries, Anglo-American civic humanism, particularly its American variant, had become obsessed with the corruptive potential of an alliance of commerce and power. The relevance of this pattern of discourse to Lower

Canada should be apparent. Here the socio-political context created the classic civic humanist confrontation. On one side stood the elected representatives of a largely rural population, on the other the appointed representatives of the urban merchant class, allied, most frequently, to the governor. Surely any country politician drawn from eighteenth-century Britain or Jeffersonian America would have recognized the potential for corruption and degeneration inherent in such a situation.

That Lower Canadian politicians came to recognize the same potential is hardly surprising. Not only did they have access to the works of authors from the mainstream of the civic humanist tradition, but they shared in common with most educated westerners of their time a grounding in classical thought and history that in itself provided a basis for the civic humanist view of history. As one might expect, classical allusions occurred frequently in discussions of current political problems, particularly when the texts in question were highly theoretical. From D. B. Viger's *Considérations*, published in 1809, which cited the fall of Rome as an example of corruption and degeneration, to articles in *la Minerve* of the 1830s that restated the argument, the classical view of history and its relevance in interpreting social and political change appears almost as an article of faith.[18] The cycle of corruption and degeneration was also emphasized through references to more recent history. The Italian city states of the renaissance and eighteenth-century Britain were used in the very first issue of *le Canadien* as examples of societies that had been or were in danger of being corrupted.[19] Indeed, by the 1830s Europe as a whole was being portrayed as being well along the downward slope of historical decline, with its societies marked by the twin characteristics of political corruption and social degeneration.

Canadien politicians, of course, defined their own people as virtuous. In the period before 1815 this was often done to contrast the habitants' qualities with the defects of American migrants moving into the Townships. The latter appeared in the pages of *le Canadien* as a morally inferior and politically corrupt people. As to the source of the Americans' corruption, the paper's political writers were quite explicit: the American had fallen through the influence of commerce.[20] By the mid-1820s French Canadian political discourse had turned that argument on its head while remaining in the civic humanist paradigm. To put it simply, virtue became North American in the decade following the end of the War of 1812. Now, the social basis of French Canadian political virtue acquired a historical and geographic explanation, and one that helped reverse the position of external political models to the benefit of America and the prejudice of Great Britain.

Implicit in that view was a redefinition of Lower Canadian society as distinctly North American. The argument that the colony was different in its social organization from European models was made first in light of the Union Crisis, when it seemed that Great Britain was interfering in the colony's internal affairs without its consent. In time, however, the same pattern of discourse would serve as a rationale for demanding change in the very constitution the *Canadiens* had sought to protect in 1823. Lower Canadian political institutions, it was argued, had to conform to North American society, where disparities in wealth were less pronounced, because of widespread land ownership, and where aristocracies had failed to take root. In short, North American political institutions had to reflect the democratic ethos of the New World.

This pattern in French Canadian political discourse will certainly be familiar to students of the early national period in American history. Indeed, since the early moments of the Revolution, Americans had believed in their particular destiny as a North American nation to preserve liberty from the corrupt governments of the old world. It was in this vein that Thomas Paine, for example, had proclaimed America the final asylum of liberty, and that Jefferson had dreamed of an empire for liberty stretching across the continent.[21] This element in American discourse, argues Pocock, accounted for the continued relevance of civic humanist forms in the new Republic. The dream of North American liberty was tied up with the concept of land ownership as a basis for political virtue and the vision of a vast agricultural republic.[22] The democratic and republican destiny of the United States and of the continent as a whole was rarely more evident in American discourse than in the years following the end of the War of 1812. Most historians consider the "Era of Good Feelings" as one marked by the rise of American nationalism and as one where dreams of Manifest Destiny took root.[23] Indeed, defending the particular character of North American politics even became official policy with the proclamation of the Monroe Doctrine in December of 1823. For Monroe's message was more than a warning that new European military incursions would not be tolerated in the western hemisphere; it also proclaimed that European political systems were no longer suitable to the New World.

Significantly, French Canadian discourse began to emphasize the distinctively North American nature of Lower Canadian
society at about the same time that Monroe was reading his message
to the American Congress. Indeed, a pronounced shift occurred in
1823-1824, as more and more French Canadian political texts made
the link between North American society and democratic institutions. Still, intercultural transfers are rarely so mechanistic as the
timing here might suggest, and, while Monroe's speech was fully
reprinted in the colony, many French Canadian allusions to the same
theme predated it.

The contrast between Europe and America was vividly
drawn in *le Canadien* in the early months of the struggle against the
Union:

En Europe il y a une dépendance continue depuis le plus grand jusqu'au plus
petit. En Amérique il y a des forêts immenses qui attendent un maître ou des
bras pour les cultiver; il n'y a ni lord, ni seigneur; le mérite individuel est ce qui
forme la règle de conduite pour la masse du peuple. La force n'y fait rien, parce
que tout homme qui travaille est toujours à même de s'y soustraire. Ainsi donc,
tout système de gouvernement qui n'a pas pour but le bien-être général, ne peut
durer longtemps.[24]

By 1823 an article in the same paper stated that the *Canadiens* were
"descendants de Français, mais ils sont natifs et habitants de
l'Amérique; ils ne veulent plus être entraînés dans les guerres de
l'Europe contre l'Amérique."[25] Later the same year the paper commented that "il y a encore dans le vieux continent des millions
d'hommes sans existence politique; selon moi ce ne sont que des
troupeaux de bétails, destinés à porter le joug."[26]

It was also in 1823 that Papineau, writing from Europe, commented on the social inequality and degeneration that marked life
in Britain and France. The implication of his analysis was that North
American society was free of those abuses. For although Papineau
found that England had maintained a free government despite these
social ills, he noted that "le peuple n'est ni aussi heureux ni aussi
content comme il l'est en Amérique."[27] Pierre de Sales Laterrière,
living in Great Britain at the time, expressed the contrast in terms
of the cycle of corruption and degeneration so common in the civic
humanist view of history: "On voit . . . l'Amérique régenérer et en
imposer par la libéralité qui existe dans toutes ses institutions, à

toutes ces vieilles machines européennes," he wrote in August of 1823.[28] Inevitably, such a view led commentators to predict that the United States would rise to become a great nation. Papineau expressed that view in one of his letters from London: "À quel degré de prospérité ne sont donc pas appelés les États-Unis qui avec le même caractère d'industrie et d'activité de ce pays sont affranchis de presque tous les abus qui règnent ici."[29]

Despite these private predictions that the American form of government would combine with the natural state of North American society to surpass the political achievements of Europe, America did not immediately become a positive political model in French Canadian discourse. The notion of democratic or representative government as the form most appropriate to North America, however, made significant inroads into that discourse before 1830. Increasingly, as reform of the legislative council became an important topic of discussion, *canadien* political writers rejected the upper chamber's aristocratic underpinnings. An early and radical statement of that view came in a pamphlet from the pen of François Blanchet attacking the council. Blanchet's argument rested squarely on the notion that North American society differed essentially from that of Europe, and that, as North Americans, the *Canadiens* could never accept a landed aristocracy. The pamphlet even provided a historical backdrop for the argument, maintaining that the *Canadiens* had acquired a different character from the French long before the Conquest. In New France the habitants had been able to get the tithe reduced, the *censitaire* had become as prosperous as the *seigneur*, and the church had been democratized through the role of elected syndics. As a North American people the *Canadiens* had evolved to a point where European institutions were no longer acceptable:

Le continent d'Europe diffère essentiellement de l'Ancien Continent sous presque tous les rapports. Le climat, la nature du sol, les productions naturelles, les végétaux, les animaux, tout y diffère. Les hommes y sont aussi différemment modifiés, et vouloir leur faire trouver bon en Amérique, ce qu'ils trouvent bon en Europe, est une absurdité complète . . . . Croit-on que lorsque l'opinion publique dans tout le vaste continent de l'Amérique est en faveur des gouvernements représentatifs, il soit bien facile d'établir et de maintenir en Canada une noblesse dégénérée. L'idée est vraiment des plus ridicules. Telle est la tournure de l'esprit humain qu'il semble qu'il faille tout le contraire dans le nouveau monde. En Amérique il suffit de travailler pour être heureux.[30]

The rejection of degenerate European aristocracies in Blanchet's argument did not mean that the emerging *patriote* party's philosophy was wholly dedicated to democratic institutions in the modern sense. Indeed, Papineau still argued in 1826 for an appointed council, modified by the admission of rich, independent, and thus, virtuous, landholders.[31] Suggestions for reform of the council were made within the framework of a social analysis that stressed the egalitarian nature of North American society.

Jacques Labrie's constitutional discussion of 1827, for example, argued for change in the council along these same lines. Labrie made the point that English politicians debating the Lower Canadian constitution's merits in 1790 had seen the need for institutions more in keeping with conditions in the New World. According to Labrie, Fox and other opposition critics,

suggérèrent que l'on pourrait confier à un peuple de pères de familles, tous propriétaires, et qui en conséquence auraient des habitudes morales et paisibles, et souvent étrangères à des prolétaires, une action plus directe dans sa législation, que ne s'était réservé même le peuple le plus libre des nations européennes; ils souhaitèrent que le Conseil Législatif, qui en Canada devait tenir lieu de la Chambre des Lords, fut électif à vie.[32]

The distinction made here between "prolétaires" and "propriétaires" is significant. The discourse of *canadien* political writers assumed that land ownership conferred qualities consistent with the virtuous practice of politics, and North America was a society of landholders. Papineau in an address to his electors made the point in more lyrical, and distinctively Jeffersonian, language:

Nous avons tous une mise à peu près égale dans le fonds social, nous ne devons pas souffrir que des sociétaires privilégiés emportent tous les profits à discrétion et sans être tenus de nous rendre compte de leur administration. La nature, ou plutôt le Dieu de la nature, en donnant aux hommes à une époque où ils sont aussi éclairés qu'en la présente, les terres fertiles et d'une étendue illimitée de l'Amérique, les appelle à la liberté, à l'égalité des droits aux yeux de la loi, sur toute l'étendue de plus vaste des continents, depuis les rives de la Baie d'Hudson, jusqu'à la terre de feu.[33]

Such an emphasis on the political destiny of the North American continent inevitably implied a re-evaluation of the image of the

United States. Indeed, by 1827, Papineau's admiration for the American republic, expressed in the same document, was clear:

Il n'y a pas sur la surface du globe une société plus belle, mieux réglée, plus prospère où les peuples soient aussi contents, aussi universellement admirateurs de leurs institutions politiques, comme ils le sont dans toute l'étendue de cette puissante confédération. Elle fait en Europe l'admiration des plus grands hommes d'état. . . . Elle est appelée, même avant cette génération passe, à devenir le plus utile des alliés ou la plus formidable des rivales de l'Angleterre.[34]

Such comments marked an important transition in Papineau's thought. For although the Speaker's public utterances still occasionally praised the British constitution, the political crises of the 1820s were pushing him closer to openly advocating republican government. Before 1830, however, the *patriote* movement had not progressed to that point and consequently the image of the United States had not yet become a central part of its discourse. Still, the changes in that discourse, particularly the distinction between North America and Europe, were accompanied by the elaboration of a far more favourable image of the United States than that which had existed before 1815.

In the years leading up to the Rebellions, the image of the American remained firmly rooted in the civic humanist archetype of the ideal citizen. As the battle between the assembly and imperial authorities intensified, discussion of the United States and of the American character became a central component of political discourse within the colony. Much of that discourse continued to point out the differences between North America and Europe. Papineau, for example, speaking in favour of the Ninety-two Resolutions in the assembly, could not resist making the comparison between the state of public opinion and enlightenment in the American republic and in European monarchies:

Dans un temps où des gouverneurs militaires couvrent l'Europe de sang, les États-Unis, sans alarme, sans trouble, ouvrent leurs ports comme l'asile du malheur, où viennent se froisser et se briser toutes les opinions contre des opinions bien meilleures et bien plus profondément gravés dans les coeurs. C'est pourquoi ils ne craignent pas les sentiments des généraux de Bonaparte, qui s'y sont réfugiés. Toutes les opinions, tous les préjugés de la vieille Europe viennent tomber auprès du républicanisme de l'Union. On n'y a pas besoin d'armée, ni de censeur de la Presse. Chacun peut tout dire, tout écrire, et l'intérêt de tous assure qu'il n'y a pas de danger que les erreurs y prennent racine, et s'étendent au point de devenir contagieuses.[35]

The basis of this ability to shape the new immigrants into virtuous North Americans came from the particular democratic ethos of the American people, which, in turn, was derived from the particular social conditions of the New World. This was again highlighted in 1835 when a correspondent for *l'Echo du pays* published his impressions of Vermont society. Writing from the tiny community of Montpelier, Vermont, he argued that "l'égale répartition de la propriété en Amérique est une forte et puissante barrière opposée à l'oppression que facilitent tant dans la vieille Europe les fortunes colossales de l'Aristocratie." The author went on to draw the obvious conclusion for Lower Canada, declaring that "l'état de société y étant le même, il doit également jouir des avantages d'un gouvernement représentatif, responsable et soumis à l'opinion publique. Ce gouvernement, je le répète, est le seul possible en Amérique."[36] Americans and French Canadians shared the common distinction of being North Americans, and as such were inherently more virtuous than the impoverished European masses.

Still, despite the assumption inherent in the logic of North American specificity, there remained room for commentary on the character of the American people in the political discourse of the 1830s. In some cases that discussion was prompted by the criticism of newspapers opposed to the *patriote* cause who now saw the necessity of discrediting both the Americans as a people and their form of government. Having adopted the Americans as a model, the *Patriotes* were now forced to defend their choice.

On one level, the *patriote* press in the 1830s continued the tendency of the earlier decade, which emphasized the virtue of the American farmer. In fact, *la Minerve* even reprinted texts that had been published in the 1820s that underlined his virtue and good manners. One such text appeared in June of 1836, based ostensibly on the unpublished account of a *canadien* traveller. Here, as it had in the 1820s, the French Canadian press heralded American farmers (in this case New England farmers) as "des hommes éclairés et vertueux, remplis de force et d'énergie, pénétrés d'amour pour leur pays, capables par cette raison de tous les sacrifices nécessaires pour en cimenter l'indépendance."[37]

The American people did not, however, always live up to the image that was being drawn of them in the *patriote* press. The 1830s were years when the political effervescence that characterized Jacksonian democracy was often expressed in mob action. Riots broke out in New York City in opposition to the growing abolitionist movement, while in Baltimore the people took to the streets in protest against the activities of the Bank of the United States. The *Gazette de Québec*, which had followed John Neilson in his opposition to the *patriote* movement, saw the activities of the mob as evidence of the instability of American political institutions. The *patriote*-press, on the other hand, tried to explain the rioting in American cities as either the healthy expression of democratic life, the result of foreign intrigues, or a temporary aberration in the otherwise orderly progress of republican institutions.

The idea that political unrest in the United States was the result of European influence gained wide currency in the French Canadian press of the 1830s. Riots in Baltimore directed at the Bank of the United States prompted the editor of *le Canadien* to write of the foreign contamination of American politics through European immigration:

L'Amérique étant devenue l'égout du rebut des peuples de l'Europe elle doit s'attendre au renouvellement fréquent de pareilles scènes; et elle doit prendre ou prendra promptement, nous n'en doutons pas, des mesures énergiques pour réprimer les violences populaires dont elle est devenu le théâtre au grand scandale du monde entier, et au détriment des institutions libérales qui y règnent.[38]

Significantly, these comments came at a time when the *Patriotes* themselves were highly critical of foreign immigration. In addition, they again underlined the European origin of political trouble in North America and the fact that such subversion could even operate in the American republic. Reporting the same riots, *l'Echo du pays* saw the activities of the mob in Baltimore as evidence that the American people were ever vigilant in guarding against the activities of institutions that might infringe on their liberties. Not unlike Lower Canadians, the good people of Baltimore had risen up against a local oligarchy:

Si l'on en cherche la source on trouvera qu'ils remontent à l'époque où l'opinion publique se déclara contre la banque des États, établissement qui eût fini par faire perdre à nos voisins leur liberté et à les mettre entre les mains d'une oligarchie puissante . . . . Ils [le peuple] prirent en horreur plus que jamais la tyrannie et les hommes qui voulaient la favoriser. Tout ce qui avait quelque rapport avec la banque excitait leur indignation, et le peuple une fois excité a peut-être été trop loin en quelques circonstances. On voit du moins que la faute n'est pas dans les institutions américaines bien dans l'aristocratie ministérielle des États-Unis.

In the same article the journalist left no question of the support for this "aristocratie ministérielle": "il est même à notre connaisance que l'Autriche soudoie des hommes qui se vendent à tout prix pour exciter des troubles chez nos voisins."[39] Thus, the source of political troubles in the United States could again be traced back to European interests and their subversive activities in North America.

If the political difficulties of the United States gave the *Patriotes* cause for concern, there was by the 1830s very little dissent from the view that American government embodied the form of political organization that was thought to be best suited to a North American society. Further, the *Patriotes* viewed the United States very much as a loosely knit federation of independent republics. In this they were consistent with the classical theme that republics could not be too large, because the common good would become unidentifiable in a large heterogenous country. The American experience seemed, then, to be the fulfilment of the Enlightenment ideal of the republic, an ideal made reality by the peculiar social conditions of the New World. Of course, this interpretation of American government was not unique to the *Patriotes.* One finds it in the writings of the French americophiles, and, indeed, in the political discourse of the Americans themselves.[40]

The theme of North American specificity and the emphasis on the United States as a political model merged in the *patriote* discourse of the early 1830s. Papineau openly avowed his republican beliefs in 1831 in speeches before the assembly that stressed the importance of making the elective principle the basis of Lower Canadian government. The Speaker made the explicit link between the social state of the colony and the need for political reform, and, increasingly, cited the United States as a model for political change in the colony. Thus, speaking on reform of the legislative council in March of that year, he referred to the American government as "le gouvernement où le système représentatif produit de si heureux effets, qui est le thème constant des hommes éclairés en Europe, et dont l'organisation sociale si sagement composée est vantée même par des ministres anglais."[41] Speaking of American political institutions a few days later, Papineau declared that "à peu d'exceptions elles sont parfaites, et les habitans des États-Unis sont sans comparaison les mieux gouvernés qu'il y ait sur la surface du globe."[42]

By late 1832 and early 1833, reform of the constitution in order to create an elected legislative council became part of the *patriote* program, and was enshrined as such in resolutions passed by the assembly.[43] At this point *patriote* papers openly began to refer to the United States as the only acceptable political model for the colony. Here again the emphasis on the American political system was justified by the argument that it was in harmony with the special nature of North American societies. In the summer of 1833 *la Minerve* argued that only the American form of limited government could apply in a situation where "un peuple est composé d'existences homogènes, c'est à dire, qu'il n'y a pas une énorme disparité de droits, de devoirs, de fortune, d'intelligence, de connaissances, d'occupations, et de respectabilité morale entre ceux qui le composent."[44] *Le Canadien* made the same point in an editorial published a few weeks later. Citing the egalitarian state of Lower Canadian society as incompatible with aristocratic institutions, the editor declared, "Le seul modèle que nous avons à suivre, ce sont les États-Unis où la société ressemble à la nôtre."[45] Yet another editorial in *la Minerve* dealt with the differences between European and North American political institutions in an article titled "Deux systèmes opposés." Arguing that the despotism that characterized European government fed on ignorance, inequality, and fanaticism, the author noted that, with the exception of the British North American colonies, such forms of government had almost disappeared in the New World: "Partout ailleurs les privilèges aristocratiques et les monopoles d'argent et de pouvoir, décrédités, honnis, ont disparu avec l'expulsion de ceux qui les exploitaient."[46] The reference, of course, was to the United States, which, according to *le Canadien*, "possède la civilisation la plus avancée; j'entends par civilisation, les meilleures lois, le gouvernement le plus libre et le mieux organisé; la population la plus heureuse et la plus généralement éclairée."[47]

The assembly's resolutions calling for constitutional change and the emphasis on the United States as a model for those changes were but a prelude for the more complete statement of the *patriote* position, which came, in February of 1834, in the form of the

Ninety-two Resolutions. Indeed, the Resolutions themselves, albeit in rather veiled language, rejected the British political model in favour of the American. Thus, the forty-first resolution reminded the British government of the Colonial Secretary's admission that the colony's inhabitants should have nothing to envy in the political arrangements of their neighbours, adding that there remained a great deal worthy of envy in the American form of government:

Les États voisins ont une forme de gouvernement très propre à empêcher les abus de pouvoir et très efficace à les réprimer; que l'inverse de cet ordre de choses a toujours prévalu pour le Canada, sous la forme actuelle de gouvernement; qu'il y a dans les pays voisins un attachement plus universel et plus fort pour les institutions que nulle part ailleurs, et qu'il y existe une garantie de perfectionnement progressif des institutions politiques.

The forty-third resolution rejected the British political tradition as the sole source for constitutional reform in the colony. Rather, it suggested that consideration be given to the more liberal regimes that had been granted the American colonies, as well as to "des modifications que des hommes vertueux et éclairés ont fait subir à ces institutions coloniales, quand ils ont pu le faire avec l'assentiment des parties intéressés." The forty-fourth resolution cited the "consentement unanime avec lequel tous les peuples de l'Amérique ont adopté et étendu le Système électif" as proof that "il est conforme aux voeux, aux moeurs et à l'état social de ses habitants."[48] If the resolutions themselves left any doubts on the matter, Papineau dispelled them in his energetic defence of the *Patriotes'* political manifesto. The speaker predicted that before long "toute l'Amérique doit être républicaine" and praised the government of the United States as far more liberal than the military despotisms of Europe.[49]

The Ninety-two Resolutions firmly established the idea that the United States was the only appropriate model for reform of the Lower Canadian constitution. This view was echoed by *la Minerve*, which, in its New Year's Day edition for 1835, again contrasted the sorry political state of Europe with the prosperity and stability of the American republic.[50] Later the same year the paper explained that representative government had evolved naturally out of the peculiar social conditions of the New World, and that North Americans had begun to teach the lessons of liberty to old Europe. Only the continued existence of European institutions in the colony had prevented it from reaching the same degree of prosperity as its southern neighbour.[51] For its part, *l'Echo du Pays* made no bones about where Lower Canadians should look for examples of improved political institutions: "L'exemple du gouvernement modèle, les États-Unis, les a convaincu qu'il est celui qui offre le plus de garanties au sujet. Ce qu'ils voient faire le bonheur d'un peuple et lui procurer un état de prospérité inconnue encore chez aucune autre nation, ils le regardent avec raison comme ce qui approche le plus de la perfection."[52]

By 1835, the same sentiments were being expressed in public meetings across the province. Thus, a reform dinner held in Stanstead toasted the United States, and proclaimed, to the air of "Hail Columbia," that the *Canadiens* should have nothing to envy their neighbours.[53] At the St. Jean-Baptiste celebrations held in St. Denis the same year, two toasts were drunk to the United States, the first celebrating the liberty and prosperity of the American republic, the second calling for reforms in the colony that would leave Lower Canadians with nothing to envy their neighbours.[54] Much the same sentiment was expressed the following year at celebrations held at St. Jean and St. Charles.[55] When news of the Russell Resolutions reached the colony, the emphasis on the United States as a political model intensified. Papineau, speaking before a patriotic assembly held at St. Laurent in May of 1837, was unreserved in his praise of the American form of government, calling it "la structure de gouvernement la plus parfaite que le génie et la vertu aient encore élevée pour le bonheur de l'homme en société."[56] Similarly, toasts made at public assemblies on the eve of the Rebellions praised the American Constitution as "un modèle de sagesse que nous envions."[57]

The *Patriotes'* admiration for American government, then, grew out of the fact that its democratic institutions were more in keeping with the particular nature of North American society. It would be a grave error to believe, however, that French Canadians viewed the United States as a unitary government, or that when they referred to American constitutions they had only in mind the federal constitution. In fact, one of the most attractive elements of American political institutions for the *Patriotes* was the autonomy of state governments, which they saw very much as independent republics within the federation. The genesis of the state governments lent credence to this view. New states, after all, adopted their own constitutions in democratically elected conventions before joining the Union.

When Papineau, in 1837, praised the American form of government as the most perfect known to man, the process for the admission of new states was one aspect listed in support of his argument.[58] Papineau used this example less than a year after the admission of the new state of Michigan. Nor had the process of constitution-making in the Michigan territory gone unnoticed in the *patriote* press. *Le Canadien*, for one, produced a detailed report on the constitutional convention's activities. Moreover, the sight of a free people adopting their own form of government moved the paper's editor to reiterate the theme of North America as the cradle of political liberty.[59]

Of course, by the time these comments were made, the idea of revising the Lower Canadian constitution through a popularly elected convention had been around for some time. The assembly had even formally called for a convention as early as 1833. While this call might not have been inspired by an American constitutional convention, there was one compelling example of the American people acting in convention at the state level early in the period. In 1832, after years of political struggle over the issue of federal tariffs, the state of South Carolina took the drastic step of calling a convention to deal with the issue. This provoked the so-called "Nullification Crisis," a test of strength between the federal government and a renegade state that ended with President Jackson declaring South Carolina to be in a state of rebellion and dispatching federal troops to enforce the tariff. Although the Nullification Convention failed in achieving its goals, it was a stunning and well publicized example of direct participation in American politics. As such it was not lost on the *Patriotes*. The incident was widely reported in the press, with Lower Canadian papers reproducing the Nullification Ordinance and Jackson's Nullification Proclamation.[60] A month after the first reports of the South Carolina convention voting the nullification ordinance appeared in the colony, the assembly passed resolutions calling on Great Britain to give an elected convention the power to amend the Lower Canadian constitution.[61] The debates over the issue leave no doubt of the American inspiration of the measure.[62]

While the debates in the Lower Canadian assembly took place before the dénouement of the nullification crisis, the *Patriotes* had to admit that the actions of this particular convention had put the Union in peril.[63] When the issue was resolved, the *patriote* press rejoiced, arguing that such a crisis, defused through compromise in the United States, would surely have provoked a war in Europe.[64]

Further, the nullification debate did little to cool *patriote* enthusiasm for the notion of a constitutional convention. Indeed, the example of South Carolina pointed out that the people of a state could meet in convention to alter existing political arrangements. Papineau made this point in 1834, when he argued that political institutions could be perfected and revised in the republican system "au moyen de conventions du peuple, pour répondre sans secousses, ni violences aux besoins de toutes les époques."[65]

Jackson's actions in the midst of the nullification crisis and in other instances led some to question the extent of executive power in the United States. When the American whigs raised the spectre of executive abuse and insisted on the role of the legislature in preserving the people's liberties, their message was received wholeheartedly by the Lower Canadian *Patriotes*. For the French Canadian political movement, the struggle was similar and the stakes just as high. In advocating an elected legislative council, the *Patriotes* were seeking to wrest control of the colonial government from the hands of the Governor and what they considered to be his corrupt entourage of appointed officials. In this sense the American model was a compelling one, for, at both the state and federal level, popularly elected bicameral legislatures watched vigilantly over the actions of the executive. The essential quality of American government in the *Patriotes'* eyes then, was popular participation at all levels of the legislative process. Thus, Denis-Benjamin Viger, speaking as a member of the legislative council he sought to abolish, pointed out that nowhere in the United States could there be found a legislative body immune from the influence of the people. Consequently no legislative body could, as was the case in the colony, stifle the will of the people's elected representatives.[66]

When French Canadian papers favourable to reform discussed changing the legislative council, the American model was invariably invoked. Even before the passage of the Ninety-two Resolutions, an article in *le Canadien* argued that the reformed upper house should be patterned after the American Senate, with councillors serving six-year terms, and with a third of the house elected every two years. The author also suggested that election to the council be reserved for those owning land in the colony.[67] Linking the council to land ensured that it would be composed of virtuous and independent members. Indeed, this was the only way to ensure the independence of councillors in a society where "les fortunes sont mobiles, où l'homme qui était indépendant hier peut devenir dépendant demain." Thus, the new council had to be clearly linked to property, "comme on l'a fait dans presque tous les États-Unis."[68]

The *Patriotes* also envisaged an upper house that would act as a balance against the will of the people expressed in the assembly. Indeed, the very call for a reformed council rather than for abolition of the upper house indicates the importance still attributed to the idea of balance in political institutions. Yet, having pronounced North America as antithetical to aristocracy, the question became what order in society would be represented in the council. To this the *Patriotes* replied that the council would be made up of the "aristocratie des talents et vertus," or the "aristocratie naturelle," within Lower Canadian society. In describing the political balance established by the American constitution, *patriote* papers noted that while the Americans had rejected the idea of a hereditary aristocracy, they had created "une aristocratie élective."[69] Indeed, this was one of the primary advantages of the American system: it allowed men of virtue, independence, and talent—the "natural" aristocracy—to take their rightful place in the political order.[70] The example of virtuous and moderate upper houses in the United States, both at the state and the federal level, seemed to indicate that such a body might restore the balance that had been so long absent from the Lower Canadian legislative process.[71]

The *Patriotes'* very open advocacy of an American form of government did not go unchallenged. Indeed, their political opponents reacted, particularly after 1834, with a scathing critique of the United States and its constitution. *Le Canadien*, while it opposed the *patriote* leadership after 1836, rarely attacked the American form of government *per se*, preferring to harp on the dangers presented by the prospect of annexation to the republic. The *Gazette de Québec*, however, felt the need to rebut the *patriote* position more directly. To this end it highlighted disorder and conflict in the United States and proclaimed that the republic was but an experiment in government that was inevitably doomed to failure. Thus, on the occasion of squabbles between two states in 1835, the *Gazette* predicted that the union "n'existera certainement pas cinquante années de plus."[72] When some slave owners in Louisiana put a price on the head of a leading New York abolitionist, the paper mocked the vaunted perfection of American institutions: "Vraiment, la république parfaite commence à offrir des traits qui répugneraient aux noirs de l'Afrique, dont ils [sic] tiennent un si grand nombre en esclavage."[73] When feeling against the Bank of the United States excited American mobs to riot, the *Gazette* termed American government "une expérience en embrion," predicting "ces étoiles et ce drapeau rayé ne flotteront pas pendant cinquante ans sur ce continent, sans qu'il se passe des scènes de carnage qui feront la honte de la liberté et de la raison."[74] When the American economy was plunged into disorder in 1837, the Quebec paper believed the crisis to be imminent: "Le peuple souverain demande à hauts cris une réforme radicale du gouvernement modèle; on parle d'assembler une convention nationale, et de lever à New York une armée de 10,000 hommes pour aller assiéger le Président à Washington."[75] In short, the *Gazette* argued that the *Patriotes* were blind to the republic's faults and that in choosing it as their political model they had demonstrated their own political ineptitude.

The attacks of the anti-*patriote* press are a powerful testimony to the central place of the American model in French Canadian political discourse of the 1830s. By then, in order to discredit the *Patriotes* one had to attack the society they sought to emulate, to discredit the Americans and their institutions. Although the *Patriotes* fought back energetically and their tone was generally optimistic when they discussed the American republic, their discourse also manifested a certain sense of urgency. To be sure, it was difficult to counter the *patriote* insistence on the excellence of American institutions and the material as well as political achievements of republican government; indeed, this positive view of the United States was supported by the work of European commentators. Still, the political events of the 1830s in the United States seriously challenged the vision of a stable and virtuous agricultural republic populated by independent landholders. For the *Patriotes'* political enemies, the Bank War, anti-abolitionist riots, and, particularly, American manifestations of anti-Catholicism, were powerful arguments against the republic. While all these events could be explained away as examples of European influence in the New World, the increased frequency of political upheaval in America was an ominous sign that the "Machiavellian moment," as Pocock called it, was at hand. The New World stood at a crossroads, with one path leading in the direction of degeneration and corruption, the other to the maintenance of virtue and liberty.

It is from this civic humanist perspective of the evolution of society and politics that the *Patriotes* viewed the historical and geopolitical significance of their own movement. For, as they made clear time and time again, corrupt European institutions had but one significant foothold in the New World: British North America. It followed that the destruction of European influence on the continent in the 1830s was as necessary to the preservation of liberty as the stand of the American patriots had been sixty years earlier. In preserving the liberty of their distinctly American society, the *Patriotes* would help guarantee its future in the hemisphere. To a certain extent this argument rested on an analysis of imperial policy that emphasized its tyrannical and aristocratic objectives, one that British attempts at compromise in the early 1830s seemed to belie. When news of the Russell Resolutions reached the colony in early 1837, however, there could be little doubt concerning the intention of European legislators.

In the context of 1837, the American image acquired its full significance. The Revolution, whose meaning had been highly ambiguous even in the early 1830s, now began to be cited as an example of armed colonial resistance. In the tense summer leading up to the Rebellion, the Revolution was invoked time and time again. In his first speech after news of the Russell Resolution reached the colony Papineau recalled the example of the First Continental Congress's economic boycott and the memory of the patriots of 1774. Yet, this oft-cited example of the early phase of American resistance was followed in his speech by references to the sword of Washington and to the defeat of British regulars by virtuous North American farmers. Over the summer, short articles on Washington now appeared beside the more traditional profiles of Franklin in the *patriote* press. In Montreal, young *Patriotes* organized themselves under the name *Fils de la liberté*, and their manifesto began with a literal translation of the Declaration of Independence. Across the province patriotic assemblies expressed solidarity with the Americans, their government, and their revolution. In the countryside committees of safety and vigilance organized in conscious imitation of those founded in Massachusetts on the eve of the Revolution. By the time more moderate leaders such as Papineau tried to regain control over the meaning of the American Revolution and use it to support economic strategies of resistance, radicals had used it to push the movement to the brink of rebellion.[76]

101

When the *Patriotes* met at St. Charles in the last days before armed conflict broke out, they spelled out the logic that led them to rebellion in clear terms. In the "Adresse de la confédération des six comtés" we find again a literal translation of Jefferson's Declaration. Like the Declaration, the "Adresse" enumerated British abuses and spoke of the government's will to impose tyranny on the people by force. In addition, however, there is an expression of solidarity with the peoples of the Americas, and particularly with the citizens of the United States. The Americans, stated the "Adresse," would recognize the similarity of the Lower Canadian situation to that which had brought on their own Revolution, and would understand that the establishment of a tyrannical government on their northern border would serve as the instrument "de l'introduction du même gouvernement arbitraire dans d'autres parties du continent américain."[77] European corruption could no longer be tolerated in the New World; what had begun at Lexington and Concord would be completed on the banks of the St. Lawrence.

As we know, the Rebellions failed, the French Canadian republic was never created, and the forces of corruption triumphed. For their part, the Americans proved indifferent to the cause, and their good republican first magistrate moved quickly to declare his country's neutrality in the conflict. In the *patriote* refugee community of northern Vermont and New York, America's positive image gave way to disillusionment and eventually resentment, but this is another story. For twenty years America's image as a sister North American society and eventually a political model had been carefully cultivated. The significance of that image, however, can only be understood in reference to definitions of French Canadian collective identity that emerged in the same period. This first definition of the distinct society was marked by an emphasis on its North American nature and was constructed in the language of civic humanism. North Americans, quite simply, lived in a social context that favoured the preservation of virtue and offered the possibility of checking the growth of commerce and its attendant threat of political corruption.

This is not to say that language, institutions, and religion, the traditional triumvirate of early French Canadian nationalism as described by historians, were not part of the first distinct society. Their inclusion in a civic humanist distinct society, however, is far less contradictory than their presence in a liberal one. In this civic humanist perspective on early French Canadian political discourse the divided souls of traditional historiography appear far less tormented. Moreover, such an explanation in no way divorces the social motivations of political actors from their political discourse. Further, it clearly situates French Canadian political discourse in a North American context, rejecting an interpretation that relies on notions of French Canadian particularism in favour of one that highlights similarities with the discursive context. Finally, the classical form of French Canadian political discourse enhances our understanding of its final and unequivocal rejection by the *Patriotes*, who could no more compromise with constitutionalism than they could with the devil.

NOTES

* This article was originally presented at a conference in Ottawa, November 1991, sponsored by the Canadian Study of Parliament Group to mark the bicentennial of the Constitutional Act of 1791.

1. NA, *Fonds Famille Papineau* 2162-2165, Louis-Joseph Papineau to Marshall Spring Bidwell 16 April 1836.
2. For a classic theoretical statement of this view see Quentin Skinner, "Meaning and Understanding in the History of Ideas," *History and Theory* 8 (1969): 3-53.
3. Yvan Lamonde, "L'histoire culturelle et intellectuelle du Québec: tendances et aspects méthodologiques," in his *Territoires de la culture québécoise* (Québec 1991) 12.
4. On the historiography dealing with French Canadian political discourse before 1837 see Louis~Georges Harvey, "Importing the Revolution: The Image of America in French Canadian Political Discourse, 1805-1837," diss., University of Ottawa, 1990, Introduction and chapter 1. See also L.-G. Harvey and M. V. Olsen, "French Revolutionary Forms in French Canadian Political Discourse 1805-1835," *Canadian Historical Review* (1987): 374-92.
5. Cited by Janet Ajzenstat, *The Political Thought of Lord Durham* (Kingston: McGill-Queen's University Press, 1988) 80.
6. André Vachet, "L'idéologie libérale et la pensée sociale au Québec," in C. Panaccio and P. A. Quintin, eds., *Philosophie au Québec* (Montréal 1976) 113-26.
7. Peter Smith, "The Ideological Origins of Canadian Confederation," *Canadian Journal of Political Science* 20.1 (1987): 3-29.
8. J. G. A. Pocock, *The Machiavellian Moment: Florentine Political Thought and the Atlantic Republican Tradition* (Princeton 1975).

9. Pocock, vii.

10. ———, vii.

11. ———, vii.

12. ——— 384, 386.

13. ——— chapters 14, 15.

14. J. G. A. Pocock, "The Mobility of Property and the Rise of Eighteenth-Century Sociology," in his *Virtue, Commerce, and History* (Cambridge 1985) 108.

15. Pocock, "Authority and Property: The Question of Liberal Origins," *Virtue, Commerce, and History* 48.

16. Bernard Bailyn, *The Ideological Origins of the American Revolution* (Cambridge, MA 1969); Gordon Wood, *The Creation of the American Republic* (New York 1972). Wood, however, argues that the adoption of the Federal Constitution marked the "end of classical politics" and the beginning of a more indigenous and modern conception of politics based on the balance of interests within the state as embodied in the constitution itself. This is a view that Pocock challenged in his *Machiavellian Moment*, and that has come under fire in more recent studies. See Wood, chapter 15; Pocock 513-52. On Jeffersonian thought see Lance Banning, *The Jeffersonian Persuasion* (Ithaca 1978), chapters 5-9. On the whigs and Democrats see Daniel Walker Howe, *The Political Culture of the American Whigs* (Chicago 1979) and Robert Remini, *Andrew Jackson and the Course of American Freedom* (New York 1981). The historiography of "Republican Revisionism" and the liberal critique of that view has recently been summarized by Banning, "Jeffersonian Ideology Revisited: Liberal and Classical Ideas in the New American Republic," *William and Mary Quarterly* (1988): 3-19.

17. On the diffusion of American news in the colony see Harvey, "Importing the Revolution" ch. 2.

18. Denis-Benjamin Viger, *Considérations sur les effets qu'ont produit en Canada . . .* (Montréal 1809), reprinted in Viger, *Oeuvres Politiques* (Montréal 1970). On the history of Rome, Viger writes, "Ce qu'il y a de plus surprenant dans le tableau de leur histoire; c'est que le temps de la dépravation fut celui des plus affreuses révolutions . . . . Gangrénée intérieurement, elle [Rome] tomba pour ainsi dire d'elle-même, affaisée par son propre . . . . L'épicurisme moderne a produit les mêmes effets chez les nations qui ont eu le malheur de se laisser entraîner par leur exemple."

19. *Le Canadien* 22 November 1806.

20. See, for example, the articles on American migrants to the Townships published in *le Canadien* 8 November 1807, 28 November 1807, and 26 December 1807.

21. Banning, *Jeffersonian Persuasion* 82-83.

22. Pocock, *Machiavellian Moment* chapter 15.

23. On this theme see Fred Somkin, *Unquiet Eagle: Memory and Desire in the Idea of American Freedom, 1815-1860* (Ithaca 1967), and George Dangerfield, *The Awakening of American Nationalism*, 1815-1828 (New York 1965).

24. *Le Canadien* 28 August 1822; cited by Philippe Reid, "Représentations idéologiques et société globale: le journal *le Canadien* (1806-1842)," diss., Université Laval, 1979, 209-210, and Benoit Bernier, "Les idées politiques d'Étienne Parent, 1822-1825," thesis, Université Laval, 1971, 36.

25. *Le Canadien* 1 January 1823.

26. *Le Canadien* 12 November 1823; cited by Reid 193.

27. RAPQ (1953-1955) 205-210, Papineau to Julie Papineau 27 June 1823.

28. NA, *Fonds Les Eboulements* MG8 F131 1313-1317, Pierre de Sales Laterrière to Paschal de Sales Laterrière 25 August 1825.

29. NA *Fonds Famille Papineau* MG24 B2 vol. 1 486-489, Papineau to Julie Papineau 23 September 1823.

30. François Blanchet, *Appel au Parlement impérial et aux habitants des colonies angloises* . . . (Québec 1824) 11. Blanchet discusses changes to French Canadian society before the Conquest on pages 34-35.

31. NA *Fonds Famille Papineau* MG24 B2 vol. 1 669-674, Papineau to Sir Francis Burton November 1826; see also vol. 1 640-659, Papineau to Sir James Mackintosh 25 April 1826.

32. Jacques Labrie, *Les premiers rudiments de la Constitution britannique* . . . (Montréal 1827) 39.

33. Louis-Joseph Papineau, *Addresse à tous les électeurs du Bas Canada* (Montréal 1827) 3-4.

34. *Adresse* 18-19.

35. Papineau, speech in the Assembly 18 February 1834, reprinted in *État de la province* (Québec 1834) [8].

36. "Situation de Montpelier: État de société en Amérique et aristocratie en Europe," *l'Echo du pays* 3 September 1835.

37. "Extrait inédit d'un voyage aux États-Unis," *la Minerve* 1 June 1836.

38. *Le Canadien* 21 August 1835.

39. *L'Echo du pays* 27 August 1835.

40. For a discussion of European sources of the same view and of their availability in the colony, see Harvey, "Importing the Revolution . . ." 2.

41. Papineau, speech to the Assembly, *la Minerve* 17 March 1831.

42. ———, *la Minerve* 28 March 1831.

43. The Assembly voted a resolution on 15 January 1833 asking that a convention be called to amend the constitution in order to make the Legislative Council more compatible with the state of Lower Canadian society.

44. "Société politique," *la Minerve* 25 July 1833.

45. Parent, *le Canadien* 12 August 1833.

46. "Deux systèmes opposés," *la Minerve* 26 August 1833.

47. Parent, *le Canadien* 20 September 1833.

48. The text of the "Quatre-vingt-douze résolutions" (1834) appears in T. P. Bédard, *Histoire de cinquante ans* (1791-1841) (Québec 1869) 334-62. The resolutions cited appear on 345-46.

49. See Papineau's speech in the Assembly 14 February 1834, reprinted in *État de la province* (1834) [7].

50. *La Minerve* 1 January 1835.

51. *La Minerve* 23 November 1835.

52. *L'Echo du pays* 31 December 1835.

53. This was the 8th toast of the reform dinner held at Stanstead in January of 1835, reported in *l'Echo du pays* 29 January 1835.

54. Reported in *le Canadien* 6 July 1835.

55. Reported in *la Minerve* 27 June 1836.

56. Comité central de Montréal, *Procédés de l'assemblée des électeurs du comté de Montréal tenue à St. Laurent le 15 mai 1837* (Montréal 1837) 10.

57. See reports of the proceedings of the "fête champêtre" held at l'Acadie and at Lavaltrie in *la Minevre* 5 October 1837.

58. The American Constitution, Papineau explained, "pourvoit d'avance a ce qu'un territoire dès qu'il y a 60,000 habitans puisse se constituer en état libre et indépendant. Il devient le maître et l'arbitre absolu de son sort." See his speech in *Procédés de l'assemblée* 10.

59. *Le Canadien* 13 July 1835.

60. The Nullification Ordinance was published in full in la Minerve 13 December 1832 and in *le Canadien* 14 December 1832. Jackson's proclamation appeared in *le Canadien* 21 and 24 December 1832 and in the *Gazette de Québec* 22 December 1832.

61. JHALC 42 (1832-33) 307-308.

62. See the text of Papineau's speech of 10 January 1833, reproduced in *la Minerve* 17 and 24 January 1833, cited by Fernand Ouellet, *Le Bas-Canada 1791-1840: Changements structureaux et crise* (Ottawa: Éditions de l'Université d'Ottawa, 1976) 353. Joseph Gugy, an opponent of the measure invoked the nullification convention as an example of political discord in the United States; see the report of his speech in the *Gazette de Québec* 22 January 1833.

63. *Patriote* papers recognized this when they first reported the actions of South Carolina's convention. Parent, in *le Canadien*, wrote of "la position menaçante dans laquelle ces deux pièces [South Carolina's Nullification Ordinance and Jackson's Nullification Proclamation] mettent le gouvernement général des

États-Unis vis-à-vis d'un des états de cette vaste et florissante république." See the paper's 14 December 1832 issue.

64. See *l'Echo du pays* 28 March 1833; also *le Canadien* 30 April 1834, where Parent argues that "La question des états du sud, qui a été réglée à l'amiable, aurait certainement causé des bouleversements en Europe."

65. Speech reported in *la Minerve* 24 March 1834; cited in Ouellet, *Bas-Canada* 353. Papineau was citing the 41st of the Ninety-two Resolutions. Privately, Papineau predicted that the American federation might one day break into several smaller federations, but believed that this would be effected through conventions of the various states involved rather than through war. Papineau made the comment in a letter to Arthur Roebuck. See NA, *Roebuck Papers* MG 24 A19 file 5 47-48, Papineau to Roebuck 13 March 1836.

66. Denis Benjamin Viger, *Observations de l'hon. D. B. Viger contre la proposition faite dans la conseil Législative...* (Montréal 1835) 31.

67. *Le Canadien* 12 August 1833.

68. *Le Canadien* 10 May 1833.

69. The term appears in "Réflexions sur l'administration générale des colonies," *la Minerve* 4 July 1831.

70. See, for example, Papineau's description of American government in his speech at St. Laurent in May of 1837: "Toutes les charges y étant électives, elles y sont exercés par l'aristocratie naturelle"; see the report of his speech in *Procédés de l'assemblée* 12.

71. Étienne Parent continued to believe this even after he had broken with the *patriotes*. Applauding the creation of an upper house in Vermont, the editor remarked "Une seconde chambre avec certaines conditions d'âge ou d'expérience et de propriété, nous parait un modérateur nécessaire dans un gouvernement représentatif." See *le Canadien* 26 October 1836. There were those, however, who argued for the abolition of the upper house, and predicted the disappearance of the House of Lords in England, as well as the American Senate. This view, a rather isolated one, appears in an article published in *l'Echo du pays* 16 October 1834.

72. *Gazette de Québec* 14 May 1835.

73. *Gazette de Québec* 3 September 1835.

74. *Gazette de Québec* 20 February and 30 April 1836.

75. *Gazette de Québec* 27 May 1837.

76. These developments are described in detail by Harvey, "Importing the Revolution" ch. 6.

77. "Adresse de la confédération des six comtés au peuple du Canada," published in *la Minerve* 2 November 1837.

CHAPTER FIVE

CIVIC HUMANISM VERSUS LIBERALISM:
FITTING THE LOYALISTS IN

Peter J. Smith

For nearly two decades scholars have been vigorously debating the place of John Locke and liberalism in eighteenth-century Anglo-American political thought.[1] The debate, particularly heated among historians and political scientists, centres on the question of which language or political discourse was dominant in the eighteenth century, liberalism or civic humanism. Closely related is the question of how liberalism arose. Was it a response to civic humanism and a defence of commercial society, or did it emerge independently of civic humanism, from its roots in the Western natural law or jurisprudential tradition? Merely posing these questions points to an extraordinary upheaval in the historical interpretation of American political culture.[2] In questioning the place of Locke and liberalism in American history one is questioning the very basis of American historiography.

The thesis that Locke and liberalism dominate not only eighteenth-century Anglo-American political thought but also the subsequent development of American political culture has been most ably put by Louis Hartz. Hartz formulated a theory about the development of new societies, applying it to the United States and, along with colleagues, to other societies. Hartz maintained that whenever a "fragment" of Europe separates itself from its European context and takes root in its new environment, it thereby loses the stimuli for change that the wider spectrum of political ideologies found in Europe provides. According to Hartz, "there is nothing mysterious about this mechanism of fragmentation. . . . A part detaches itself from the whole, the whole fails to renew itself, and the part develops without inhibition."[3] Thus, in Hartz's view, in breaking away America had escaped the dialectic, and Americans have always been Lockeans. Hartz's theory has also been employed to account for the roots of English-Canadian political culture. According to K. D. McRae, Hartz's Canadian counterpart, "as the central figure of the English-Canadian tradition we encounter once again the American liberal." In McRae's opinion, "the bulk of the Loyalists in British North America were predominantly Lockean and liberal."[4] Gad Horowitz, however, asserted that Lockean liberalism was not hegemonic in Canada, that "non-liberal British elements [had] entered into English-Canadian society *together* with American elements at the foundation." The result, in Horowitz's opinion, was a greater diversity in English Canadian political culture. A "tory touch" carried by the Loyalists prepared the way for a significant "socialist touch." Horowitz noted, however, that he did not intend "to deny that liberalism is the dominant element in the English-Canadian political culture, [but] to stress that it is not the sole element."[5]

In questioning the dominance of Locke, therefore, one is challenging our understanding of the formation not only of American but also of English Canadian political culture. Despite criticisms over the years, the Hartz-Horowitz thesis continues to be widely taught in Canada, serving as a basis for explaining not only Loyalist political thought but also subsequent English Canadian political culture.[6] The thesis deserves serious reconsideration. This paper reexamines the roots of Loyalist political thought and, implicitly, English Canadian political culture, arguing against both a Lockean dominance of Loyalist political thought and the existence of a precapitalist tory "touch." It begins by summarizing the major debates that have arisen among students of Anglo-American political thought. Second, it situates Loyalist political thought within this debate. Third, it outlines some of the possible implications of the debate for our understanding of the formation of English Canadian political culture.

THE CIVIC HUMANIST CRITIQUE

The existence of civic humanism, or, as American scholars call it, republicanism, has been thoroughly documented as a prevalent form of discourse throughout the eighteenth-century Anglo-American world.[7] Civic humanism was a post-feudal ideology; its inspiration lay in the works of classical historians, philosophers, and rhetoricians who stressed the possibility of liberty and virtue in a republic. Virtue referred primarily to the practice of citizenship in the classical, or Aristotelian, sense of the term. Man was a political animal (*zoon politikon*) who fulfilled himself by living a public life dedicated to civic concerns and the public good. Virtue necessitated certain moral qualities, for example, the ability to act selflessly for the public good. It also required a material base, preferably land, which gave individuals not only freedom and independence but the stake in one's country necessary to motivate them to act on its behalf. Virtue, however, was always difficult to establish and maintain. It was continually liable to corruption, from new forms of property and from the pursuit of selfish ends, whether they be wealth, pleasure, or power. The result, if not checked, would lead to a degeneration into despotic rule and the loss of political liberty.

The cure for corruption was not so much a reformation of human nature as good political and social institutions. Drawing from Polybius it was argued that each of the simple forms of constitution, where rule was exercised for the good of all, tended to degenerate into its corrupt form, in which rule was exercised for the selfish ends of the rulers—monarchy into tyranny, aristocracy into oligarchy, and law-abiding democracy into mob rule and thence to anarchy, from which, in turn, a single ruler would arise. This process could be avoided, however. Through a system of balanced government, that is, a mixed constitution that balanced classes or constitutional elements, the tendency of constitutions to degenerate could be slowed or arrested. Power would counter power. Rome in the ancient period and Britain in the modern era had such constitutions. Citizens could also be motivated to sacrifice through military service, while property qualifications could be required for citizens and rulers, thus ensuring at once their independence and their immunity from bribes.

Civic humanism in the modern world had been revived through the works of Machiavelli and James Harrington. According to some commentators, civic humanism "was the prevailing

111

ideology"[8] framing the political debate in eighteenth-century Britain and serving as a basis of the Country party's criticism of the established or Court whigs. Particularly feared was the financial and commercial revolution sweeping England, which had created not only a new class of moneyed men but also a vast expansion of state administration and public credit. The latter provided the means, the places and pensions, the political patronage used to "entice" members of parliament into supporting ministers of the Crown.

The acceptance of the civic humanist critique was widespread. One finds it discussed in Montesquieu's *The Spirit of the Laws*. It is deployed in the American colonies during the revolutionary period and beyond, in Jefferson's and Madison's criticisms of Hamilton's economic program, and in the nineteenth century as well.[9] Moreover, the survival of civic humanist themes in nineteenth-century Europe, especially Britain and France, has been well documented.[10]

DEFENDING COMMERCE AND THE WHIG REGIME

The ideological defence of the Court whigs is typically viewed as enjoying a symbiotic relationship with civic humanism, recognizing but recasting and transforming its themes so as to provide, as it did so, an articulate defence of modernity. It is debatable whether this transformation represents a difference in degree or in kind. Some, like M. M. Goldsmith, argue that civic humanism was sufficiently elastic to accommodate the defence of the Court whigs; they maintain that "ministerial writers responded to the Opposition by attacking their pretensions to virtue and by asserting the Ministry's civic humanist credentials." Court whigs, Goldsmith further claims, tended to invoke the post-Aristotelian, Stoic, and Ciceronian additions to civic humanism that stressed the private, social sphere, with its emphasis on personal freedom from authority rather than public participation.[11] In *The Machiavellian Moment* Pocock sketched an ideology of the Court that, he asserted, exhibited a clear interdependence with civic humanism. This ideology, derived from the writings of Jonathan Swift, Daniel Defoe, and others, strongly defended both commercial society with its luxury, refinement, and system of credit and the whig regime with its increasing administrative complexity, patronage, standing armies, and National Debt.[12]

Subsequent to the publication of *The Machiavellian Moment* Pocock and others modified this thesis by portraying Scottish political economy as the most effective alternative to civic humanism.[13] In brief, virtue was redefined and commerce defended by the Scottish political economists. Virtue was reinterpreted by placing the emphasis on the social, not the political. At the same time, commerce, with its attendant luxury, was depicted as refining passions and manners.[14] According to this interpretation liberty no longer meant the freedom to participate in public decisions; it meant a social liberty, the freedom to add to one's economic and cultural resources. Commerce was thus the parent of politeness and implied a new conception of liberty. If the rise of the social sphere over the political sphere is accepted as a defining characteristic of liberalism then "the liberal paradigm thus made its appearance in answer to the civic."[15]

EIGHTEENTH-CENTURY POLITICAL THOUGHT: CIVIC HUMANISM OR NATURAL JURISPRUDENCE?

In the approach to political thought sketched above there is no room for Locke. Liberalism, in brief, had non-Lockean roots. However, this interpretation is by no means universally accepted. There are students of political thought who assert that civic humanism is not central to an understanding of the development of eighteenth-century political thought. Those subscribing to this perspective argue the centrality and autonomy of the natural jurisprudence or natural law perspective from which liberalism is claimed to have evolved. In the opinion of Donald Winch, "there are those on the natural jurisprudential side of the divide who find it unnecessary to mention the civic tradition."[16]

In brief, these writers employ another vocabulary of thought and argue that the natural law tradition, which is virtually as old as Western political thought itself, has an existence independent of its role as a rebuttal to the criticism of the civic humanists. The basic concept of this tradition is *ius* (or right) as compared to virtue. *Ius* has as its central concern the possession, distribution, and administration of things. Man is viewed as a creature with "rights" to things that must be defined and protected by public law. In the natural jurisprudential paradigm man is a legal or juristic person very much unlike the citizen-warrior of the civic humanist tradition. The primary concern of man is not participation in ruling (*imperium*) but rather the rational pursuit of his private concerns and interests. One has liberty, but in a negative sense, that is, as the liberty to enjoy

113

one's life and to acquire and dispose of one's property without arbitrary action by one's rulers. The end of the state is not to encourage political participation but to protect the liberty and property of its subjects.[17]

From Grotious to Pufendorf to Locke and the Scottish political economists, it is argued, the concerns of the jurisprudential tradition remained the same—law and justice, the origins, rights, and duties of government, the protection of property, and the enforcement of contracts. For those subscribing to this tradition, "the child of jurisprudence is liberalism."[18]

There is a great deal to be said for the centrality of the natural jurisprudential perspective. Many American historians continue to view the development of the United States as occurring essentially within this paradigm, with Locke as the dominant thinker.[19] One would be remiss not to acknowledge evidence of this same perspective in the works of the Court whig pamphleteers. According to H. T. Dickinson:

among all the defenders of the Whig establishment there prevailed the firm conviction that authority could be maintained and liberty preserved only by the rule of law. . . . The aims and purposes of civil government—to maintain public order, to protect private property and to preserve the liberty of the subject— could only be achieved when the rule of law operated.[20]

A similar view of the state was evident in the works of Scottish theorists like Gershom Carmichael, Francis Hutcheson, Hume, and Smith, who, as M. M. Goldsmith argues, employed the vocabulary of natural jurisprudence.[21] Yet as they did so they gradually transformed and modernized that vocabulary, using history to show the growth of property relations and rejecting, as a consequence, Locke's jurisprudential contract theory based on a state of nature.

What results is a continuing puzzle for students of political and social theory. As Jeffrey C. Isaac writes, "there is a consensus on the absence of consensus among political theorists."[22] Political theorists are divided on the question of whether civic humanism or natural jurisprudence was the dominant approach in the eighteenth century. They are also divided on the question of which of the two was the parent of liberalism. A further question that arises is whether, in fact, one approach should be chosen over another. Goldsmith, when discussing eighteenth-century Britain, makes the case that

114

civic humanism was the dominant ideology. In the United States the debate is particularly fractious; competing claims are made for the pre-eminence of either civic humanism (republicanism, as American historians label it) or natural jurisprudence (in the form of Lockean liberalism in the eighteenth and nineteenth centuries).[23] Perhaps the last word on this subject should be left to Gordon S. Wood, who, referring to revolutionary America, writes:

> None of the Founding Fathers ever had any sense that he had to choose or as choosing between Machiavelli and Locke. We ought to remember that these boxlike traditions into which the historical participants must be fitted are essentially our inventions, and as such distortions of past reality.[24]

In effect, contemporary historians and political theorists may be looking for consensus or synthesis when none, in fact, existed.

For those who prefer boxlike certainty the absence of consensus is a problem. For others it represents an opportunity to reassess the foundations of eighteenth- and nineteenth-century political culture in the Anglo-American world. It is appropriate in this light to turn to a reassessment of Loyalist political culture in eighteenth-century America.

THE LOYALISTS AND CIVIC HUMANISM

There is considerable evidence that the Loyalists who participated in the debates over colonial independence were familiar with the language of civic humanism as well as the language of natural jurisprudence. Some preferred the language of one over the other, while others mixed the two, depending on the context of the argument. Typically, their defence of the empire along with their notions of liberty and property were likely to be taken from the rhetoric of natural jurisprudence, with its emphasis on regular government, sovereignty, order, and justice. In contrast, their defence of commerce, luxury, Crown patronage, and the system of public credit was derivative of the Court whig response to the civic humanist critique of the political and moral excesses of the whig regime. In the end the Loyalists had to defend a society that was becoming increasingly modern, commercial, heterogeneous, and hierarchical.

In particular, the Loyalists demonstrated a willingness to endorse the advantages of commerce. Unlike the Patriot literature of the American revolutionaries, which extolled "agrarianism" and a homogeneous society, the Loyalists extolled the advantages of a commercial society. In general, writes Hendrik Hartog,

Tory [i.e., Loyalist] arguments articulated values of a capitalist state. Whigs [i.e., Patriots], by contrast, reflected an earlier, largely agrarian tradition—even if only sentimentally. Their vision of decentralized, local institutions resistant to external authority would be antithetical to the expanding centrally controlled interdependency and the utilitarian calculation which we have learned characterizes the capitalist state.[25]

A representative example of the Loyalist defence of commerce came from the pen of James Chalmers, a Maryland landowner who during the war raised and commanded the Maryland Loyalist Regiment.[26] On the eve of the Revolutionary War Chalmers wrote a rebuttal to Thomas Paine's pamphlet, *Common Sense*, entitled *Plain Truth*.[27] Unlike many contemporary scholars, he interpreted Paine as a civic humanist and offered a spirited defence of commerce.

Chalmers was particularly intent on rebutting Paine's assertion that commerce had negative effects on the human personality. Like so many others in the civic humanist tradition, Paine had argued that "commerce diminishes the spirit both of patriotism and military defence." Furthermore, Paine insisted, "with the increase of commerce England had lost its spirit."[28] On the contrary, argued Chalmers, the spirit of commerce was entirely positive. "I do most fervently pray," he wrote, "that we may never exchange the spirit of commerce for that of military defence." Chalmer's authority for the advantages of commerce was Montesquieu, whom he quotes at length. In *The Spirit of the Laws* Montesquieu had described how *"doux commerce"* refined and moderated behaviour. Commerce was a civilizing process in history, making men and nations less rude and barbaric. In Chalmers's opinion nothing but calamities had befallen peoples possessed of a military spirit, and he concluded that "commerce has most happily humanized mankind." Moreover, he maintained, England had not lost its spirit. Rather, the English were the "lords and factors of the universe," joining "to the commerce of Tyre, Carthage, and Venice, the fire of old Rome."[29]

Daniel Leonard, a Massachusetts Loyalist, echoed Chalmers on the blessings of commerce.[30] Leonard linked commerce and progress, contrasting progress with the disadvantages of an agri-

116

cultural economy. In his estimation, "exclusive of commerce, the colonists would this day have been a poor people, possessed of little more than the necessaries for supporting life: there would have been but little or no resort of strangers here; the arts and sciences would have made but small progress; the inhabitants would have degenerated into a state of ignorance and barbarity." Instead of such a sorry state of affairs, Leonard drew attention to

the effects of our connection with, and subordination to Britain. Our merchants are opulent, and our yeomanry in easier circumstances than the noblesse of some states. Population is so rapid as to double the number of inhabitants in the short period of twenty-five years. Cities are springing up in the depths of the wilderness. Schools, colleges, and even universities are interspersed through the continent: our country abounds with foreign refinements, and flows with exotic luxuries. These are infallible marks not only of opulence but of freedom.[31]

In political terms many Loyalists expressed the need for strengthening the position of the executive in colonial societies. American society and, consequently, its constitutional order had become unbalanced. The people were becoming too powerful and there was no aristocracy to counter popular encroachments on the Crown. Joseph Galloway, a prominent Pennsylvania Loyalist, was alarmed at the increasing power of the democratic branch of government in the New England colonies, a power that was threatening to destroy the balance of the constitution. In Massachusetts, he wrote, "the executive power is bound in the chain of democratical influence in such manner that it cannot appoint a single officer of the Government without the assent of a popular assembly." The second or aristocratic branch was similarly weak. In sum, the two highest branches of government had become "dependent on the lowest and meanest."[32]

Ten years before, the governor of Massachusetts had made virtually the same point: "There is no Government in *America* at present, whose powers are properly balanced; there not being in any of them a real and distinct third legislative power mediating between the *King* and the *People*, which is the peculiar excellence of the *British* Constitution."[33] As a consequence, the scales had tipped in favour of the democratic branch and against the royal branch. Other Loyalists argued in much the same way. According to Jonathan Boucher, "too much weight was from the beginning . . . thrown into the popular scale." In Boucher's opinion the weakness of the executive stemmed from the fact that in too many colonial governments the people had too much patronage and the governors too little. This was no small matter, for "a man has, or has not, influence, only as he has, or has not, the power of conferring favours."[34] James Chalmers agreed. "It is often said," he wrote, "that the Sovereign, by honour and appointments, influences the Commons." There was, he maintained, nothing wrong with this. On the contrary, it was a laudable activity. Hence, he continued, "the profound and elegant Hume agitating this question, thinks, to this circumstance, we are in part indebted for our supreme felicity; since without such control in the Crown, our Constitution would immediately degenerate into Democracy, a Government, which . . . I hope to prove ineligible."[35]

Only the British Constitution with its equipoise of powers could maintain stability and prevent a degeneration into chaos. A democratic, republican government was destined to end in chaos, and the rule of one man. Charles Inglis of New York, later Bishop of Nova Scotia, wrote that in England "once, indeed, republicanism triumphed over the constitution; the despotism of one person ensued; both were finally expelled." Moreover, the most sophisticated political science of the century, as expressed best but not exclusively by Montesquieu, told Inglis that the republican form of government could not be applied to the entire body of America. America, Inglis wrote, "was too extensive for it." While the republican form might do well enough for a single city, or small territory, America was "too unwieldy for the feeble dilatory administration of democracy."[36]

Such sentiments were similar to those expressed by William Smith, Jr., former Chief Justice of New York and later Chief Justice of Quebec. Democratic republics, he warned, were inherently unstable and unsuited for large areas of territory. The governments established by the revolutionaries were weak internally because of the powers possessed by popularly elected assemblies. The American colonies from the very outset had been "abandoned to Democracy."[37] Before the war, Smith proposed a federal union of the colonies, to counteract the power of the provincial assemblies. His proposal bears a strong resemblance to David Hume's "Idea of a Perfect Commonwealth," which argued that there was a clear relation between representation, the public interest, and extent of territory. In Hume's opinion, the further one is removed from the people, that is, the more refined the choice of representative, the better the chance of acting in the public interest.[38] The problem with the current system for Smith was that "many assemblymen represent obscure little Counties" and were prone "to frequent Bickerings and Discords in which the common Interest is too often sacrificed to private Piques or partial aims." Matters would be different in a continental parliament: "In a parliament, chosen not by the Counties, but by the Representatives of the Colonies, we shall collect the Wisdom of the whole Continent, and find the Members acting upon Principles, doubly refined from popular Lees, and with a Liberality unbiased by the partial Prejudices, prevalent in the little Districts by which they were sent."[39]

Smith's sentiments reveal an ideological shift in emphasis, for earlier in his career he had been strongly identified with the "Country party" in New York politics.[40] During the 1750s he had been one of the three editors of the *Independent Reflector*, an essay magazine that mirrored the radicalism of the English "commonwealth-men," notably John Trenchard and Thomas Gordon.[41] His gravitation from the oppositionist whig politics of the Country party to the Loyalist cause defies simple explanation. His motives—personal, material, ideological—were no doubt as complex as the man himself. One could view his early oppositionist politics as merely reflecting a desire to advance his family, which previously had been excluded from influence. Subsequently successful as a lawyer, land speculator, and office-holder, Smith, like many Court whigs and Loyalists, may have realized that loyalty brought rewards, with the result that his oppositionist ardour cooled. Yet, despite his changing political position, one could argue that he remained faithful to one key concept in his political writings, that of balance. Smith, Leslie Upton notes, "spoke often of the need for balance in political society, for monarchy, aristocracy, as well as democracy."[42] Early in his career he saw the executive (or monarchical) element in New York as threatening the democratic element of the constitution. Later he saw a need for a strong central government and aristocracy to balance the excesses of democracy, views that he carried to and promoted in the remaining British North American provinces in the 1780s and 1790s.

Beyond critiquing the excesses of republican government and democracy, the Loyalists were also intent on exposing what they saw as the false patriotism of the revolutionaries. Charles Inglis, for

119

example, distinguished between "true" and "false" patriotism. "True patriotism," he wrote, consisted "in a desire . . . to promote the welfare and happiness of our country, without injury or injustice to others." "Virtue" and "rectitude" were "its inseparable attendants." The false patriotism of the revolutionaries was little more than "local prejudice and pride" mixed with insatiable ambition.[43] These sentiments were echoed by Jonathan Sewell, a former Attorney General of Massachusetts.[44] James Chalmers also asserted that the revolutionaries were false patriots. The truly virtuous were those who maintained their loyalty to the Crown and constitution. The most patriotic person in the realm was, of course, the king, "revered by his grateful countrymen . . . for his true patriotism and . . . unbounded benevolence."[45]

In another forum, London, Joseph Galloway wrote a blistering attack on the false virtue of the whig leader, Charles Fox, for advocating withdrawal of British troops from the American colonies. The title of Galloway's pamphlet, *Letters from Cicero to Catiline the Second*, is revealing. The Court whigs, in their attempts to rebut the indictment of their Country critics, searched for a symbol from the Roman Republic that could be used to defend their power. They settled on a figure who had demonstrated his love of liberty and country, Cicero, the most famous Roman republican of them all.[46] Cicero possessed the qualities the Court whigs desired in a symbol. He had, for example, supervised the successful defence of Rome against Catiline and his fellow conspirators. He had also sought to preserve the old balanced constitution from the demagoguery of the *populares*. In addition, he had fought for the rights of property, and for all of this he had suffered at the hands of the mob. Therefore, as Cicero denounced Catiline for his intrigues, so does Galloway denounce Fox, Catiline the Second. Galloway quotes Cicero at length, redirecting his indictment of Catiline against Fox. "What pity," Galloway wrote, "that your conduct is not directed by virtue, and a love for your country." This, to his mind, was proven by Fox's advocacy of troop withdrawals from America, an action that showed that Fox had "lost all sense of public virtue, and love for the true interest" of his country. Fox, wrote Galloway, was not motivated by virtue but by ambition and love of office. Such was demonstrated by Fox's efforts to wrest from the king "his constitutional right of appointing his own servants, and to compel him to place you and your confederates in their office, that you and they may command the purses, and riot in the wealth of your fellow-citizens."[47] Galloway's pamphlet persists in pulling the cloak of virtue from Fox's shoulders and placing it on the shoulders of the established whigs.

LOYALISM AND NATURAL JURISPRUDENCE

If one were only making a case for the Loyalist response to the civic humanist indictment of the revolutionary Patriots one could stop here. However, an equally strong case can be made for Loyalist connections with the natural jurisprudential tradition. While it is safe to say that the Loyalists took a conservative stance toward natural law, using it to support established government, they were hardly united in its actual interpretation. There were, for example, some Loyalists who relied upon Lockean contract theory as a basis for asserting their loyalty to the Crown; others repudiated the social contract and the notion of a state of nature, but continued to work within a natural jurisprudence paradigm.

Peter Van Schaack, who had studied law under William Smith, Jr., was one Loyalist who, having accepted Lockean contract theory and the idea of a state of nature, turned them against the Patriots. According to Van Schaack, if the compact binding rulers and ruled had been dissolved as the Declaration of Independence supposed, then "we must have been reduced to a State of Nature, in which the powers of Government reverted to, as they originated from, the People." However, given that man was "by Nature, free, equal, and independent," upon the dissolution of the compact he now regained "that Portion of his natural Liberty which each Individual had surrendered to the Government . . . and to which no one Society could make any Claim until he *incorporated* himself in it."[48] If the compact had, in fact, been dissolved, it was up to each individual to choose the government to which he would give his allegiance. Van Schaack chose England.[49]

The tendency of historians to depict Van Schaack as entirely Lockean must be qualified, however. A close reading of Van Schaack's writings indicates that they were interspersed with the vocabulary of civic humanism that would eventually be used to critique British institutions. Not long after he went into exile in England, Van Schaack indicated his belief that America would maintain its independence, but that independence would inevitably lead to

121

corruption. Yet in doing so he indicated his unease with English society and politics:

America will perhaps never see such happy days as the past. They may be a great empire, and enjoy opulence; but that mediocrity between extreme poverty and luxurious riches made their condition substantially happy. There being but few offices, there was no scope for bribery, corruption, and the numerous train of evils which attend the venality of this country. Henceforth, having an empire of their own, the numerous train of offices will produce the same effects as the same causes do here.

By 1780 Van Schaack had come to the conclusion that corruption, luxury, and dissipation were the leading characteristics of British government. In a language that is quintessentially civic humanist he delivered a sharp indictment of British government and society. The government, he argued, was engaged in efforts "to enhance the influence of the crown," and desired "to establish in the Colonies the system of corruption by which their government is carried on." Viewing this sorry state of affairs, Van Schaack concluded, "I see the British Constitution in its most essential principles totally lost. I find the British spirit extinct. I see luxury its predominant character, and power in almost every department centred in those who are most abandoned, that class of people who might have virtue to rescue the government from its abuses, excluded from office because they have not the means of corruption." As a consequence of this corruption Van Schaack in Lockean language concluded that he was "absolved, therefore, from the ties of allegiance" to the British Constitution. He had, so to speak, reverted to a state of nature and had become "a citizen of the world, and to my native country I am determined to return," which he did in July 1785.[50]

Elsewhere, Joseph Galloway accepted the theory of a social contract, but gave it a non-Lockean twist. On the one hand, Galloway agreed that when governments are established the rulers and ruled enter into a reciprocal agreement, the rulers to protect, the ruled to obey. On the other hand, he disagreed with Locke in that he did not believe that man's innate natural rights endured following the establishment of society. Rather, he argued that men surrender their natural rights upon the adoption of the social contract. Upon the surrender of their natural rights, the rights that men have are derived from the state.[51] Furthermore, while the state has an obligation to offer security to men and their property, it has another purpose, to promote the "happiness of the people."[52] Galloway's primary source for his position on natural law was the eighteenth-century Swiss jurist, Jean-Jacques Burlamaqui, whom he quotes at length. Burlamaqui's view of happiness, which he in turn took from Francis Hutcheson, is distinct from the utilitarian doctrine of happiness for the greatest number.[53] Rather, according to Burlamaqui, "by *Happiness* we are to understand the internal satisfaction of the soul, arising from the possession of good, and by good, whatever is suitable or agreeable to man for his preservation, perfection, conveniency, or pleasure." Moreover, Burlamaqui argued that society was perfectly natural: the "nature of man is such that he has no desire to avoid society." Men preferred the friendship and esteem of others; only in society could men approximate their ultimate purpose, happiness. Society was thus complementary to the individual. Burlamaqui viewed civil society as only "natural society itself, modified in such a manner, that there is a sovereign presiding over it, on whose will . . . the welfare of the society ultimately depends; to the end that, by these means, mankind may attain, with greater certainty that happiness to which they all naturally aspire."[54] Galloway adhered, then, to two purposes of the state: one negative, to restrain men's individual freedom and offer "protection . . . against the private injustice of individuals," the other positive, to promote the public good and happiness.[55]

As Janice Potter's work illustrates, Galloway's views were similar to those of many other Loyalists. According to Potter, the Loyalists had both negative and positive views of freedom. First, the Loyalists believed that to allow unrestrained freedom "would be to invite disorder, instability, and irrationality." The positive view of liberty was "based on two main ideas, of institutions generally, of government specifically. One idea was that institutions were essential to the happiness and freedom of individuals; the other was that institutions and their authority were seen not as potentially threatening but as benign or salutary."[56]

While there was agreement with Galloway on the positive nature of institutions, the Loyalists tended to view man and society as very much historical products "formed," in the words of Charles Inglis, "by the wisdom of the ages." Daniel Leonard argued that a state of nature was a "condition of darkness where . . . man had to conceal himself from his fellow men, inhabit his own cave, and seek his own prey."[57] Among the Loyalists Inglis voiced the most pointed rebuttal to those adhering to contract theory. Man, he argued, was a social creature, society was natural, and government was not a source of tyranny and evil, but a means of guaranteeing liberty and order and promoting happiness. History, moreover, told us that the origins of government were dependent on a variety of causes. Wrote Inglis:

A state of society is the natural state of man; and by the constitution of his mind and frame he is fitted for it. Not only his wants and weaknesses require it, but his inclinations, his noblest faculties impel to it; and the more perfect these faculties are, the better is he fitted for society. As nature has thus made us members of society, without any choice or will of ours; so, whatever happiness or perfection we are capable of, can only be attained in society.[58]

As much emphasis as the Loyalists put on happiness as an end of government, they were concerned more immediately about order and the growing violence in the colonies. In the minds of the Loyalists, the social institutions that the Patriots were threatening to destabilize and overturn could not be easily replaced. The state, in this situation, had a special duty to act as a policeman, imposing order, ensuring social cohesion, and protecting the lives, liberty, and property of citizens. Such a view of government is particularly modern, in keeping with the jurisprudential view of the state held by the Court whigs and the Scots. According to the New York Loyalist, Samuel Seabury, it was clearly the task of government to provide "for the security of those who live under it; to protect the weak against the strong;—the good against the bad;—to preserve order and decency among men, preventing every one from injuring his neighbour. Every person, then, owes obedience to the laws of the government under which he lives and is obliged in honour and duty to support them." Like Adam Smith he believed in the necessity for a proper administration of justice: "the grand security of the property, the lives of Englishmen, consists in the due administration of justice. While the courts are duly attended to, and fairly conducted, our property is safe."[59]

Consistent with their jurisprudential view of the state, the Loyalists defended the British constitution, parliamentary sovereignty, and the right of Parliament to legislate and apply its laws to the colonies. In the end, parliamentary sovereignty became a divide between the Loyalists and Britain on the one hand, and the Patriots on the other, that could not be bridged. Prior to the Glorious Revolution of 1688 the threat to the freedoms and rights of the subject had been the Crown. In the eighteenth century the guarantor of these rights and freedoms became the sovereign Parliament. The Parliament in London was now the "the supreme uncontrollable power" with "an absolute authority to decide and determine."[60] The supreme authority of Parliament extended over the entire empire, America included, and it was not constitutionally possible to have *imperium in imperio*, two absolute and distinct powers in one government. The Patriots, on the other hand, worked from a seventeenth-century constitutional theory, "which," according to John Phillip Reid, "for a time, had made 'law'—the law of custom, community consensus, and right reason—supreme over the royal prerogative." The result was that in the later eighteenth century "the guarantor of rights at home became the threat to freedom in America."[61]

There is every reason to suggest, then, that the Loyalists were participants in the natural jurisprudence tradition. They were clearly familiar with its traditional concerns, the origins, rights, and duties of government, as well as the protection of lives, property, and contract. Nevertheless, many of them adhered to a modern, historical-sociological view of the origins of the state, eschewing the idea of a state of nature and the social contract. The state had a familiar end, to protect the lives, liberty, and property of its subjects. This, however, was not the possessive individualism depicted by C. B. MacPherson, for the state had a positive end, the promotion of happiness.

One finds, then, in the thought of the Loyalists the simultaneous encounter of two languages of political thought, one that responded to the civic humanist indictment of the whig regime, the other that relied upon the natural jurisprudence tradition to defend law and order in the empire. As intellectually incompatible as these languages may have been, they coincided to provide a means of defending a society and state increasingly modern in its outlook.

THE LOYALISTS AND ENGLISH CANADIAN POLITICAL CULTURE: WHICH LANGUAGE?

The preceding discussion raises once again the question of how the formation of English political culture may be best understood. First, what should we conclude about the Lockean connection to Loyalism? Second, what are the implications of Horowitz's claim that the Loyalists brought to Canada a tory streak, an element of precapitalist organic conservatism? Finally, how are we to understand the Loyalist legacy?[62]

In regard to the first question, it has been argued that Locke was not the central figure in the formation of Loyalist political thought. This is not to say that Locke was not a presence, but only that eighteenth-century political discourse was much more diverse and encompassing. What Isaac Kramnick, a scholar sympathetic to Locke, has to say about the American founding is true of the Loyalists as well. According to Kramnick, "there was a profusion and confusion of political tongues among the founders." Moreover, the founders "lived easily with that clatter; it is we two hundred years later who chafe at this inconsistency."[63] Similarly, Loyalism was much broader than Locke. Even Loyalists such as Peter Van Schaack, customarily depicted as Lockean, demonstrated their familiarity with other modes of discourse. Admittedly, there was a strong element of what we now describe as liberalism among the Loyalists, who believed that the state had an obligation to protect the lives, liberty, and property of its citizens. Yet they were also skeptical of natural rights and contract theory. Many Loyalists, influenced by thinkers such as Montesquieu and the Scottish social theorists, were to utilize a more sociological and historical explanation of the nature of man and the origins of society, thus permitting them to adhere to a more conservative interpretation of whiggism than their Patriot counterparts.[64]

This leads to the second question, the merit of Gad Horowitz's assertion that the Loyalists brought a tory streak to Canada. This is no small matter, since Horowitz argues that the organic collective nature of toryism contributed to the growth of socialism and a Canadian political culture distinct from that of the United States.[65] Horowitz's claim that the Loyalists had a tory touch is difficult to analyze and sustain, for we are only given some of the characteristics of toryism, never its specific intellectual progenitors.

The evidence indicates, however, that there was no continuity between an ancient, precapitalist toryism and the British (or Canadian) conservatism of the late eighteenth and early nineteenth centuries. There is, for example, little connection between the late-seventeenth-century tories who supported James II and advocated absolute monarchy, non-resistance to governments, and passive obedience, and the later tories of the eighteenth century. The Jacobites disappeared early in the eighteenth century. One finds the Hanoverian tories under Bolingbroke emerging as a political force early in the eighteenth century, but by the 1720s these tories had accepted the Revolution Settlement and formed an alliance with the Country whigs to condemn the established whigs, who were perceived as governing through corruption. Throughout much of the eighteenth century the term tory was used in a different context, to describe those whigs in power or their supporters who advocated the role of the Crown versus the legislature in the British Constitution. Lord North, for example, was labelled a tory, as were the American Loyalists, although most preferred to be called, and indeed were called, whigs. Only following the French Revolution was the term tory used favourably for the first time by those whigs who identified with the Crown.

An excellent example of a Loyalist who has been identified as a tory when he was, in fact, a whig, was Charles Inglis. Wallace Brown and Hereward Senior, for example, claim "that of the two Loyalists who exercised the greatest influence in the surviving colonies, William Smith, who became Chief Justice of Quebec, was an unrepentant Whig, and Bishop Charles Inglis was a true Tory." William Nelson also argues that Inglis was a tory who had "rediscovered medieval social theory."[66] No doubt Smith was a whig, but was Inglis a tory? If Inglis is allowed to speak for himself he most assuredly was not. He declared, and the emphasis is his, that "I am none of your *passive obedience* and *non-resistance men*. The principles on which the glorious Revolution in 1688 was brought about, constitute the article of my political creed."[67]

In summary, the Loyalists were not carriers of a precapitalist toryism, having accepted what their American counterparts feared—trade, commerce, and empire. No doubt many of the values Horowitz labels as precapitalist—order, authority, hierarchy—were accepted by whigs, but these values were the very elements that conservative whigs were trying to uphold in a society becoming increasingly modern and commercial. No less a whig than Adam Smith recognized the importance of the psychological ties that bind people together in every society. Smith was acutely aware that every independent state was divided into different orders and ranks, each with its own privileges, powers, immunities, and interests. Moreover, he recognized that "the political community found in a commercial society [arose] out of the natural disposition in individuals to defer to others in positions of authority."[68] The problem was that deference was more uncertain in a commercial society. Smith's priority was to maintain those conditions most conducive to the continuance of existing authority relations. Similarly, the Loyalists demonstrated their concern over the problem of deference in a colonial society becoming increasingly modern.[69]

The problem Horowitz and others have in their use of the term "tory" stems from the failure to recognize that whiggism was heterogeneous, possessing its own dialectic and ideological diversity and tension. While all whigs insisted they were defenders of freedom—for example, the mixed constitution, the limited power of the state, and the rule of law—they differed profoundly on the proper balance in the British Constitution, the meaning of the rule of law, liberty, and the implications of commerce and modernity for society and politics.

Once in Canada, many of the Loyalist leaders set about rectifying the mistakes of imperial governance of the American colonies. Both William Smith and Jonathan Sewell, for example, sought to restore balance to the governments of the remaining British North American colonies by advocating more power for the colonial executive, along with the encouragement of an aristocracy through a system of public rewards and distinctions. The attempt to create an aristocracy failed, but the demand of Loyalist leaders that they be appointed to the key posts in the new governments led to a repetition of many of the quarrels over patronage that had occurred in the rebellious colonies. This time, however, the imperial government was to be the mediator, not the focus of protest.[70]

As part of their attempt to strengthen the power of the executive, some Loyalists proposed federal union. These ideas were passed on from one generation to another. For instance, both Smith and Sewell proposed highly centralized schemes of federation. The son of Jonathan Sewell, Justice Sewell of Quebec, married into the family of William Smith and became familiar with Smith's ideas, publishing two plans of federation similar to Smith's.[71] Sewell's plans were eventually used as the basis of a plan for federal union proposed by John Beverley Robinson. Robinson and Bishop John Strachan later collaborated and proposed a similar plan for union. In 1849, Strachan's son, James, repeated his father's plan almost verbatim at one of the two meetings of the British North American League where the subject of federation was actively considered. In brief, Canadian tories were inclined to believe that a strong, centralized federation would eliminate the instability that marked the American colonies and led to their severance from Britain.

While there was a continuity between the proposals for union advanced by the Loyalists and those suggested by Canadian tories, historians caution us not to view all Loyalists as tories. Neil Mackinnon, Wallace Brown, and Hereward Senior point out that in Nova Scotia, for example, the newly arrived Loyalists, confronted with the fact that the pre-Loyalist element dominated the executive council, were perfectly willing to adopt the classical role of a Country party, championing the power and rights of the assembly, invoking the rhetoric of the opposition whigs in England.[72] The rhetoric softened once the Halifax oligarchy made room for the more noted Loyalists in the 1790s. Loyalists in Nova Scotia politics soon became divided, one element supporting the executive, the other the assembly.

Elsewhere, Paul Romney inverts my arguments and those of Gordon Stewart on the strength of Court whig values in nineteenth-century English Canadian political life.[73] It is Romney's contention that the late Loyalist arrivals, immigrating to Upper Canada before the War of 1812, were instrumental in injecting the Upper Canadian Reform ideology and politics with the country ideology of the eighteenth-century radical whigs. Romney traces the transformation of the Upper Canadian ideology, focusing on the contradictions in whig constitutionalism between the constitution and the law. In Romney's version it is the Reformers that triumph with the advent of responsible government, thus contributing in their own way to emphasis on the community and state in Canadian politics.[74]

However different in interpretation and emphasis is the work of Romney, Stewart, and myself, each calls into question the commonly accepted notion of the conservative-liberal antithesis of Horowitz as a means of understanding Loyalism and the formation of Canadian political culture. We are thus led to consider the formation of English political culture within a broader framework, emphasizing a liberal-community antithesis as a defining characteristic. Thus, we are just beginning to unpack the "cultural baggage" in Canada's past. Much more work remains to be done.

NOTES

*I would like to thank the Social Science and Humanities Research Council for funding part of the research for this article, and Gordon Stewart and Barry Cooper for their helpful comments.

1. For an overview of the issues see Gordon S. Wood, "Ideology and the Origins of Liberal America," *William and Mary Quarterly* 44.3 (1987): 628-40; Jeffrey C. Isaac, "Republicanism vs. Liberalism? A Reconsideration," *History of Political Thought* 9.2 (1988): 349-77; M. M. Goldsmith, "Regulating Anew the Moral and Political Sentiments of Mankind: Bernard Mandeville and the Scottish Enlightenment," paper presented at Conference for the Study of Political Thought, University of Edinburgh, 25-28 August 1986; Istvan Hont and Michael Ignatieff, eds., *Wealth and Virtue: Shaping of Political Economy in the Scottish Enlightenment* (Cambridge: Cambridge University Press, 1983).
2. On this point see Richard Nelson, "From Empire to Antipode: Liberalism, Republicanism, and Reinhold Niehbuhr's Jeremiad On Recent American Historiography," *The Canadian Review of American Studies* 20.1 (1989): 1-16.
3. Louis Hartz, *The Founding of New Societies* (New York: Harcourt, Brace, 1964) 3, 9.
4. K. D. McRae, "Louis Hartz's Concept of the Fragment Society and Its Application to Canada," *Études Canadiennes/Canadian Studies* 5 (1978): 21. See also David V. J. Bell, "The Loyalist Tradition in Canada," *Journal of Canadian Studies* 5 (1970): 25.
5. Gad Horowitz, *Canadian Labour in Politics* (Toronto: University of Toronto Press, 1968) 19.
6. See, for example, H. D. Forbes, "Hartz-Horowitz at Twenty: Nationalism, Toryism, and Socialism in Canada and the United States," *Canadian Journal of Political Science* 20.2 (1987): 287-315; Ian Stewart, "The Study of Canadian Political Culture," in Alain-G. Gagnon and James Bickerton, eds., *Canadian Politics* (Peterborough: Broadview Press, 1990); W. Christian and C. Campbell, *Political Parties and Ideologies in Canada*, 3rd ed. (Toronto: McGraw-Hill Ryerson, 1990) chap. 2.
7. See, for example, M. M. Goldsmith, "Liberty, Luxury and the Pursuit of Happiness," in Anthony Pagden, ed., *The Language of Political Theory in Early-Modern Europe* (Cambridge: Cambridge University Press, 1987); J. G. A. Pocock, *The Machiavellian Moment* (Princeton: Princeton University Press, 1975).
8. Goldsmith, "Liberty, Luxury" 234.
9. Lance Banning, *The Jeffersonian Persuasion* (Ithaca: Cornell University Press,

1978); David W. Noble, *The End of American History* (Minneapolis: University of Minnesota Press, 1985).

10. Isaac, "Republicanism vs. Liberalism."

11. Goldsmith, "Liberty, Luxury" 234.

12. Pocock, *Machiavellian Moment* 487.

13. J. G. A. Pocock, "Cambridge Paradigms and Scotch Philosophers: A Study of the Relations Between the Civic Humanist and the Civil Jurisprudential Interpretation of Eighteenth-century Social Thought," Hont and Ignatieff, *Wealth and Virtue*.

14. On this point see Goldsmith, "Regulating Anew" 25.

15. Pocock, "Cambridge Paradigms" 241.

16. Donald Winch, "Adam Smith's 'enduring particular result,'" Hont and Ignatieff, *Wealth and Virtue* 264.

17. For a comparison of civic humanism and natural law see Richard F. Teichgraeber III, *"Free Trade" and Moral Philosophers* (Durham: Duke University Press, 1986) 21-26.

18. Pocock, "Cambridge Paradigms" 249.

19. Joyce Appleby, *Capitalism and a New Social Order: The Republican Vision of the 1790s* (New York: New York University Press, 1984); John Patrick Diggins, *The Lost Soul of American Politics* (New York: Basic Books, 1984).

20. H. T. Dickinson, *Liberty and Property* (London: Weidenfeld and Nicolson, 1977) 159.

21. The presence of the natural jurisprudence theme in the thought of these thinkers is summarized by Goldsmith, "Regulating Anew."

22. Isaac, "Republicanism vs. Liberalism" 349.

23. Isaac Kramnick argues that both forms of discourse were present in 1787. Thomas Pangle's recent attempt to reassert Locke as the primary thinker supporting the principles of the American Founders has met with mixed reviews. Joyce Appleby argues that Lockean liberalism triumphed in the nineteenth century, a claim denied by David W. Nobel and Michael Fores, who maintain that civic humanism was "the dominant political philosophy in the United States during the nineteenth century." Isaac Kramnick, "The 'Great National Discussion': The Discourse of Politics in 1787," *William and Mary Quarterly* 45.1 (1988): 3-32; Thomas Pangle, *The Spirit of Modern Republicanism: The Moral Vision of the American Founders and the Philosophy of Locke* (Chicago: University of Chicago Press, 1988); for a critical review of Pangle see Richard Ashcraft, *Political Theory* 18.1 (1990): 159-62; Appleby, *Capitalism and a New Social Order*; David Nobel and Michael Fores, *Soundings* 68.2 (1985) 160.

24. Wood, "Ideology and the Origins of Liberal America" 634.

25. Hendrik Hartog, "Losing the World of the Massachusetts Whig," and

"Distancing Oneself from the Eighteenth Century: A Commentary on Changing Pictures of American Legal History," in Hendrik Hartog, ed., *Law in the American Revolution and the Revolution in the Law* (New York: New York University Press, 1981) 146, 147, 240.

26. Following the war Chalmers was part of the Loyalist migration to Canada, but subsequently moved to London, where he died in 1806. Details on his time in Canada are sketchy. See Thomas R. Adams, "The Authorship and Printing of *Plain Truth* by 'Candidus,'" *Bibliographical Society of America Papers* 49 (1955): 230-37.

27. James Chalmers, *Plain Truth* (Philadelphia, 1776), reprinted in Merrill Jenson, ed., *Tracts of the American Revolution, 1763-1776* (New York: Bobbs-Merrill, 1967) 447-88.

28. Thomas Paine, *Common Sense* (Philadelphia, 1776), reprinted in Michael Foot and Isaac Kramnick, *The Thomas Paine Reader* (Harmondsworth: Penguin Books, 1987) 99. These are the quotations that Chalmers cites.

29. Chalmers, *Plain Truth* 476, 477.

30. Daniel Leonard, like many Loyalist leaders, settled wherever a suitable position could be found, in this case as Chief Justice of Bermuda. Earlier he had agreed to serve as a principal officer in a contemplated province to be called New Ireland in what is now Maine, a plan that never came to fruition.

31. Daniel Leonard, *Massachusettensis* 20 March 1775, reprinted in Bernard Mason, ed., *The American Colonial Crisis* (New York: Harper and Row, 1972) 85.

32. Joseph Galloway, *Historical and Political Reflections on the Rise and Progress of the American Rebellion* (London: G. Wilkie, 1790) 38, 39. Galloway went into exile in England, a land in which he was never very happy, and died in Wafford, England, in 1803. In 1785 he had sought, unsuccessfully, the post of Chief Justice of Nova Scotia.

33. Francis Bernard, as quoted in Pierre Tousignant, "Problématique Pour Une Nouvelle Approche de la Constitution de 1791," *Revue d'Histoire de l'Amérique Française* 27.2 (1973): 2.

34. Jonathan Boucher, *The Causes of the American Revolution* (London: G. G. and J. Robinson, 1797) 44: 218. Boucher, a Maryland Loyalist, has customarily been described as a high Tory who derived his ideas entirely from Robert Filmer, an interpretation debunked by Anne Young Zimmer and Alfred H. Kelly, "Jonathan Boucher: Constitutional Conservative," *Journal of American History* 58 (1972): 897-921.

35. Chalmers, *Plain Truth* 451.

36. Charles Inglis, *The True Interest of America Impartially Stated* (Philadelphia: Jeffrey Humphrey, 1776) 52. James Chalmers's analysis of republicanism very much parallels Inglis's in its use of Montesquieu.

37. William Smith, Jr., "Letter to Dorchester," Quebec, 5 February 1790, in W. P. M. Kennedy, ed., *Documents of the Canadian Constitution 1759-1915* (Toronto: Oxford University Press, 1918) 204.

38. David Hume, "Idea of a Perfect Commonwealth," *Essays, Moral, Political, and Literary*, Vol. 1, ed. T. H. Green and T. H. Grose (London: Longman, Green, 1875).

39. William Smith, Jr., "Thoughts Upon the Dispute between Great Britain and her Colonies," quoted in Robert M. Calhoon, "William Smith, Jr.'s Alternative to the American Revolution," *William and Mary Quarterly*, ser. 3, Vol. 22 (January 1965): 1. While Smith does not cite Hume, he was very familiar with the leading figures of the Scottish Enlightenment, and patterned his history of New York after Hume's *History of England.* Michael Kammen, Introduction to William Smith, Jr., *The History of the Province of New York* (Cambridge, MA: Belknap Press, 1972) 1: xliii, xliv.

40. Kammen, Introduction xix.

41. Milton M. Klein, "The Independent Reflector," in Milton M. Klein, *The Politics of Diversity: Essays in the History of Colonial New York* (Port Washington, NY: Kennikat Press, 1974).

42. L. F. S. Upton, *The Loyal Whig: William Smith of New York and Quebec* (Toronto: University of Toronto Press, 1969) 219.

43. Inglis, *True Interest* 111.

44. See Philalethes (Jonathan Sewell), *Massachusetts Gazette* June 1773. Sewell was appointed to the Council of New Brunswick in 1787, assuming at the same time duties as Judge of the Vice-Admiralty Court.

45. Chalmers, *Plain Truth* 479, 480.

46. For more on this point see Reed Browning, *Political and Constitutional Ideas of the Court Whigs* (Baton Rouge: Louisiana State Press, 1982), Chap. 8, "The Ciceronian Vision," 210-57.

47. Joseph Galloway, *Letters from Cicero to Catiline the Second* (London, 1781) 10, 34.

48. Peter Van Schaack, as quoted in William Allen Benton, *Whig-Loyalism* (Rutherford: Fairleigh Dickinson University Press, 1969) 181.

49. An excellent example of how Locke could be interpreted in a conservative manner may be found in Thomas Hutchinson, *A Dialogue Between An American and a European, 1768* 1, ed. Bernard Bailyn; reprinted in Donald Fleming and Bernard Bailyn, eds., *Perspectives in American History* 9 (1975): 343-411.

50. Peter Van Schaack, "Journal" November 1779, January 1780, in Henry Cruger Van Schaack, *The Life of Peter Van Schaack* (New York, 1842) 244, 263.

51. Joseph Galloway, *A Candid Examination of the Mutual Claims of Great Britain and the Colonies: With a Plan of Accommodation, On Constitutional*

Principles (New York: James Rivington, 1775) 16. See also John Ferling, *The Loyalist Mind* (University Park: Pennsylvania State University Press, 1977) 67-81. Galloway did believe, however, that the contract could be nullified if the ruler acted arbitrarily or failed to protect the people.

52. Joseph Galloway, *Claims of the American Loyalists—Reviewed and Maintained Upon Incontrovertible Principles of Law and Justice* (London, 1788) 16. Numerous references are made in Galloway, *Candid Examination*, as well.

53. Jean-Jacques Burlamaqui, *The Principles of Natural Law* (London, 1748), Part 2, Chap. 3, Par. 1 and 2, 146.

54. Burlamaqui, *Natural Law*, Vol. 1, Part 2, Chap. 4, Par. 12, 167; Part 1, Chap. 1, Para. 1, 1; Burlamaqui, *The Principles of Political Law* (London, 1752), Part 1, Chap. 1, Par. 3, 8.

55. Galloway, *Candid Examination* 15.

56. Janice Potter, *The Liberty We Seek: Loyalist Ideology in Colonial New York and Massachusetts* (Cambridge: Harvard University Press, 1983) 56. While I concur with Potter's conclusion that the Loyalists drew upon Court literature, her depiction of Court and Patriot literature as essentially Lockean (85) considerably oversimplifies its true character. Potter's own work clearly reveals the civic humanist strains in the Patriot literature and the non-Lockean strains in Court literature.

57. Inglis, *True Interest* 52; Daniel Leonard, *Massachusettensis* 6 February 1775, 57.

58. ———, *True Interest* 115.

59. Samuel Seabury, "The Congress Canvassed: or, an Examination into the Conduct of the Delegates at their Grand Convention" (1774), and "Free Thoughts on the Proceedings of the Continental Congress at Philadelphia, Sept. 5, 1774," in Clarence H. Vance, ed., *Letters of a Westchester Farmer, 1774-1775* (White Plains, NY: Westchester County Historical Society, 1930) 90, 58.

60. Letter from the Earl of Dartmouth to Governor Thomas Hutchinson, 9 December 1772, as quoted in John Phillip Reid, *The Briefs of the American Revolution* (New York: New York University Press, 1981) 10.

61. Reid, *Briefs of the American Revolution* 30, 163. For an interpretation of how this clash of ideas unfolded within a Canadian context see Paul Romney, "From the Rule of Law to Responsible Government: Ontario Political Culture and the Origins of Canadian Statism," *Historical Papers Presented at the Annual Meeting of the Canadian Historical Association, Windsor, 1988*, 86-119.

62. I am indebted in this section to Janet Ajzenstat, "Durham and Robinson: Political Faction and Moderation," *Journal of Canadian Studies* 25. 1 (1990), which briefly compares the Hartz-Horowitz approach to that of Gordon Stewart and my own.

63. Kramnick, "The 'Great National Discussion'" 4.

64. On this phenomenon in late eighteenth-century England see Dickinson, *Liberty and Property* 317.

65. By toryism Horowitz "meant the British conservatism which has its roots in a pre-capitalist age, the conservatism that stresses prescription, authority, order, hierarchy, in an organic community." Gad Horowitz, "Tories, Socialists and the Demise of Canada," in H.D.Forbes, ed., *Canadian Political Thought* (Toronto: Oxford University Press, 1985) 352.

66. Wallace Brown and Hereward Senior, *Victorians in Defeat: The American Loyalists in Exile* (Toronto: Methuen, 1984) 134; W. H. Nelson, *The American Tory* (Boston: Beacon Press, 1961) 186, 187.

67. Inglis, *True Interest* 3.

68. Edward J. Harpham, "Liberalism, Civic Humanism, and the Case of Adam Smith," *American Political Science Review* 78.3 (1984): 770.

69. Potter, *Liberty* 26.

70. Anne Gorman Condon, *The Envy of the American States: The Loyalist Dream for New Brunswick* (Fredericton, NB: New Ireland Press, 1984); David Bell and Lorne Tepperman, *The Roots of Disunity* (Toronto: McClelland and Stewart, 1979); Gordon Stewart, *The Origins of Canadian Politics: A Comparative Approach* (Vancouver: University of British Columbia, 1986); Peter J. Smith, "The Ideological Origins of Canadian Confederation," *Canadian Journal of Political Science* 20.1 (1987): 3-29.

71. W.H. Nelson, "Last Hopes of the American Loyalists," *Canadian Historical Review* 32 (1951): 22-42.

72. Neil MacKinnon, *This Unfriendly Soil: The Loyalist Experience in Nova Scotia 1783-91* (Kingston and Montreal: McGill-Queen's University Press, 1986) 123-35; Brown and Senior, *Victorians in Defeat* 154-56.

73. Stewart, *Origins of Canadian Politics*; Peter J. Smith, "Ideological Origins of Canadian Confederation."

74. Romney, "Rule of Law."

IV
Liberal Roots

STANDING IN A FIELD. **CANADA** IS A
LAST CIGARETTE. **CANADA** IS SCRAP
METAL. **CANADA** IS A PINE TREE –
BURNING. **CANADA** IS A MINNOW IN
A METAL BUCKET. **CANADA** IS A

CHAPTER SIX

DURHAM AND ROBINSON:
POLITICAL FACTION AND MODERATION

Janet Ajzenstat

What is perhaps the most widely accepted thesis in Canadian political thought supposes that, until well into the twentieth century, Canada's political culture exhibited traces of a conservatism that originated with the United Empire Loyalists. Gad Horowitz, whose exposition of the thesis is always the starting point for debates on Canada's national identity, argues that the Loyalists and their tory party heirs in English Canada rejected aspects of the American liberal ideology, especially the liberal emphasis on individual freedoms. They had a vision of the political community as "organic," and "hierarchical"; they were willing to entertain the idea that the common good may sometimes require the sacrifice of individual objectives and private desires.[1] As a result, the argument goes, Canada throughout her history has been less hostile than the United States to measures restraining individual ambition and more open to the possibility of legislating for the community and for collective interests.

A substantial challenge to this thesis has been mounted recently by Peter J. Smith and Gordon T. Stewart, under the influence of J. G. A. Pocock's interpretation of seventeenth- and eighteenth-century political thought in England and the United States. Applied to Canada, the Pocock model turns Horowitz upside down.[2] In this new view the Loyalists and tories appear as champions of an individualist ideology, willing—only too willing—to sacrifice the common good to party and career. It is the British North American radical parties, not the tories, that exhibit a sense of collective interests, according to the new line of thought.[3]

Pocock sees the political cultures of Britain and the United States as the product of a debate between, as Smith argues, "the defenders of classical republican values and the proponents of a rising commercial ideology formulated during the Enlightenment."[4] Classical republicanism, he says, is distinguished above all by an idea of public "virtue," drawn originally from the ancient world and developed in the modern context by Britain's eighteenth-century "Country" party. It demands a principled, participatory citizenry and scorns the "new forms of property, finance and commerce."[5] Both Smith and Stewart describe Canadian radicals like Mackenzie as drawing on "Country" party ideas.[6] The Canadian tories in contrast are said to have been influenced by the commercial ideology of the British "Court" party. In nineteenth-century Canada, argues Stewart, "the 'court' orientation developed into a statist outlook by which administrations of the day deployed patronage and influence to shore up their positions, stimulated and participated in economic growth, and tried to free themselves as much as possible from close legislative supervision."[7]

Both the Horowitz and Pocock schools have much to say about the propensity of tories, especially in Upper Canada, to undertake great public works with public funds. But whereas Horowitz cites this as evidence that the heirs of Loyalism could legislate for the common good, the new school argues that the tories were merely building private fortunes at public expense.[8] Horowitz describes the nineteenth-century tories as representing (admittedly only to a degree) a high-minded tradition of thought that finds expression ultimately in Canada's twentieth-century socialist parties. The new interpretation depicts them as decidedly low-minded graspers.

Moreover, for the new school the United States is not the home of unbridled individualism, as seen by Horowitz. The argument rather is that the United States was heavily influenced by the tradition of public "virtue," giving American political thought and political institutions a profoundly anti-individualist thrust.[9] In

Stewart's description, the "country" ideology triumphs in the United States, and the "court" ideology in tory Canada. For Horowitz, the British North American tories are distinguished by a bent toward collectivism; the United States, in contrast, is purely individualist. For the new school the tories are individualist; it is the United States that tends toward collectivism. Both models suggest that the Canadian political culture differs from the American in small but nevertheless significant ways, and both single out the tory influence in British North America as crucial; however, the one promotes the idea that as a result of that influence Canadians are more community-minded, more "virtuous" than the Americans, the other that we are considerably less community-minded and "virtuous."[10]

What is needed to assess the Pocock and Horowitz schools on Upper Canada is a thorough exposition of the documentary history—an impossible task in a short paper. Only two documents from the crucial years are considered here, admittedly two of the most famous: Lord Durham's *Report on the Affairs of British North America* and John Beverley Robinson's *Canada and the Canada Bill*.[11] The latter is the most complete statement we have from the man who was Upper Canada's leading tory during the years of the Family Compact. We shall see that neither Durham nor Robinson focuses directly on the role of the individual in relation to society and government, the topic of such interest to the aforementioned commentators. The immediate and important matter was to understand what had led to the colonial rebellion and the suspension of the constitution. Both Durham and Robinson address themselves primarily to what we might call the problem of political faction. Nevertheless, in the course of their arguments both draw on assumptions about the individual and government current at the time. With a careful exploration of their views on faction we can hope to bring those assumptions to light. It is argued here that, although the new-school understanding of nineteenth-century tory acquisitiveness provides a salutary corrective to Horowitz's picture of toryism informed by an idea of the common good, Smith and Stewart are wrong to see Upper Canada's conservatism as little more than a justification of patronage and privilege. Men like Robinson did not believe that a prior high-minded idea of the common good—a sense of republican "virtue," we might say—should constrain the individual citizen or limit political deliberation. Nevertheless, they argued that the clash of selfish interests under constitutional government would yield legislation and policies in the public interest, and thus benefit all, regardless of rank. This is not a position that can be reduced to an argument for the promotion of class or special interests at the expense of the community.

Moreover, it is a position that may as properly be attributed to Durham. The comparison of Durham and Robinson will show that, for all their differences on concrete issues, the British whig and the Canadian tory share considerable theoretical ground. Both distrusted popular parties and popular leaders in British North America, both argued that the intransigence of colonial reformers was an important factor in the Canadian crisis, and both entertained the idea of constitutional "checks and balances" as remedy. Horowitz, Smith, and Stewart all fail to do justice to the nineteenth-century argument for restraining popular participation, and so miss an important element of Durham's liberalism—and the liberal heart of Canadian toryism.

Both Durham and Robinson call attention to the role the colonial Reform parties played in bringing on the Rebellion. Robinson described Papineau and his associates in the lower province as "wicked and dangerous men" who were corrupting their countrymen and poisoning the public mind in order to gratify their own "insane ambition." The "Mackenzies, the Papineaus and the Nelsons," he argued, would sacrifice the public interest rather than allow the "friends of Government . . . by successfully promoting it, to strengthen their claims upon the good will of the community."[12] It would indeed be easy to interpret Robinson's tirade against popular parties and leaders as mere partisan prejudice, in line with the new-school supposition that the tories were arrogantly eager to free the executive from legislative control, or Horowitz's belief that the toryism of the period had a "hierarchical" inegalitarian component. A recent biographer, arguing along such lines, states that Robinson supposed gentlemen to have "a natural right to govern," while the "lesser born" had "a duty to obey."[13] But it becomes more difficult to take Robinson's views as simple prejudice or a defence of class interests when we see how similar Durham's were.

Durham was one of Britain's leading advocates of parliamentary reform in the 1820s and 1830s. Closely associated with the British Philosophical Radical party during the fight for the Great

Reform Bill, he argued over the years for measures to curtail the powers of the Crown, and for frequent parliaments, an extended franchise, and the secret ballot.[14] His proposal for colonial "responsible government" would have enabled the majority party leaders, including radicals like Mackenzie and Papineau, to take their places in the colonial Executive Councils. His liberal credentials are impeccable. The fact remains that he took the colonial reformers to task in very much the way Robinson did. The Assembly of Lower Canada, he argued, had "endeavoured to extend its authority in modes totally incompatible with the principles of constitutional liberty." It had "transgressed our notions of the proper limits of Parliamentary interference."[15] He proposed measures to limit the "present powers of the representative bodies in the colonies," and, like Robinson, spoke of curbing "popular excesses."[16] Robinson argued that the leaders of the majority parties were "the cause of infinite evil and suffering to the people themselves."[17] Durham in similar fashion referred to the French Canadian leaders as "demagogues" and "agitators."[18] Both suggested that the *patriote* leaders were using appeals to nationality to manipulate the populace.[19] Unlike Robinson, Durham argued that the English-speaking leaders in Lower Canada and the tories in Upper Canada were exploiting their followers in the same way that the French leaders were exploiting theirs. But both argued that the majority party leaders in the two provinces bore considerable responsibility for the crisis. Durham was no more obviously on the side of the reformers than Robinson was.

Their distrust of popular parties and popular leaders sounds a note that echoes throughout the nineteenth century. It may indeed appear on first reading to be a simple rejection of democracy. But closer examination shows that the view expresses fear of democratic tyranny, rather than of democracy *per se*. Those who make this argument are not rejecting the idea of a political system in which leaders and parties alternate in office competing for the electorate's favour, but the form of government in which popular leaders claim absolute title to rule. Durham and Robinson give us a picture of the colonial Assembly parties as factions claiming to represent the majority, a permanent majority, the "people," rather than the kind of temporary majority that forms and reforms with each election, in the manner of the liberal democratic parties of today. Did they see the radicals correctly?[20] The new-school argument that the radicals

143

espoused an idea of public "virtue" suggests that indeed there may have been an absolutist streak in the radical parties. Peter J. Smith describes Papineau as dreaming of a Canada that would be a "one-class democracy."[21] Such a dream would go a long way toward justifying one-party government. In any event we may say that Durham and Robinson were alarmed by their perception that Mackenzie and Papineau were advancing absolute claims. It was the threat of absolutism, not the popular character of radical claims, that aroused them.

Durham stresses, as Robinson does not, that the intolerant claims of the majority parties were met by the intolerance of imperial rule (and the intolerance of colonials who claimed the imperial mantle). But clearly both are looking at the same bleak picture: parties and political leaders no longer able to participate in the give and take of parliamentary debate, unable to accept defeat on issues, and unable to compromise even when compromise would further the interests of those they represented—parties in the process of transforming themselves into armed camps. The partisan quarrel was dividing the colonies from Britain, a dreadful prospect in Robinson's eyes and an unfortunate one in Durham's, but worse, it was destroying civil peace and authority in each province. Looking back through the years of peace in Canada it is perhaps easy to underestimate the crisis of the 1830s. To observers of the day it must have seemed to have the proportions of a situation like Ireland's today. Citizens were carrying arms against their government and against fellow citizens. In liberal doctrine there is no greater political evil.

The problem for both men, then, was to find means to moderate the intransigent passions and claims of the quarreling factions. Both suggested that in the ordinary course of events moderation in politics is furthered by a form of government that encourages citizens in the acquisition of property. Both adhered to the nineteenth-century faith in economic progress, believing that mankind profits as international trade flourishes and as new scientific discoveries and technologies are disseminated. The new-school suggestion that men like Robinson belong in the "commerce" and not the "virtue" camp has, as I have said, its merits. Side by side with the bleak picture of the contemporary disorders in British North America, Durham and Robinson sought to outline prospects for a gloriously wealthy future.

Robinson argued that Upper Canada had already made considerable progress "in regard to trade, revenue, cultivation of soil, construction of public works and the advancement of civil institutions." His vision of the province's future included a "prodigious increase in population, in wealth, in trade, in all that constitutes power."[22] Discussing the deadlock in colonial politics, Durham contrasted the relative poverty of the Canadas with the rising prosperity of the northeastern United States. He argued that the poverty of the British colonies stemmed from deficient political institutions and practices, and that with reform would come a prosperity to rival that of the American states.[23] Indeed, throughout the Report he argued that the economy of the Canadas was declining, while Robinson, in contrast, stoutly maintained that the affairs of Upper Canada were flourishing.[24] As we shall see, Robinson was unwilling to entertain the suggestion that the political institutions of Upper Canada were in any way defective. But both men were working from the same underlying assumption, that citizens would be wealthy under good political institutions and poor under imperfect institutions. Both suggested as well that it is chiefly the individual's hope of acquiring property and improving his prospects that grounds his loyalty to nation and his obedience to law.

As part of his plea for measures to promote emigration from Britain, Robinson described how the starving paupers of the home country, prone to discontent and disaffection in the crowded conditions of British cities, were transformed into "peaceful, industrious and respectable yeomen" in the colonies. They became "useful, independent and happy members of society."[25] Both Durham and Robinson argued that the experience of poverty breeds discontent and rebellion. Both believed that rebellion in turn brings poverty.[26]

At times Robinson wrote with apparent nostalgia about Britain's "ancient and venerable institutions," and the influence in British politics of "the traditionary respect for rank and family—with all the substantial power of wealth and control of numerous landlords over a grateful tenantry."[27] We catch a glimpse in these passages of an older, more traditional society, a society that might deserve the name "tory" as Horowitz uses it, where the respect and deference of a populace habituated to obedience grounds political obligation. But we ought not to conclude from what Robinson wrote in such passages that he hoped to inculcate such traditions in

Upper Canada. His point is precisely that there was no such tradition of deference and respect in British North America, where, as he argued, every farmer was "an independent freeholder and every adult male a voter." Convinced of North America's economic potential, he suggested that, although habits of deference had moderated political debate in the past, institutions promoting wealth would serve the same purpose in the future. Civil peace is possible—perhaps even more likely—when individuals are engrossed in obtaining a good living and all are hopeful about the future. On the subjects of political obligation, the objectives of good government, and rebellion and civil peace, Robinson is not noticeably more conservative than Durham. It is certainly a mistake to suppose that his thought is informed by "feudal" notions of hierarchy or dreams of community and collectivity, as the Horowitz thesis would assert.

But if the argument is that loyalty to government and obedience to law result from the individual's satisfaction with the way in which the laws secure his property and prospects, it would seem to follow that something was very wrong with law and government in the Canadas. Durham argued outright that the colonial constitution and colonial political practice were deficient. The "official" parties (in Upper Canada the Tories) were more or less permanently ensconced in the Executive Councils (but—especially in the case of Lower Canada—without effective control of public moneys), while the radicals sulked in Legislative Assemblies, their hopes of government office constantly frustrated, turning over dangerous dreams of a popular coup. The partisan quarrel was bound to escalate under these conditions, Durham argued; it was bound to be the more heated exactly because neither faction was able to promote the policies needed to further the economic affairs of the colonies.[28] His remedy for moderation was two-fold. He prescribed the political reforms, including responsible government, that he believed were necessary to promote moderate behaviour and moderate claims in the legislature. Moreover, he expected that as a result, leaders in the reformed parliament would be able, at last, to turn their attention to measures needed to better economic conditions.

Robinson could not take such a line, although it would seem to have suited his own suppositions. The stumbling block for him was responsible government. He could not accept it, and for a very simple reason. He was convinced that it would lead to the severing of the imperial connection, and he believed that his beloved Upper

Canada could not realize its future wealth and power without the assistance of British trade preferences and the security afforded by the British forces in North America. In Robinson's opinion the Executive Councils of the colonies had the function of representing the imperial interests.[29] Expecting the Executive to curry favour with the majority in the Assembly, as the principle of responsible government requires, would mean that imperial interests had no forum in colonial affairs; the formal, institutional connection between Britain and the colony would be lost.

Durham, by contrast, argued that responsible government and empire could be reconciled. He suggested that a severing of the institutional connection would not destroy the empire, because British North Americans would always continue to find it to their advantage to endorse measures agreeable to the home country. Colonists and the home country were bound to think alike on the constitution, immigration, trade, and defence.[30] It is perhaps not hard to see why some observers of the time found Durham's position on empire unconvincing. Certainly Robinson was not the only one to argue that the kind of airy tie between Britain and the colonies that Durham was proposing would not suffice, and that a firm institutional connection was required.[31] Smith and Stewart see evidence of tory "statism" in the fact that the Upper Canada tories rejected responsible government. They describe the tories as merely trying to consolidate their position as the party that dominated in the Executive Councils. But when we add Robinson's argument against responsible government, that it would deprive the province of the support of the imperial connection, to his position on popular absolutism, we are far indeed from being able to say that tory thought on the constitution was formed chiefly by party or "statist" ambitions.

Because he rejected the idea that the provincial constitution required such reforms as responsible government, Robinson was left with virtually no explanation for the raging discontent of the 1830s. Moreover, he had virtually no remedy. He was largely reduced to arguing that the institutions established in the Canadas in 1791 ought to have been good enough for anyone. The province had flourished, the discontent was unfounded, and, in any event, reforms would not improve things. It is, perhaps, not a very satisfactory position. Nevertheless, the fact that Robinson could reconcile himself to living in a dependency, the fact that he could praise a political constitution that was little more than oligarchy, itself tells us a good deal about his political thought. He could give up the idea of responsible government without great grief because in fact he did not hold that furthering the participation of the ordinary rank and file in government affairs was the highest political good. The highest good in his eyes, as we shall see, was the protection of individual rights; this, in his opinion, was not always easily guaranteed in a participatory society.

Both Durham and Robinson are liberals. But they are liberals of different stripes. Both held that it is the purpose of government to guarantee individual rights and freedoms. But Durham undoubtedly leaned toward the view that political rights, that is, the rights enabling citizens to participate in the affairs of government, are the most important rights. The franchise, problems of representation, and "responsible government" preoccupied him. In contrast, Robinson held that individual rights, the rights that protect a citizen from government, such as the right to own property and security from arbitrary arrest, are the most important.

The difference is significant, but it will not do to exaggerate it. Robinson, for his part, despite his distrust of the democratic element, knew very well that in a free country popular claims must have a voice and that opposition to government must be allowed. "There is in all free countries a party in opposition to the Government," he wrote.[32] To be sure, he emphasized the problems that such opposition might entail: "Who can hope to set bounds to its desires, or to limit its attempts?" But like Durham he was pleading for moderation in political debate; he did not support outright suppression of free political speech. He was willing (more willing than Durham, it is true) to curtail the effectiveness of the popular house and political opposition, but he was not proposing to deprive the popular house and opposition of all constitutional powers. Although he rejected responsible government, he defended the right of the colonial popular house to vote money bills ("long usage has established [this privilege] on a firmer footing perhaps than any other"). The practice prevailing in the colonial assemblies whereby "measures of public utility are taken up by any of the members indifferently" was acceptable to him.[33]

Durham, it is argued, was far less enamoured of political participation than were the colonial and British radicals. Although he was proposing to open new opportunities for the radicals (the very men who, in his own analysis, had done so much to bring on the

Rebellion), he was not proposing to give them unrestricted political freedom. He meant to allow the radicals power within a "balanced" political constitution, in which the powers of the democratic branch of government were offset by the powers of the political executive and the upper legislative house.

It was important in Durham's view that, although the leaders of the party securing the largest number of seats in the lower house become the polity's governors under responsible government, they do not govern from the lower house, in the people's name. They govern, rather, as members of the political executive, that is, as Ministers of the Crown. Radicals like Mackenzie and Papineau insisted that the lower house was the proper seat of government power. Durham firmly opposed that idea. He regarded the principle of responsible government as one aspect of the mixed or "balanced" political constitution; that is, he thought in terms of a Parliament with three branches: the "monarchic" branch (the political executive, the Ministers of the Crown), the "aristocratic" branch (the upper legislative chamber), and the "democratic" branch (the lower chamber), each having distinct powers under the constitution.[34] What is important here is that he believed that the political executive and the popular house should be inseparable yet distinct. Although the cabinet has to secure a majority vote in the lower house on matters of importance (responsible government), the lower house has its own resources and traditions that allow opposition and dissent.

The result is that the branch truly representing the nation, the lower house, does not govern. In the argument of the eighteenth and nineteenth centuries, this safeguard protects the people from democratic tyranny. But just as important, the branch that governs, the cabinet, does not represent all political opinions, and as a result is never free from challenge. This, it was held, is what secures the people from oligarchy. The minority in the lower house can never be eradicated or silenced, because the lower house does not govern. No party can claim absolute title to rule, because the executive branch is not representative. Power is no party's permanent possession.[35] Durham thus proposed to allow new avenues for participation—he would give political passions more rein—but within a political system that rewards only those prepared to be moderate.

Robinson understood the uses of institutions to curb immoderate political demand as well as Durham. In the language of the day, he praised "checks and balances" and the "balanced" constitution, just as one would expect. Indeed, he provided a fair description of responsible government as it operated in Britain, and seems not to have objected to it in the Mother of Parliaments.[36] But desirable or not, he could not accept responsible government for the British North American colonies, because he believed it would lead to outright colonial independence. He had to defend the status quo. The result is an argument for accepting limits on political rights coupled with a defence of the measures and principles necessary to protect individual rights.

Contrary to what the Horowitz thesis might suggest, Robinson was not defending the sacrifice of individual rights for collective political ends. He considered it of the first importance, for example, that, although the suspension of the constitution had deprived the inhabitants of Lower Canada of representative government, they had not lost their individual rights. The government of Lower Canada (then comprised of a Governor and an appointed Council of twenty) "is fully adequate to protect all classes, to redress all grievances, to promote all improvements, and to answer every end for which societies are formed," he argued; "It is very far from being a despotic government." He continued:

It is a written constitution conferred by Parliament, in which the limits of executive and legislative authority are defined, and the laws are as supreme as in any other country . . . nothing can be done contrary to law, and . . . the law, so far from depending on the will of the executive, can only be changed with the concurrence of a council of twenty members, taken from the worthiest . . . inhabitants of the province. . . . It is merely reverting to the form of constitution established by Parliament for the province of Quebec in the year 1774.[37]

Robinson was not arguing that the French Canadians should be deprived of their Assembly for more than a few years. It was important in his view to restore the franchise and political rights to the inhabitants of the lower province.[38] But maintaining the present system would not be intolerably unjust as long as the individual was protected from government.

The constitution of 1791, in Robinson's view, gave the British North American colonies laws "better calculated than those of any other country to secure the best interests and promote the happiness of the human race."[39] It is significant that he wrote of the human race in this connection. He was not praising laws peculiarly fitted for a particular people, such as the British. His argument rather is that British laws and the British constitution are best in a universal sense, because they are suited to human nature. They provide individuals with what they most want from government. They promote "happiness," as he argued repeatedly, meaning exactly that they secure the individual from arbitrary interference by government or by fellow citizens, leaving him free to pursue his own ends. As he argued in a statement of 1838:

To protect life, liberty and property laws are necessary; and these laws can only be enforced by officers clothed with regular and defined authority . . . . When attempts are made to overturn this Government by force . . . from that moment, property ceases to be secure; the independence accumulated by industry may be swept from its possessor in a moment; life and liberty have no protection; the most bold, and worthless, and cruel, become for a time, the instruments of power, as arbitrary as their will.[40]

It has been argued here that the Pocock school is correct insofar as it leads us to see tories like Robinson as endorsing commerce and acquisitiveness. What we fail to get from that interpretation is a sense of the tories' defence of individual opportunities and rights for all citizens regardless of rank. And Pocock's model is as unhelpful as others when it comes to explaining the nineteenth-century whig and tory arguments for restraining popular participation within a balanced constitution.

In the Horowitz interpretation the tories are endowed with a benign "feudal" touch that makes them at times capable of acting for the common good. In the new-school view the tories are mere purveyors of a "statist" élitism; it is the radicals who are the spokesmen—benign spokesmen—for the common good. Both perspectives regard the collectivist, "organic," "virtuous" thrust in political thought with uncritical favour. For this reason, neither is able to recapture or assess the argument against allowing a privileged idea of the popular interest or the common good in political debate.

Durham as a liberal is assumed to be the outright friend of political participation. His argument for limitations on popular participation has been virtually ignored. While Gordon Stewart notices aspects of it, he concludes that Durham must be a covert tory, arguing, as Stewart believes tories do, for measures to support the hegemony of an official party. As an opponent of responsible government Robinson is seen as the enemy of all liberal freedoms. His conviction that individual freedoms are more secure in a less participatory regime, if it is noticed at all, is dismissed as just so much more tory rhetoric in aid of party ambition.

Both Robinson and Durham believed that civil war and loss of all political and individual freedoms follow when absolute demands enter politics. Both saw in the demands of the popular, democratic parties of British North America the threat of just such an absolutism. Indeed, if we take "virtue" to refer to collective sentiments that are privileged in politics because they are deemed to represent what the "people" really want, then we may say that Durham and Robinson feared above all in the British North American context the consequences of "virtue."

We are left with questions about Canadian political culture in relation to American. But to see this matter clearly would require a fuller account of Canadian attitudes to the United States in the nineteenth century as well as an exploration of the American political culture and the American founding. Neither can be undertaken here.[41] Nevertheless, we must ask whether we should accept the Hartz-Horowitz view of the United States as largely formed by Lockean liberalism, or Smith's and Stewart's suggestion that ideas of public "virtue" inform the American political culture.

We can say that Durham saw little difference between the two nations during those crucial years of the early nineteenth century. He argued that the English-speaking population of the Canadas, and the inhabitants of the northern states of the Union, "speak the same language, live under laws having the same origin, and preserve the same customs and habits." He spoke of two divisions of an "identical population."[42] It is the more interesting then that he believed it worthwhile to establish a separate nation in the northern half of the North American continent, as a "counterbalance" to the United States. Like Robinson, he hoped for a federation of all the British North American colonies, to form a new and separate British nation.[43] But there is nothing to suggest that he thought this proud new North American federation would have a cultural or national character markedly different from that of the United States, or indeed other modern liberal nations.[44]

And Robinson the Loyalist? It goes without saying that he preferred British political institutions to the American alternative and that he hoped for a strong imperial connection exactly because he treasured the British political heritage. But did he see a real difference in national character between Canada and the United States, a difference in political culture, as we say today? He noted at one point that the Americans exhibit a laudable spirit of enterprise, and concluded that this "has resulted from the characteristics of their race which we share with them." By "race" he meant, in its nineteenth-century usage, not a people that share a genetic heritage, but a people that share political traditions and have similar institutions. His argument here is that the political constitution of the United States has resulted in prosperity and is admirable on that score.[45] We understand Robinson best, I think, if we see him as a loyalist rather than a nationalist. He does not have to justify a blind allegiance. He does not have to put his allegiance above a shrewd appreciation of his own interests. He gave his loyalty to British political institutions exactly because, as his argument tried to show, they gratified individual aspirations in exemplary fashion. And on this count he is surely, again, like Durham.

Durham reminds us of the legitimate avenues open within the parliamentary system for moderate political participation. Robinson reminds us of the value of the private life, secure from the political realm. These are shrewd, hard-headed political insights—both liberal.

NOTES

*The author is grateful to R. C. B. Risk for ideas, references, and a challenge.

1. See Gad Horowitz, "Conservatism, Liberalism, and Socialism in Canada: An Interpretation," *Canadian Journal of Economics and Political Science* 32.2 (1966). The article has been reprinted many times. Horowitz draws on arguments about political ideology and political culture in North America developed by Louis Hartz in *The Founding of New Societies* (New York: Harcourt, Brace and World, 1969). It is worth noting that Kenneth McRae, whose arguments also derive from Hartz's thesis, suggests that exactly because the Loyalists were refugees from the United States it has to be supposed that their political ideology was largely American Lockean liberalism. McRae, "The Structure of Canadian History," in Hartz, *The Founding of New Societies.* H. D. Forbes describes Canadian political scientists' fascination with Horowitz's views in "Hartz-Horowitz at Twenty: Nationalism, Toryism and Socialism in Canada and the United States," *Canadian Journal of Political Science* 20.1 (1987). Forbes's notes provide a full bibliography. If further proof is needed

that the debate is perennial, see Nelson Wiseman, "A Note on 'Hartz-Horowitz at Twenty': The Case of French Canada," *Canadian Journal of Political Science* 21.4 (1988) and Forbes's reply in the same issue.

2. Gordon T. Stewart, *The Origins of Canadian Politics: A Comparative Approach* (Vancouver: University of British Columbia Press, 1986), a "new school" survey of Canadian history from 1791, draws chiefly on John M. Murrin, "The Great Inversion, or Court versus Country, a Comparison of the Revolution Sentiments in England (1688-1721) and America (1776-1816)," in J. G. A. Pocock, ed., *Three British Revolutions, 1641, 1688, 1776* (Princeton: Princeton University Press, 1980), and Bernard Bailyn, *The Origins of American Politics* (New York: Knopf, 1968). See Stewart's bibliography, *The Origins* 117. Peter J. Smith, "The Ideological Origins of Canadian Confederation," *Canadian Journal of Political Science* 20.1 (1987), cites Pocock, *The Machiavellian Moment* (Princeton: Princeton University Press, 1975) among others. See Smith's bibliography on page 4. "My debt to Pocock's work is obvious," he writes.

3. For a balanced discussion of "court" and "country" in nineteenth-century Canadian politics that does not force all facts into the one model, see Phillip A. Buckner, *The Transition to Responsible Government: British Policy in British North America, 1815-1850* (Westport, CT: Greenwood Press, 1985), especially chap. 2, "The Old Representative System in Theory and in Practice."

4. Smith. "Ideological Origins" 4.

5. ———, "Ideological Origins" 5-9. "Virtue" in one new-school description of the American founding is the concept of "furthering the public good" through the "constant sacrifice of individual interests to the greater needs of the whole." (Robert E. Shallope, "Republicanism and Early American Historiography," *William and Mary Quarterly* 39: 335-36, cited in Thomas L. Pangle, *The Spirit of Modern Republicanism: The Moral Vision of the American Founders and the Philosophy of Locke* [Chicago: University of Chicago Press, 1988] 28). I am greatly indebted to Professor Pangle for his discussion of "classical republicanism" and the Hartz thesis. *The Spirit of Modern Republicanism* provides a convincing critique of classical republicanism at which I can only hint in this paper.

6. Smith, "Ideological Origins" 12; Stewart, *The Origins* 28.

7. Stewart, *The Origins* viii. "The debate between wealth and virtue . . . is critical to comprehending the clash between Reformer and Tory in nineteenth-century Canada," says Smith. "Against the Tory system of centralized elite control and influence Reformers posed democracy." "Ideological Origins" 5, 13.

8. For the suggestion that the tories' public works were at least in part an expression of genuine public-spiritedness and sense of the common good, one could follow up the literature on "red toryism" in Canada. Forbes, "Hartz-Horowitz

at Twenty," again provides a bibliography. Stewart at one point tries to assimilate his views to those of Hartz-Horowitz by using "statist" for both interpretations. He utterly misses the way in which his line of thought overturns Horowitz.

9. See Peter J. Smith's summary of Bernard Bailyn on the Americans as "virtuous." "Ideological Origins" 9.

10. G. Blaine Baker rings the changes again. He accepts the picture of the United States promulgated by the Pocock school, but argues that the Upper Canada tories resembled the Americans. Robinson and his peers, he says, were "animated by classical notions of public virtue." "So Elegant a Web: Providential Order and the Rule of Secular Law in Early Nineteenth-Century Upper Canada," *University of Toronto Law Journal* 38 (1988): 185.

11. C. P. Lucas, ed., *Lord Durham's Report on the Affairs of British North America*, 3 vols. (Oxford: Clarendon Press, 1912). References will be given first to the text in the second volume of this edition and then to the widely-used Carleton Library paperback, Gerald Craig, ed., *Lord Durham's Report: An Abridgement of Report on the Affairs of British North America by Lord Durham* (Toronto: McClelland and Stewart, Carleton Library, 1968). The Report was first published in London in 1839. John Beverley Robinson, *Canada and the Canada Bill* (East Ardley, Yorkshire: S. R. Publishers [Johnson Reprint], 1967) (first published in London in 1840). Robinson meant *Canada and the Canada Bill* to give a tory picture of the colonies to counter the false impressions left by Durham and his whig and radical associates in the Report. See his scathing comments on Durham and Durham's radical connections, 54-55, 63, 151-52, 169.

12. Robinson, *Canada and the Canada Bill* 109, 30, 93, 145, 111.

13. Patrick Brode, *Sir John Beverley Robinson, Bone and Sinew of the Compact* (Toronto: University of Toronto Press, for The Osgoode Society, 1984) 119; see also 35, 36. Brode is merely expressing the standard view of Robinson. S. F. Wise, for example, calls Robinson a "high tory," and refers to the regime of the Upper Canada tories as "standing testimony to the weaknesses and dangers of government by an authoritarian and paternalistic elite." "Upper Canada and the Conservative Tradition," in Edith G. Frith, ed., *Profiles of a Province: Studies in the History of Ontario* (Toronto: Ontario Historical Society, 1967). Blaine Baker speaks of Robinson's "revulsion" toward equality, in "Providential Order and the Rule of Law" 194.

14. See Janet Ajzenstat, *The Political Thought of Lord Durham* (Montreal: McGill-Queen's University Press, 1988) chap. 1, "Durham's Liberalism." For Durham on parliamentary reform in Britain see Ajzenstat, *Political Thought* 53, 64-66.

15. Lucas, *Report* 84, 81; Craig, *Report* 60, 58.

16. Lucas, *Report* 286, 155; Craig, *Report* 114, 84. See the discussion in Ajzenstat, *Political Thought* chap. 6, "'Responsible Government' in the Colonies." Stewart indeed comments on just these passages in the Durham report, in *The Origins* 43, 44. The point he makes about the way in which Durham's commentators have overlooked them is well taken. But Stewart simply takes these passages as reason to enlist Durham in the "court" camp. He does not put what Durham says about restricting the assemblies together with the overall liberal thrust of Durham's thought, and as a result he does not see the scope of the argument that supports Durham—or the tories—on this issue.

17. Robinson, *Canada and the Canada Bill* 93; see also 95, 116-17, 126.

18. Lucas, *Report* 33, 58; Craig, *Report* 30, 43.

19. See Ajzenstat, *Political Thought* chap. 7, "The Assimilation Proposal: Durham's Analysis."

20. For the colonial and British radicals on democracy see Ajzenstat, *Political Thought* chap. 6, especially 55, 57-58; and Ajzenstat, "Modern Mixed Government: A Liberal Defence of Inequality," *Canadian Journal of Political Science* 18.1 (1985).

21. Smith, "Ideological Origins" 13.

22. Robinson, *Canada and the Canada Bill* 99, 100, 39. Analyzing Robinson's judgments in such areas as property law, bills, notes, franchises, debtor-creditor relations, and the law of transportation, Bernard J. Hibbitts shows just how much Robinson himself did to promote commercial enterprise in the province ("The Legal Thought of Sir John Beverley Robinson, Chief Justice of Upper Canada, 1829-1862," manuscript). It is Hibbitts's argument indeed that his analysis goes a long way toward showing the deficiencies of Horowitz's "tory-touch" argument (see page 73).

23. Lucas, *Report* 90, 206, and elsewhere; Craig, *Report* 60, 112. See Ajzenstat, *Political Thought* 27-29.

24. The immensely detailed picture of the life and the economy of Lower Canada in the 1830s that is being built up by Serge Courville, Jean-Claude Robert and Normand Séguin provides an important corrective to the idea that Lower Canada was in decline. See especially their paper, "La Vallé du Saint-Laurent à l'époque du rapport Durham: économie et société," *Journal of Canadian Studies* 25.1 (1990). Courville, Robert, and Séguin argue that even those historians who wish to quarrel with Durham's recommendations for French Canada have tended to accept his assessment of the economy of that period uncritically.

25. Robinson, *Canada and the Canada Bill* 50-51. For Durham on "independence" see Ajzenstat, *Political Thought* 25.

26. Ajzenstat, *Political Thought* 32-33. For Robinson's best statement on the effects of rebellion see his *Charge to the Grand Jury at Toronto, March 8, 1838,*

pamphlet (n.p., n.d.) 9, 10. In these pages he gives a stirring short lecture on political obligation.

27. Robinson, *Canada and the Canada Bill* 122. It seems likely that passages like this have led to the idea that Robinson advocated social hierarchy.

28. See the analysis in Ajzenstat, *Political Thought* chap. 6.

29. Robinson, *Canada and the Canada Bill* 17-23, 40, 46, 73, 96, 116-17. On the idea that the Assembly leaders would combine forces after union, see 73, 93, 111. Robinson saw the imperial connection as one means by which immoderate political demands in the colonies could be tempered. The argument is that some issues, perhaps the most contentious, would not enter the political arena in the colony because they are determined by the British Parliament, and that, as a result, it would be possible to debate local affairs more freely, with greater hope of settlement. Durham, in contrast, could not accept the idea that the colonists would be better off if imperial power in colonial affairs were enlarged.

30. For Durham on the imperial connection, see Ajzenstat, *Political Thought* chap. 5, "'Responsible Government' and Empire."

31. Robinson was certainly not the only one to see the problem in this way during these years. Lord John Russell, a whig very much of Durham's kind, opposed responsible government on grounds like Robinson's. See *Hansard*, Series 3, 36 (March 6, 1937) 1295ff.; and Russell's letter of instruction to Governor Poulet Thompson in W. P. M. Kennedy, ed., *Documents of the Canadian Constitution 1759-1915* (Toronto: Oxford University Press, 1918) 522-54.

32. Robinson, *Canada and the Canada Bill* 123; here and on page 33 he notes that the number of places of honour and influence in government will always be limited. The suggestion is that opposition rises in part out of jealous competition for places. This argument is as old as Machiavelli. See Ajzenstat, "Modern Mixed Government."

33. Robinson, *Canada and the Canada Bill* 189, 192. What Robinson would not accept was the introduction in the colonies of the constitutional principle requiring that money bills originate with the ministers of the Crown.

34. See Ajzenstat, "Modern Mixed Government," and *Political Thought* chap. 6.

35. See Frank MacKinnon, *The Crown in Canada* (Calgary: McClelland and Stewart West, 1976) 15-16. See also Ajzenstat, "Comment: The Separation of Powers in 1867," *Canadian Journal of Political Science* 20.1 (1987); and Ajzenstat, "Canada's First Constitution: Pierre Bedard on Loyalty and Dissent," manuscript, for a discussion of Blackstone on the principles grounding political opposition in the parliamentary systems.

36. Robinson, *Canada and the Canada Bill* 143, 152, 188-89.

37. ———, *Canada and the Canada Bill* 136, 138.

38. ———, *Canada and the Canada Bill* 121, 136.

39. Robinson, *Canada and the Canada Bill* 22, 23; and see 95, 156. The Constitution of 1791 was as "liberal, as just, as unexceptionable a constitution as any colony has ever enjoyed" (119).
40. Robinson, *Charge to the Grand Jury at Toronto*. Hibbitts's analysis of the Chief Justice's decisions, in "The Legal Thought of Sir John Beverley Robinson," amplifies this picture of Robinson as a defender of the rule of law. Rule by individuals, no matter how gentlemanly, no matter how well-educated, is mere tyranny if unconstrained by law.
41. On Canadian attitudes to the United States in the nineteenth century see Jane Errington, *The Lion, The Eagle, and Upper Canada* (Kingston and Montreal: McGill-Queen's University Press, 1987). Errington maintains that historians, especially S. F. Wise, have greatly overrated anti-Americanism among the Upper Canadian élite. See also Carol Wilton-Siegel's review of *The Lion, The Eagle*, "Upper Canadian Politics Revisited," *Journal of Canadian Studies* 23.4 (1988-89) 137-40. Both Baker and Hibbitts argue that differences between British North America and the United States have been exaggerated, Baker because he believes tory Upper Canada to have been as communitarian as the United States, Hibbitts because he is convinced that tory Upper Canada was very nearly as liberal as the United States (Baker, "Providential Order and the Rule of Law"; Hibbitts, "The Legal Thought of Sir John Beverley Robinson.") Hibbitts demonstrates the similarity between the legal thought of Robinson and that of American judges like Joseph Story, James Kent, and Lemuel Shaw.
42. Lucas, *Report* 267-68; Craig, *Report* 132-33. Did Durham really understand the people and institutions of the United States? I have argued elsewhere that his information was at least in part derived from Alexis de Tocqueville. Ajzenstat, *Political Thought* chaps. 3 and 4. Tocqueville too saw no difference between the English-speaking colonies of British North America and the northeastern United States. Durham takes phrases like "identical population" directly from Tocqueville.
43. Lucas, *Report* 305, 309; Craig, *Report* 158, 160; Robinson, *Canada and the Canada Bill* 71.
44. See the argument in Ajzenstat, *Political Thought* chap. 3, "Durham and Tocqueville on Society."
45. Robinson, *Canada and the Canada Bill* 57, 54-55, 59.

CHAPTER SEVEN

THE TRIUMPH OF LIBERALISM IN CANADA:
LAURIER ON REPRESENTATION AND
PARTY GOVERNMENT

Rainer Knopff

Modern party government as we know it in the West rests on
liberal foundations. Only with the development and general acceptance of liberal principles did it become possible to conceive of
parties as normal and legitimate political phenomena, and to establish a system of party government in which self-consciously competitive parties alternate peacefully in office.[1] In previous eras politics was often a battle between what Tocqueville called "great
parties."[2] Based on competing visions of the best way of life or the
true road to salvation, "great parties" tended to see each other not
as legitimate opponents in a game whose rules were understood
and accepted by all sides, but as heretics whose victory would sub-
vert the highest truths and most important human pursuits, and
who thus had to be suppressed. This was a recipe for the kind of
civil strife, even civil war, that liberalism was designed to overcome. The liberal solution was to turn the question of the best
way of life into a matter of private choice and to limit the public
sphere to securing the conditions of life itself.

Although modern party government rests on foundations
laid down by liberal theorists, its practical establishment was often

assisted by the work of political statesmen.[3] This paper explores the contribution made in Canada by Wilfrid Laurier in his famous 1877 speech on "Political Liberalism."[4] The "silver-tongued" Sir Wilfrid is generally acknowledged as one of the finest orators this country has produced, and his 1877 speech epitomizes his rhetorical artistry. A close analysis of the speech underlines the rhetorical difficulties involved in establishing modern party government against the opposition of an influential exponent of traditional "great party" politics. It also reminds us of why the liberal solution, in its fully developed (i.e., liberal *democratic*) version, entails both the formalistic understanding of political representation first propounded by Thomas Hobbes and the separation of church and state associated with the writings of Locke.

POLITICAL CONTEXT

A rising star in Canada's Liberal party, Laurier gave his 1877 speech to rescue his party from the charge of heresy levelled against it by the politically influential ultramontane wing of the Catholic church in Quebec. The ultramontanes were theocrats who believed that the secular and political realms were properly subject to the superintendence of the church, and who thus vigorously rejected modern notions of popular sovereignty and the separation of church and state, the very notions propounded by the *Patriotes* in the period leading up to the 1837 Rebellions, and by the Rouges after 1848.[5] In the early 1870s this theocratic opposition to liberalism was formalized in the so-called "Catholic Programme," a document inspired by the ultramontane Bishop Laflèche, which argued that Quebec Catholics should make opposition to the heresy of liberalism their first political priority. Calling the separation of church and state "an absurd and impious idea," the Programme advised the faithful always to vote against Liberals. This generally meant voting for the Conservatives, though only if the latter accepted the theocratic principles spelled out in the Programme; if they did not, Catholics were advised to abstain from voting altogether. In effect, the Catholic Programme was the blueprint for a Catholic party in Quebec.[6]

The Catholic Programme clearly implied that the clergy should play a significant role in electoral politics, using the pulpit to advise parishioners about how to cast their votes. This view was made explicit in an 1875 joint pastoral letter of Quebec's bishops. According to this pastoral, it is a "monstrous error" to say "that the clergy has functions to fulfill only in the church and sacristy, and that in politics the people ought to practise moral independence."[7] This led to considerable "pulpit politics" in the elections of 1876, in which parishioners heard their priests condemn liberalism as "the serpent which crept into the terrestrial paradise to tempt and lead the human race to fall," and advise them that if they did not wish to give their votes to "deceitful men" they "ought not give [them] to a Liberal."[8] In response, Liberal party supporters went to court, charging that this pulpit rhetoric constituted "undue influence" under the terms of the Controverted Elections Act of 1874. The very premise of this charge, that church and state should be separated, was precisely the liberal heresy so offensive to the ultramontanes. The courts upheld the claims of "undue influence," but the cases simply confirmed the ultramontanes in their suspicion of liberalism and hardened their opposition.

By this time the political influence of the ultramontane wing of the church had reached the point where the Liberal party was in real danger of extinction in Quebec. The decisions in the undue influence cases, however, gave pause to the more moderate elements within the hierarchy, and these, led by Archbishop Taschereau (brother of the judge who decided one of the undue influence cases), began to oppose the extremism of the ultramontanes.[9] The escalating battle between these two wings of the Quebec clergy finally led to the intervention of Rome, which appointed the Irish Bishop Conroy to travel to Canada and investigate the problem. Conroy's report would be decisive. If he sided with the ultramontanes, liberalism in Quebec would have received a mortal blow; a decision in favour of the moderates would give it new life.

It was during Conroy's deliberations that Laurier was invited by the *Club canadien* in Quebec City to give his speech. As heir apparent to the leadership of the Quebec wing of the Liberal party, Laurier could not avoid saying something about the highly charged issue of undue influence that was occupying the legate.[10] But to speak on the subject was risky. Coming from a rising star in the party the speech would be well reported and Conroy would read it. If it offended him, it might lead to a fatal decision in favour of the ultramontanes. Clearly prudence was in order. Indeed, Alexander Mackenzie, the Liberal Prime Minister, was of the opinion that the most prudent speech would be no speech at all. Laurier was well aware of the problem and indicated his willingness to abandon the speech if Mackenzie insisted. "This is a subject," he wrote his Prime Minister, "which gives me a great deal of uneasiness and I feel at times sorry of having accepted to go into it. However, I am studying to make it as prudent as possible."[11]

Laurier's emphasis on caution and prudence is understandable. In order to defend his own party, he had to defend the principles of modern party government, especially the separation of church and state. Doing so openly and directly, however, would provide his opponents with exactly the evidence they needed to confirm their charge of heresy. In brief, it was the extremely delicate task of Laurier's rhetoric to promote the practical attainment of what he could not openly recommend.

POLITICAL LIBERALISM VERSUS
CATHOLIC LIBERALISM

Laurier begins his speech by distinguishing between "Catholic liberalism" and "political liberalism." He concedes that there is a species of liberalism called "Catholic liberalism" that is heretical, but denies that it has anything to do with the "political liberalism" of his own party. His party has aroused the ire of the church not because it is heretical, but because of an unfortunate coincidence in name. His manner of drawing the distinction, however, is not very satisfactory: "I know that Catholic liberalism has been condemned by the head of the church. But I will be asked: what is Catholic liberalism? On the threshold of this question I stop. This question does not come within the purview of my subject; moreover, it is not of my competence. But I know and I say that Catholic liberalism is not political liberalism."[12] This is mere assertion. Laurier says he "knows" the two forms of liberalism are not the same, but he admits to stopping "on the threshold" of the very question he must pose and answer in order truly to know. If he cannot say precisely what each one is—if this is beyond his purview—how can he know them to be different? Yet he admits that he is incompetent to define "Catholic liberalism."

This difficulty is surely explained by the rhetorical necessities of the situation. As a layman Laurier could not compete with the hierarchy in defining a religious heresy. He could not afford to become embroiled in a straightforward examination of the principles of the two liberalisms. Any distinctions he drew could be easily undermined if the church claimed that they were based on his misunderstanding of the theological definition of *Catholic* liberalism, and that a correct understanding would show the two liberalisms to be identical. Indeed, there was every probability that this would have happened: as late as 1896, when Laurier further elaborated his principles with respect to the Manitoba schools question, Bishop Laflèche was to call them the epitome of the heresy of Catholic liberalism.[13]

Because logical proof of his distinction is rhetorically precluded, Laurier resorts to an argument from consequences. Catholic liberalism and political liberalism must be different things, he says, because disastrous consequences would flow from the conclusion that they were identical. Such an argument would hardly satisfy a logician—something is not proven false just because it has negative consequences—but it has great rhetorical merit. Rhetoric persuades more by appealing to public passions than to the standards of pure reason, and Laurier seeks to persuade the public of his distinction by showing that it must be accepted to avoid what the public fears. Of course, to a considerable extent the public also fears heresy. Laurier's strategy thus depends on appealing to fears powerful enough to offset the fear of heresy. In fact, he appeals to two such fears. Over the course of the speech he gradually develops the argument that identifying political liberalism with the heresy of Catholic liberalism will lead to revolution or civil war, thus appealing to the fear of violence. First, however, he appeals to the fear of national insult.

"If it were true," says Laurier, "that the ecclesiastical censures hurled against Catholic liberalism should also apply to political liberalism that fact would constitute for us, French by origin and Catholic by religion, a state of things, the consequences of which would be painful." Hitherto, he continues, French Canadians, although a conquered race and a minority, have achieved liberty and equal rights with other Canadians because the democratic suffrage allows them to protect themselves within the Canadian family. "But it must not be forgotten that the other members of the Canadian family are divided into parties, the Liberal party and the Conservative party," and that if Catholics were prohibited from belonging to the former, they would either have to abstain from public life altogether, or become the "tools and slaves" of English-speaking Conservatives, who could take their votes for granted. Not being able

163

to use the suffrage for their own patriotic purposes, the constitution would become a "dead letter" in the hands of French Canadians. Such terrible consequences, says Laurier, "conclusively show how false is the assertion that a Catholic cannot belong to the Liberal party."[14]

THE POLITICAL STEAM ENGINE

Having made his audience receptive by conjuring up the unpalatable national consequences of identifying the political with the theological division, Laurier proceeds to more substantive theoretical demonstrations of the morally neutral nature of partisanship. Characteristically, he approaches the question obliquely, giving not an immediate explanation of the true roots of partisanship, but asking why it had been so misunderstood; why, in other words, the conflict between liberalism and conservatism had been cast in the form of a struggle between good and evil. The reason is an inadequate understanding of the newly invented principle of representation. Viewed from the perspective of this new principle, liberalism, far from being a new and heretical idea, turns out to be "as old as the world."

The liberal idea is no more a new idea than is the contrary idea. It is old as the world and is found written on every page of the world's history, but it is only in our days that we have come to know its force and its law and to understand how to utilize it. Steam existed before Fulton, but it has only been since Fulton that we have learned all the extent of its powers and how to make it produce its marvellous effects. The combination of tube and piston is the instrument by which we utilize steam and the system of representative government is the instrument which has revealed to the world the two principles, liberal and conservative, and by which we get from that form of government all its effects.[15]

Thus, just as steam drives the steam engine, the principles of liberalism and conservatism drive representative government. Just as the steam engine harnesses and puts to use the pre-existing steam, so representative government harnesses the eternal principles of liberalism and conservatism. Prior to the invention of representative government these principles at best did mankind little good, and at worst much harm, just as prior to the steam engine steam either dissipated harmlessly or caused nasty burns. To understand the morally neutral character of the partisan division, therefore, we must first understand the "political steam engine": representative government.

Laurier does not follow his own directive, however. Instead of explaining representation, the lens without which, he has argued, the true causes of the partisan division cannot come to light, he simply states these causes. The difference between liberalism and conservatism, he says, is caused first by the fact that "the same object will not be seen under the same aspect by different eyes," and that "for this sole reason, the one will take a route which the others will avoid, although both propose to arrive at the same end." Secondly, borrowing from Macaulay, Laurier tells us that the human mind by its very nature is "drawn in opposite directions by the charm of habit and by the charm of novelty." It is these ineradicable attributes of our nature that manifest themselves in politics as liberalism and conservatism. Consequently, "those who condemn liberalism as an error have not reflected that, in so doing, they condemn and attempt to suppress an attribute of human nature."[16] As Laurier later makes explicit, the attempt to suppress human nature leads to unavoidable explosions. The energy of liberalism may be harnessed by the political steam engine—representative government—but, like steam, it cannot be confined or suppressed without catastrophic consequences. This appeal to the fear of violence is, of course, the second part of the argument from consequences referred to above.

Thus, although he began by arguing that a proper understanding of representation would teach men not to cast political differences in moral terms, Laurier provides no such understanding. Instead, he makes an entirely independent argument against the moralization of politics. Can it be that one does not have to understand representation after all in order to appreciate the moral indifference of political parties?

This paradox is resolved if one considers the moral indifference of the parties as itself the key aspect of representative government. To return to the analogy, one could argue that the key element in the invention of the steam engine is a proper understanding of the nature of steam. There is, however, this difference: once the steam engine is invented it is no longer essential to understand the nature of steam; one simply applies the machine and it works. But this is plainly not the case with representative government, which, Laurier insists, has already been

Macaulay could cheerfully vote down the system of rotten boroughs by virtue of which they held their own seats. These men were admirable precisely because, despite their conservative inclination, they were able to understand the true aspirations of human nature and enthusiastically bend to them. The Macaulays of this world, argues Laurier, are the model of the Liberal party.

By suggesting that the upper-class origin of the leaders of British liberalism placed them in the category of temperamental conservatives, Laurier indicates that self-interest is one of the chief factors underlying the two partisan inclinations. This fills an important gap in his earlier argument. His claim that partisanship stems from the same object being seen differently by different eyes is unsatisfactory because he has not explained what makes one person see things differently from another. Similarly, to argue that the human mind is "drawn in opposite directions by the charm of habit and by the charm of novelty" is to say nothing about what causes the one or the other charm to attract any particular mind. By his praise of the Liberal peers of England, however, Laurier indicates that class-based interest accounts for the difference.

For Laurier the "model liberal" appears to be a temperamental conservative who understands the role of self-interest in human affairs. The crucial difference between the temperamental conservatives who led the British Liberal party and their continental counterparts is that the latter deceived themselves into believing they were defending immutable truth rather than their own interests. By contrast, the British peers appreciated the true role of self-interest in political life, and thus arrived at a more farsighted understanding of their own self-interest. Not blinded by the language of absolute truth and error, they understood that defending their present interests too vigorously would provoke a revolution that would destroy those interests completely. By disguising their self-interest under the banner of absolute truth, the continental conservatives succeeded only in bringing such disastrous consequences upon themselves.

It is the misguided political approach of the continental conservatives, moreover, that accounts for the extremism and violence of their liberal opponents. The church objected to liberalism not only because it was heretical but also because of its alleged revolutionary tendencies. Indeed, the two criticisms were often connected: liberalism was violent *because* it was heretical. Thus, in addition to distinguishing political from Catholic liberalism, Laurier distinguishes British from European liberalism. The latter is a distorted form of liberalism. If one wishes to understand true liberalism one must look to Britain:

It is true that there is in Europe, in France, in Italy, and in Germany, a class of men, who give themselves the title of liberals, but who have nothing of the liberal about them but the name and who are the most dangerous of men. These are not liberals, they are revolutionaries: in their principles they are so extravagant that they aim at nothing less than the destruction of modern society. With these men, we have nothing in common; but it is the tactic of our adversaries to always assimilate us to them. Such accusations are beneath our notice and the only answer we can with dignity give them is to proclaim our real principles and to so conduct ourselves that our acts will conform with our principles.[23]

As with his earlier dissociation of Catholic from political liberalism, Laurier simply asserts this distinction without offering any proof. In fact, the burden of his argument heretofore has run contrary to this distinction. If we accept his analysis of the causes of the partisan division, temperamental liberals on either side of the channel are indistinguishable. The continental liberals had become more revolutionary not because of any difference of principle or tendency but because they faced conservatives who tried to suppress them as purveyors of heresy and error. The true difference between continental and British liberalism is accounted for by the fact that the temperamental conservatives who mounted such an intransigent opposition to liberalism on the continent became its leaders in Britain.

Laurier seems to favour a judicious blend of both natural political inclinations, based on a realistic appreciation of the self-interest underlying both. Parties embodying this blend would recognize the irrepressible need for change and innovation in order to satisfy the eternally restless human spirit; at the same time they would be aware of the need to contain change in a framework of order and continuity, so that violence and anarchy would not destroy the ground of all aspiration. Laurier is surely not implying that there should only be one party to which all who truly understand their situation belong. Not only would this contradict his earlier praise of party alternation as the basis of liberty, but it would be rhetorically ineffective. He is trying to teach the conservatives a lesson, not to convince them to join his own party. What he appears to have in mind is two parties, differing in emphasis but both made up of the same political types, contending not on the battleground of irrevocable truth, but on the much narrower ground of interest. In another sense, however, both of the parties envisaged by Laurier contest the ground established by liberalism. From the larger perspective of "great party" politics they are simply divisions that appear within liberalism after it has completely defeated its theocratic opponents. If one focuses on "great party" issues, Laurier is indeed advocating the complete and permanent victory of one party, the party of liberalism, which will put an end once and for all to "great party" politics and pave the way for the "small parties" of modern party government.[24]

For Laurier the "small party" politics he favoured had been made difficult in Quebec by the conservative overreaction to the youthful and temporary excesses of the liberal followers of Papineau after 1837. "Hardly had they taken two steps in life," says Laurier, "when [these liberals] perceived their immense error" and became moderate.[25] Nevertheless, the damage was done, and conservatives continued to brand liberals as revolutionary heretics, deluding themselves that conditions in Canada were like those in continental Europe. In the face of extreme suppression, however, the moderation of Canadian liberalism could not be expected to persist forever. Eventually there would be an explosion that, through a kind of self-fulfilling prophecy, would vindicate the conservative view. The fault, however, would lie with the conservative attempt to suppress nature, not with the liberals.

Religion is the chief source of the destructive tendency to cast political disputes in the language of truth and heresy. It was the Catholic church that took the lead in opposing liberalism and introducing the biblical language of good and evil, and it was the church that attempted to band all Catholics together in a political fight against liberalism. By investing liberalism with a religious, or rather anti-religious, significance the church was taking the first step in making Canadian politics a religious battleground. Here we see more fully the significance of Laurier's distinction between political and Catholic liberalism. If the distinction does not hold, if the church is successful in branding one of the major political parties as heretical, then the attempt to form a Catholic party to combat it is inevitable. But such an attempt would be disastrous. Although the enemy would be liberalism, not Protestantism, a Catholic party would inescapably call forth a Protestant reaction in kind. For when the Catholic church declared that liberalism was anti-religious it meant that it was anti-Catholic, which implied that the Catholic definition of what is politically necessary for religion should rule the day. This no Protestant could accept.

You wish to organize a Catholic party. But have you not considered that, if you have the misfortune to succeed, you will draw down upon your country calamities of which it is impossible to foresee the consequences. You wish to organize all the Catholics into one party, without other bond, without other basis, than a common religion, but have you not reflected that, by the very fact, you will organize the protestant population as a single party and that then, instead of the peace and harmony now prevailing between the different elements of the Canadian population, you throw open the door to war, a religious war, the most terrible of all wars?[26]

Why the most terrible of all wars? Surely because, more than any other, it is carried out on the plane of absolute truth and goodness. Here again Laurier appeals to the fear of violence as part of his argument from consequences.

UNDUE INFLUENCE

It is important to reflect further on the fact that Laurier nowhere proves his distinctions between Catholic and political liberalism and between British and continental liberalism, but relies instead on appeals to the fearful consequences of identifying with them. It is by now apparent that his most important reason for avoiding a true examination of the differences is that they do not exist and that he is himself a Catholic liberal. His entire analysis implies the separation of church and state in the sense that the questions with which the church is most concerned—questions of good and evil, truth and heresy—cannot be allowed to become public and political questions. But for the ultramontanes this view lay at the heart of the heresy of Catholic liberalism. Thus, Laurier seeks rhetorically to promote what he cannot openly admit.

The already considerable difficulty of this task was rendered doubly acute because Laurier could not avoid a direct discussion of the propriety of the kind of pulpit politics that led to the undue influence cases. On this question, especially, he had to tread very carefully.

He had to discourage priestly involvement in politics without openly denying the right to such involvement. Not surprisingly, then, he begins his examination of the undue influence question by explicitly denying that the Liberal party wished to keep the priest out of public life: "In the name of what principle should the friends of liberty seek to deny the priest the right to take part in political affairs?" Indeed, "why should the priest not have the right to say that, if I am elected, religion will be inevitably destroyed, when I have the right to say that, if my adversary is elected, the state will go into bankruptcy?"[27] In short, it appears that the priest is perfectly free to take part in politics and even to introduce religious issues into politics.

What Laurier openly grants with one hand, however, he obliquely steals away with the other. Although the priest has as much right to take part in politics as any other citizen, this right is subject to the same limitations that apply to others: "The right of interference in politics finishes at the spot where it encroaches on the electors' independence." The Canadian constitution, according to Laurier, "rests on the freely expressed wish of each elector," which means that no vote may be forced by intimidation. Votes may certainly be changed through argument and persuasion. "If, however, notwithstanding all reasoning, the opinion of the electors remains the same, but that, by intimidation or fraud, they are forced to vote differently, the opinion which they express is not their opinion, and the constitution is violated."[28] Thus, while the priest may legitimately introduce religious questions into politics, he must not resort to intimidation. Laurier does not specify the kind of intimidation he has in mind, but it is safe to say that he is not thinking of physical force. In light of the decisions rendered in the undue influence cases it is reasonable to suppose that he means such things as the deprivation of the sacraments and religious burial, or even saying that a particular vote constitutes sin.[29]

But where does this leave us? The priest may say that a particular vote is contrary to the interests of religion, but not that such a vote is sinful, nor can he apply the sanctions normally attaching to sin, for these constitute intimidation. Laurier would surely have denied that, generally speaking, the clergy had no authority to define or punish sin; he implies, however, that it does lack this authority in the context of an election.[30] This means that in an election the private judgment of the individual on the relation of politics and religion is just as good as the judgment of the church. While the church denied the liberty of private judgment, considering it sinful to advocate it, Laurier implicitly insists on it. The theocratic alternative, Laurier repeats, "will culminate in explosion, violence and ruin," something "the clergy themselves would not want." Once again, by appealing to popular fears, Laurier attempts to encourage what he cannot openly insist upon: the retirement of the priest from political life.

This separation of the religious question of good and evil from issues of public life is essential for the peaceful party government Laurier is attempting to ensure. At stake is the justification for majority rule in a liberal democracy. Majority rule derives its moral authority from the liberal premise that all men are created equal (for politically relevant purposes), that no one rules by natural or divine right. Since none rules by right, the whole must rule itself, which in its modern version means that all must agree to be bound by the view of the majority. Majority rule remains legitimate only so long as the majority of the moment do not base their claim to rule on the issue on which they are agreed, rather than on the fact that they happen to be the majority among equals. If rule is justified by having the correct view of the issue, then those who know the truth should rule whether or not they are a majority. This implies that men are not politically equal, that those best equipped (by nature or divine revelation) to discern the truth should rule. Gaining the consent of the majority thus becomes a matter of prudence rather than principle. The argument that majority rule is right in principle stands or falls with the rejection of this pre-liberal inegalitarianism.

THEORETICAL FOUNDATIONS: HOBBES AND LOCKE[31]

One might say that majority rule stands or falls with the Hobbesian substitution of the *summum malum* of violent death for the traditional pursuit of a *summum bonum* as the primary function of government. This is not the first echo of Hobbes we have encountered in this speech (Laurier's view of man's nature as perpetual motion and restless incompletion springs to mind). This is hardly surprising. Laurier was confronting precisely the problem Hobbes was trying to overcome, and Hobbesian assumptions had become well entrenched in the liberal tradition on which Laurier drew. To understand the full implications of Laurier's rhetoric it is useful to explore its theoretical foundations, not only in Hobbes but also in Locke, who helped to transform Hobbesian liberalism into the kind of liberal democracy advocated by Laurier.

For Laurier, as for Hobbes, the opinions concerning good and bad that characterize political life and propel it into violence are merely rationalizations of selfish interests. The problem is that men deceive themselves into believing their own vain babblings about good and bad, thereby denying their essential equality. The only way to avoid this problem is to force men to tell the truth about themselves by keeping the fear of the *summum malum* constantly before their eyes, and by showing how inordinate attachment to their opinions leads to this *summum malum.* Hence, Laurier's constant development of the theme of explosion and civil war.

Laurier's view of representation and majority rule also rests on Hobbesian foundations. Laurier was quite right in calling the kind of representation he favoured a modern invention. The inventor, it is generally agreed, was Hobbes.[32] The chief characteristic of Hobbesian representation is its formalism, in the sense that it is less concerned with the substantive content of the representative's actions than with the fact that the representative has been authorized in advance to act on behalf of his constituents. Once he has been so authorized, his actions represent and obligate his constituents whether or not they agree with him.[33] The justification of majority rule implicit in Laurier's rhetoric embodies this formalism: the majority rules not because of their opinion on the issues concerned but simply because they are a majority among equals. Hobbes himself, of course, was not a democratic majoritarian, but his formalistic view of representation clearly survived the transition from liberalism to liberal democracy.

The Hobbesian view of representation has been criticized because, although it accounts for what we mean when we speak of a representative as one whose actions bind or obligate us, it does not account for what we mean when we speak of him as a servant or messenger of the people, someone whose substantive actions ought to accord with what the people want. According to Hannah Pitkin, for example, both elements must be present in a truly adequate account of representation.[34] A good representative, in short, should represent the substantive opinions of his constituents. By reminding us of the practical problem Hobbes was attempting to solve, Laurier's speech shows why this criticism misses the point. It reminds us of why the formalism of his concept of representation was essential to his solution. To represent the opinions of constituents rather than the passions they share in common is to open the door to competing claims to rule and to the civil strife attendant upon such claims. The proponents of the Catholic party in Laurier's Quebec were clearly advocates of the "representative-as-messenger-of-opinion" school, and in very Hobbesian terms Laurier shows how such an approach is fatal to civil peace in a religiously divided community. The representative is indeed the servant of fundamental and common passions, but never of opinions of good and bad.

By contrast, Laurier's emphasis on modern party government and the separation of church and state reflects Locke's modifications to Hobbesian liberalism. Hobbes himself opposed both notions. For him, the presence of political parties indicates disagreement about public matters, which in turn indicates that what is represented by the different parties is not the same. Since the passions that it is the purpose of government to represent are everywhere the same, the existence of different parties must be based on opinions of good and bad—precisely what Hobbes wished to banish from politics.

Nevertheless, although Hobbes did not himself recommend it, it is clear that party government as we know it must rest on Hobbesian assumptions. After all, the parties of modern party government do not generally engage in the kind of partisanship Hobbes deplored.[35] The characteristic of modern parties is that they give way gracefully to each other, which is possible only on the basis of the Hobbesian assumption that government should represent rather than rule. In other words, modern party government rests on the agreement that government be limited to securing rights rather than prescribing the manner of their exercise; which is to say that party government is decisively impartial, or non-partisan, concerning the questions over which partisans formerly divided: questions of good and evil. When parties are non-partisan in this higher sense, the only kind of partisanship remaining is that concerning the lower-level questions of how best to secure rights. About this goal, the only goal open to representative government, there may be peaceful disagreement.[36]

This limited partisanship assumes that it is possible to allow public disagreement about the best means to secure rights without running the risk of that disagreement transforming itself into one about the proper exercise of these rights. It depends on the agreement of private men to leave their essentially private opinions concerning the good life at home when they enter the public sphere to form political parties. Hobbes did not think this was possible. Because of his vanity, man would always transform his passions into opinions about good and evil, and given the opportunity would try to establish these opinions. Thus, for Hobbes, the only way to keep private opinions of good and bad at home was to keep the bearers of those opinions at home. Private men must not be allowed to enter the public sphere, which is to deny the very basis of political parties.

It was left to Locke to establish the possibility of private men entering the public sphere without bringing their opinions with them. This was possible for Locke because he had discovered what Hobbes had not: commerce. Locke is justly famous for two writings above all: the *Letter Concerning Toleration* and the chapter on property in the *Second Treatise*—and the two go together. With the establishment of the commercial society, men could be counted on to leave their opinions (especially their religious opinions) at home, because their attachment to those opinions would have been diluted by the material pleasures offered by commerce.[37] It was only with this Lockean transformation of the Hobbesian project that the conceptualization of party government as we know it became possible.

CONCLUSION

Although its theoretical foundations were laid by Hobbes and Locke, the institutionalization of modern party government required practical statesmanship. In Britain itself the essentials of party government were institutionalized in 1688-89, but elsewhere the proponents of "great party" politics impeded the full victory of the liberal project for much longer. In Quebec, theocrats retained considerable political influence until the late nineteenth century. At the height of their influence the ultramontanes posed a serious threat to the liberal democratic project. Laurier's attempt to meet this threat in his 1877 speech was a significant event in the history of liberal democratic statesmanship.

The speech was remarkably successful, for it seems to have influenced Bishop Conroy (as it was surely intended to do). Appearing shortly after Laurier's speech, the papal legate's report contained some of that speech's central arguments. In particular, Conroy accepted Laurier's distinction between political liberalism and the heresy of Catholic liberalism. The ultramontanes thus suffered a stinging defeat and henceforth would have to be more cautious. Their influence did not disappear overnight, of course. For some time, "the episcopacy remained conservative by personal conviction." In subsequent elections, however, the bishops "were carefully neutral when acting in an official capacity." The liberals still had considerable obstacles to overcome in Quebec, and it would be some time before they could rival the conservatives in electoral success.[38] Nevertheless, with the church no longer engaging in anti-liberal pulpit politics, the Liberal party's survival was secured. Laurier's 1877 speech played no small part in achieving this victory of liberal democratic principles in Quebec. In a sense, his speech can be seen as a successful attempt to bring to Quebec, almost two hundred years later, the Glorious Revolution of 1688.

NOTES

1. Harvey C. Mansfield, Jr., "Party Government and the Settlement of 1688," *American Political Science Review* 58 (1964): 933-46.

2. Alexis De Tocqueville, *Democracy in America*, trans. George Laurence, ed. J. P. Mayer (Garden City, NY: Anchor Books, 1969) 174-75.

3. Although Laurier is the pre-eminent Canadian example, others, such as Alexander Galt, also played an important role. See Rainer Knopff, "Religious Freedom and Party Government: The Galt-White Debate of 1876," in Stephen Brooks, ed., *Political Thought in Canada: Contemporary Perspectives* (Toronto: Irwin, 1984).

4. In Ulric Barthe, *Wilfrid Laurier on the Platform* (Quebec, 1890) 51-80; hereafter cited as "Political Liberalism."

5. Knopff, "Religious Freedom and Party Government" 24-29.

6. ———, "Religious Freedom and Party Government" 24-29.

7. Known as the "September 22 Pastoral," this document is found in *Mandements, Lettres Pastorals, Circulaires et Autres Documents Publiés dans le Diocèse de Montréal depuis son Érection* (Montréal: J. A. Plinguet, 1887) 7: 209.

8. Brassard v. Langevin (1878), 1 S. C. R. 145 at 163.

9. H. Blair Neatby, *Laurier and a Liberal Quebec* (Toronto: McClelland and Stewart, 1973) 6. Cf. O. D. Skelton, *Life and Times of Sir Alexander Tilloch Galt* (Toronto: McClelland and Stewart, 1966) 242-44.

10. Joseph Schull, Laurier: *The First Canadian* (Toronto: Macmillan, 1966) 117.

11. Schull, *Laurier* 116.

12. "Political Liberalism" 54.

13. See *Parliamentary Debates*, 1896, 2735ff.; Robert Rumilly, *Mgr. Laflèche et son temps* (Montreal: B. D. Simpson, 1945) 363-78; John Willison, *Sir Wilfrid Laurier and the Liberal Party* (Toronto: Morang, 1903) 2: 242ff.; Laurier LaPierre, "Joseph Israel Tarte: Relations Between the French-Canadian Episcopacy and a French-Canadian Politician (1874-1896)," *Canadian Catholic Historical Association Report* (1958) 37.

14. "Political Liberalism" 54-55, 56.

15. "Political Liberalism" 57-58.

16. "Political Liberalism" 58, 59.

17. "Political Liberalism" 60.

18. "Political Liberalism" 61.

19. "Political Liberalism" 61.

20. Thomas Hobbes, *Leviathan*, ed. C. B. Macpherson (Harmondsworth: Penguin, 1968) 161.

21. "Political Liberalism" 61

22. "Political Liberalism" 64-65.

23. "Political Liberalism" 67.

24. For further discussion of this point see Rainer Knopff, "Quebec's 'Holy War' as 'Regime' Politics: Reflections on the Guibord Case," *Canadian Journal of Political Science* 12 (1979): 315-31; and Knopff, "Religious Freedom and Party Government."

25. "Political Liberalism" 69.

26. "Political Liberalism" 72.

27. "Political Liberalism" 75.

28. "Political Liberalism" 76-77.

29. This seemed to be the position of many of the judges in the undue influence cases.

30. This same argument is implicit in the judgment of Ritchie J. in *Brassard v. Langevin*, 123-24.

31. The following discussion borrows heavily from the writings of Harvey C. Mansfield, Jr., especially "Party Government and the Settlement of 1688"; "Hobbes and the Science of Indirect Government," *American Political Science Review* 65 (1971): 97-110; "Modern and Medieval Representation," in Roland Pennock, ed., *Representation (Nomos* 10) (New York: Atherton Press, 1968); and "Impartial Representation," in R. Goldwin, ed., *Representation and Misrepresentation* (Chicago: Rand McNally, 1968).

32. See Hannah Pitkin, *The Concept of Representation* (Berkeley: University of California Press, 1972) ch. 2; Mansfield, "Hobbes and the Science of Indirect Government"; and Clifford Orwin, "On the Sovereign Authorization," *Political*

Theory 3 (1975): 26-44. For a discussion of the distinction between this modern form of representation and earlier forms see Mansfield, "Modern and Medieval Representation."

33. Pitkin chaps. 2 and 3.
34. Pitkin ch. 3.
35. Mansfield, "Impartial Representation" 95.
36. See, generally, Mansfield, "Party Government and the Settlement of 1688."
37. For more extended discussions of the necessity of commerce to the liberal project see Thomas Pangle, *Montesquieu's Philosophy of Liberalism* (Chicago: University of Chicago Press, 1973) chs. 7 and 8; Walter Berns, *The First Amendment and the Future of American Democracy* (New York: Basic Books, 1977) ch. 1.
38. Neatby 11, 10-11.

CHAPTER EIGHT

EGERTON RYERSON'S
CANADIAN LIBERALISM

Colin D. Pearce

Egerton Ryerson has most frequently been characterized by scholars as a Loyalist, Royalist conservative.[1] This judgment is usually
rendered even as his efforts in the direction of modernizing educational and constitutional reforms are acknowledged. Such broad
labels undoubtedly capture something of Ryerson's temperament,
but this essay will attempt to provide a more precise description of
his political principles. It will argue that the particular blend of ideas
expounded by Ryerson is connected to his awareness of the problems and weaknesses in the theory of liberal, commercial society, a
theory to which, nevertheless, he remained attached.

In general, the problem with previous scholarship has been its
overemphasis on Ryerson's Christianity. Great stress has been placed
on the influence on his thought of the Methodist theologians John
Wesley, Adam Clarke, and Richard Watson.[2] Robin S. Harris
describes Ryerson as a figure whose "religious principles were his
first principles."[3] Albert F. Fiorino says Ryerson's main concern was
"to promote Christianity as the only efficient solution to the human
condition."[4] R. D. Gidney argues that for Ryerson civil institutions
were among the means established by God to enable man to seek

sanctification in his life and everlasting happiness with God in the next.[5] Such scholars may even acknowledge Ryerson's debt to such thinkers as Locke, Paley, and Blackstone and yet still conclude that above all he was shaped by "traditional ideas."[6] I will argue that this scholarship seriously distorts Ryerson's thought. The Ryerson of life, liberty, and property, church-state separation, religious tolerance, political economy, and scientific progress becomes almost invisible in the treatment of him as "a Christian first, last and all the time."[7]

The reasons for this misperception are not hard to find. In a society that has become as secularized and as emancipated from traditional religious influences as ours, frequent references to God and expressions of submission to His will are promptly taken as symptomatic of a deeply religious, theologically traditional attitude. In the case of Ryerson a hasty conclusion as to the monolithically Christian basis of his thought is drawn. In what follows I hope to redress this imbalance and establish Ryerson's thoroughgoing liberalism. I will proceed by trying to describe Ryerson's basic responses to such fundamental questions as human nature, the roots of social existence, the ends of political society, the relation of the economic to the political world, the problem of civic virtue, and the place of religion in modern society. Ryerson's views on each of these matters would warrant a much more extended discussion than is possible here, but I will attempt to provide a survey sufficient to establish the general outlines of his thought. An excellent place to begin is with Ryerson's debt to Scottish Enlightenment thought.

THE SCOTTISH CONNECTION

The study of Ryerson lends credence to Peter J. Smith's assertion that the Scottish Enlightenment is "critical" for the understanding of Canadian political thought.[8] For Ryerson, Edinburgh was the "Athens of North Britain," and he studied the diverse teachings of the great philosophers who came out of Scotland. But the most proximate connection to Ryerson of this tidal wave in European intellectual life was the *Edinburgh Review*. He was an assiduous reader of this first of the great Victorian periodicals, along with the major philosophical works from which it drew inspiration. According to one scholar, the *Edinburgh Review* stood for a "broad intellectual and political disposition" best described as "philosophic whiggism."

Its outlook rested on "an essentially socio-economic interpretation of history" as developed by such figures as Hume, Kames, Smith, Millar, and Stewart.[9]

Of the various Scottish figures who exercised an influence on Ryerson, Henry Lord Brougham was perhaps the most significant. Indeed, it is not too much to say that Ryerson aspired to be Canada's Lord Brougham. Like this "Nestor statesman of Europe," he sought to promote moderate constitutional reform and general education, to found Mechanics' Institutes, and to establish non-exclusive university education. Ryerson's various writings include many paraphrases of Lord Brougham's voluminous arguments in favour of scientific and technological progress, the diffusion of useful knowledge, the importance of political economy, and the study of natural theology, and against high tory "ultraism," religious exclusivism, and, above all, the *summum malum* in politics, "partyism" and party spirit. Brougham's influence on Ryerson was perhaps predictable, in that the Canadian had earlier been trained in the natural theology and Christian apologetics of William Paley, and Brougham had reworked Paley's arguments for the Society for the Diffusion of Useful Knowledge in the 1830s.[10] In the one essay in which he claims to have presented an "epitome" of his "fifty years reading and meditation, and more than forty years occasional discussion respecting the first principles of government,"[11] Ryerson, who was prone to copious quotation, quotes most copiously from "the venerable Lord Brougham's" *Political Philosophy.*[12] The evidence suggests that for Ryerson the whig liberal Lord Brougham was more of an authority on "the principles of civil polity" than were the Methodist theologians on whom the scholars have placed such emphasis.

In highlighting Ryerson's debt to the Scottish intellectual tradition, I do not wish to suggest that this particularly distinguishes him. As one scholar has noted, "All educated Englishmen on both sides of the Atlantic—indeed all educated Europeans—were familiar with [the Scottish philosophers'] writings."[13] What is remarkable is that Ryerson's indebtedness to Thomas Reid, Adam Smith, Dugald Stewart, Henry Brougham, John Ramsay McCulloch, and other Scottish thinkers has received so little emphasis.[14] That Ryerson does not fit the stereotypical definition of a liberal individualist may well be due not so much to an attachment to elements of pre-modern or pre-liberal ideas as to the modifications made to the tradition of liberal political thought by the Scottish philosophers who followed in the wake of John Locke. In order to make this apparent it is necessary to examine Ryerson's views on the relation between the individual and the political community.

INDIVIDUAL AND SOCIETY

In the eighteenth century Montesquieu had said that "where we find man we find him together with others." Following this lead, philosophers such as Hume, Paley, Bentham, and Brougham rejected the idea of the state of nature as a "philosophical fiction."[15] In general accordance with this reform of the theoretical basis of liberal individualism, Ryerson professed not to be persuaded that there ever was a state of nature. Such a notion he considered to be "founded merely on conjecture." "The necessity of government is so obvious . . . that we read of no age in which it did not exist."[16]

In Ryerson's account of the origins it is the family that appears as coeval with human existence. "At the beginning there were only the children of one man, living under the care of their father."[17] The family was the first form of civil government, and as it has always existed so civil government has always existed. Ryerson, then, denied that the universal, perpetual, and absolute independence of each individual was the natural human condition. The universal natural human condition was the marital union. It is "the very law of man's constitution," "a law prior to, and stronger than all human law, that man should marry." This natural law of conjugality is evident "in the numerical proportion of the sexes—in the courage, strength, enterprise of the one, and the fortitude, susceptibility, dependence of the other—in their mutual qualities, affections and sympathies—in their adaptation to promote each other's happiness."[18]

In the family the theoretical liberties of the state of nature are as much compromised as they have to be in civil society. There is the habit of obedience and the "law of parental affection," which together tend to produce order and stability. In Ryerson's theory it is the family that provides the crucial link between the individual and society. It is the family that is "the fountain of social order and the basis of social improvement." This connecting role of the family is indispensable, because "Society assumes and demands the merging of the individual man in the social man."[19] In the family, individuals learn that they are "closely related to others" and a "constituent part of a whole." They are therefore made ready for the assumption of "civil relations" and the "mutual obligations they involve." The family is the wellspring of the individual's "social affections," and it is from this wellspring that "love of kindred, love of nation, and love of country" flow. That natural principle that ineluctably brings man and woman together ultimately issues in the social dimension to human existence. "Civil institutions are the appropriate sequel to the domestic."[20]

It would seem, then, that for Ryerson humans are not as naturally averse to each other as Hobbes, or even Locke, wished to suggest. "As man's very nature is social—as he is formed for society—he must and he will, in some form or other, fraternize with his fellow-man."[21] Ryerson clearly defended a theory of society where the individual is capable of seeing something of his own family in his fellow citizens. Following thinkers like Hume and Smith, he argued that "active sympathy" in social relations "is the arterial life of a country's social advancement."[22] But caution is necessary here. Ryerson was not for these reasons anything remotely resembling a devotee of what today we might loosely call communitarianism. He defined society as a "union of *individuals* . . . prompted by the original impulses of man and *imposed* by his necessities."[23] Thus there is an ambiguity in Ryerson's analysis of individual and society. On the one hand he starts from the basic premise of human individuality, and on the other hand he suggests that the conjunction of the individual and the social order is natural. That he thought the radically individualist propensities were the more powerful is evident when he speculates on the human condition without law.

According to Ryerson, if the laws were "thrown down," every individual could "act as his interests or his passions at the moment led him." But what would this situation ultimately mean? In Ryerson's estimation it would mean that the "whole mass of society" would be infused with "the poison of mutual distrust, jealousy, hatred and resentment." It would mean that "there would be no security against mutual invasions and injuries." It would mean in the end that "no man's property would be safe for half an hour," and the "avenues to fraud, rapine and oppression [would be] opened wide."[24] Even the "law of parental affection" could not survive the breakdown of the social order. Without the restraining force of law it would not be surprising to see "brother [armed] against brother, parents against children and children against parents." Ryerson makes clear that in the absence of government the hostile human passions will be in the ascendant over the sociable ones. Thus his allowance for humanity's sociality needs to be seen in the context of his belief in its deeply anti-social propensities.

Ryerson's theorizing as to the human condition without law gives clear indication that although he rejected the contractarian theories of society, the ends or purposes of government as he understood them are identical to those posited by contractarianism. Without government, Ryerson explains,

the arts and sciences languish, and trade and commerce decline; the wealth and resources of a people are consumed, and their might and influence among neighbouring powers are lost; the regular course of justice is obstructed, and its principles subverted . . . and that subordination among mankind which is of the last consequence to their happiness, welfare and safety, is destroyed.[25]

According to Ryerson, government exists to ward off these evils traceable to human nature itself. For him, as it was for the early modern natural law tradition, "The legitimate end of civil government is the preservation and advancement of men's civil interests, and the better security of their lives, liberty and property."[26]

This discussion tends to the conclusion that Ryerson was somehow half-way between classical liberalism with its emphasis on asocial individuality and *bellum omnium contra omnes*, and utilitarian liberalism with its greater openness to sociability, sympathy, and the irreduceable character of the family. The individual is primary in both traditions, but Ryerson betrays signs of the "softening" trends of post-Lockean thought. There is clearly a certain distance between Ryerson and what is sometimes called "possessive individualism" or "Lockeanism."[27] But it must be stipulated that this distance was not in the direction of the older pre-modern natural law tradition, with its teleological considerations and catalogues of human duties. Ryerson had little time for "the metaphysical jargon of Aristotle."[28] Rather it was in the direction of a later liberalism, with its focus on utility over abstract rights, security over theoretical liberties, and sympathy and sociability over the most naked self-interest.

Ryerson's basic modernism is clear when we remind ourselves that he speaks of individuals as social and not political animals. Ryerson's humans live contiguously to others but privately in the decisive respects. The core of their lives is not in common with their fellow-citizens; they are drawn into society by sub-political and sub-rational attachments, and these attachments find their satisfaction not in the public realm of political speech and argument but in the realm of private life. "By far the greatest amount of happiness in civilized life is found in the domestic relations."[29] This basic individualism is made politically explicit in Ryerson's firm conviction that not participatory democracy, but modern representative government is the best form of polity. In his view it is much to be preferred that the people confine themselves to judging "of the character and qualifications of the men whom [they] would trust with the immediate care of [their] interests"[30] than that they should claim a "right to active resolutions"[31] in the public sphere. In this respect Ryerson followed the critique of classical participatory republicanism developed by such thinkers as Montesquieu, Hamilton, and Madison.

CLASSICAL VERSUS LIBERAL REPUBLICANISM

Among many other things, there is to be found in Ryerson's writings a rehearsal of what one scholar has called the "debate between classical republican values . . . [and the] rising commercial ideology formulated during the Enlightenment."[32] As might be expected from what has been said above, Ryerson comes down firmly on the non-classical side.

That element in Ryerson's thought that might be described as "civic humanist" is to be seen in his repeated praise of the virtue of patriotism. Ryerson presents this virtue as most classically manifest in the heroes of antiquity such as Cincinnatus, Aristides, and Epaminondas. "Let each Canadian," Ryerson says, "love his country and seek its glory as did the ancient Greeks."[33] Ryerson even suggested that maxims from Cicero's *Republic* should be "inscribed on the doorposts of every dwelling."[34]

But when we look more closely at Ryerson's analysis of the ancient republics, we see that for all his admiration of the patriotism of their heroes, his rejection of classical republicanism is complete. With respect to religion, Ryerson does allow that the Greek philosophers such as Plato and Aristotle wrote "with considerable propriety on some of the chief doctrines of theism, such as the existence of one God and the immortality of the soul."[35] But in the end these thinkers made little headway against the prevailing religion, whose "Deities were the patrons of the worst passions and vices, and their worship an instrument of debauchery and corruption."[36] Greek philosophy did not or could not get beyond the "ethics of heathenism," and these ethics are radically deficient in the light of revealed religion, where "the love of God is everything."[37] Given this deficiency in their religion and the related limitations of their "human philosophy," Ryerson concluded that the ancients did not possess the wherewithal to construct a successful social and political order.

But Ryerson's brief against "the famed and fallen nations of antiquity" includes more than observations on the depraving features of their "heathenism" and the stunted character of their "human philosophy." They also suffered from a radically deficient political science, which meant that "their governments were either de-regulated and tumultuous democracy or military despotisms." Modern political science, by contrast, has discovered the "essential elements of durability" in politics, and these consist in the principles of "free and representative government," which is to say "a well digested and well balanced system, free from class distinctions, and based on the broad principles of public liberty."[38] In addition to this defect in their knowledge the ancients also lacked the "almost superhuman art of printing." This was a circumstance of no small import according to Ryerson, because it meant that "with them knowledge was confined to the cities, to sophists and slave-holders, while the mass of the people throughout the country, and even in the towns and cities were profoundly and brutally ignorant."[39] Again in this connection Ryerson stresses the advantages that modern man possesses in that the technological advances in printing make it possible for "the knowledge of the Statesman [to become] the common property of the country."[40]

In sum, Ryerson argues that the ancient city was devoid of constitutional stability, religious freedom, and social equality. Religion was part of the political order and enjoined on all regardless of conscience, the rulers' powers were unchecked except by rebellion, and the mobility between social classes according to the distribution of nature's gifts was hampered. Ryerson's overall perspective on the status of the modern world when contrasted with the ancient is made clear in his comparison of ancient Greece and Rome with modern Britain.

In the sublimer discoveries of the sciences, in the mightier conquests of the arts, in the more perfect systems of government and morals, and in the wider range of literature, as well as the boundless travels of commerce, Great Britain stands pre-eminent above all the admired greatness of antiquity, even in the brightest days of Grecian and Roman glory.[41]

Not ancient Greece and Rome but modern Britain, and not classical virtue but modern science and commerce, represent the best polity to Ryerson. Not the denaturing self-sacrifice of the Spartan, but the keen and intelligent activity of the Englishman, is for him most necessary in a modern nation.

Ryerson, then, was most manifestly an heir to the political thought of Bacon, Hobbes, Locke, Montesquieu, Hume, Smith, and the Scottish school, all of whom argued in some way or another for the solution of commercial or liberal republicanism.[42] He arrived at this conclusion because, like his intellectual predecessors, he not only found the arguments against the classical polis persuasive, but also found the changes in modern Europe to be fundamental. Things in Western Europe were as bad if not worse than they were in the ancient polis until "the light of modern civilization" removed it from its "unnatural state." The people existed "for the sake of government, and not government for the sake of the people."[43] But with the American and French Revolutions and the triumphs of Napoleon the "old foundations of feudalism were shaken [and] . . . rulers began to learn that they must, henceforth, govern through the understanding and affections of their subjects, rather than by the sword and bayonet."[44] With the passage of time "the light of modern civilization" has taught rulers "their relations and duties, and the people their rights and privileges."[45]

Ryerson, then, was at bottom a "modern European." He rejected the older politics of Europe, based as it was on unattainable visions of perfection and on a contempt for the common, useful, and ordinary. The older political principles sustained great levels of inequality and deprived the masses of their human dignity and basic justice. These masses "were regarded as mere machines, designed for the use and benefit of others,—as various other animals—fit only to labour and fight for their masters."[46]

In line with his rejection of the old politics, Ryerson also rejected the traditional contempt for the "improvers" of human life, and for the solid "bourgeois" virtues of patience, industry, steadiness, application, self-command, and foresight. Honour should go to those who by hard work and dedication improve their own lot and with it that of others. The most honourable individuals are those who contribute to the "wealth and enjoyment of mankind," whose discoveries are contributions of "science to the arts and comforts of civilized life"—those like Arkwright with his spinning jenny, Cartwright with his power loom, Watt with his steam engine, and Franklin and Faraday with their electrical discoveries. "The humble authors of any one of these discoveries or inventions has established infinitely stronger claims to the grateful admiration of mankind, than an Alexander or Napoleon."[47]

It is worth noting here that Ryerson was much influenced in his youth by his reading of Franklin's *Autobiography*, wherein it is argued that "one man of tolerable abilities may work great changes and accomplish great affairs among mankind."[48] In Ryerson's view, young Canadians should take note of "what has been accomplished by the zeal and intelligence of earnest men." If farmers', barbers', and printers' sons like Rumford, Arkwright, and Franklin could, through "honest and intelligent industry," rise from obscurity to fame, then others can follow suit. Some rising on the social scale is within the reach of almost everybody. Obscurity of origins will count for little in a commercial society. Those who by their steady efforts assist in meeting the real needs of people will receive enhanced social standing and respect. "The influence which a well-instructed mind,—especially among the labouring classes,—may exercise in the community, is, in its aggregate influence, beyond the arithmetic of human calculation."[49]

It was natural for Ryerson to feel a kinship with the founders and heroes of classical antiquity, given that he was absorbed in and motivated by the prospect of establishing in a "new and young country" a free and self-governing political community. But in the end his use of the models of ancient greatness was in large part rhetorical. In Bernard Bailyn's terms they contributed to the "vivid vocabulary" of his arguments, but were secondary as far as "the logic or grammar of [his political] thought" was concerned.[50] In the end, Ryerson neither expected nor desired the emergence of towering figures of political heroism or greatness in modern society. Rather he expected or desired to see industrious, frugal, "common sense practical men" held in high esteem. After all, "the pursuits and duties of our new country, under our free government, are invested with an almost exclusively practical character."[51] Ryerson was a solid defender of the sober and businesslike virtues of "the middle classes of society," with whose "happiness and well being" he was always "involved."[52]

POLITICAL ECONOMY

In accordance with his preference for modern England over the ancient polis and medieval Europe, Ryerson was a devoted advocate of the modern science of political economy. He wrote a textbook on the subject and repeatedly stressed the importance of its study in his various educational lectures and addresses. Political economy, particularly as developed in "the immortal work" of Adam Smith, was for Ryerson that branch of modern science that explains "how individuals and a nation become rich."[53] It "is one of the many branches of knowledge to which, in the process of modern civilization, the investigations of the last hundred years have given birth and raised to the dignity of a science."[54] McCulloch, Whately, Brougham, and others further persuaded Ryerson that political economy was an advancement of modern knowledge that could be and should be made accessible to the masses.

My first reason in favour of making Political Economy a branch of public education is the fact that it may be easily comprehended by all classes of society. It is true—the doctrines—the science—of Political Economy are the result of profound investigation and extensive research . . . yet every schoolboy can master the elements.[55]

In accordance with the principles of political economy, Ryerson tended to demote the conventional divisions within and among nations. Modern political economy tends to foster a "chain of dependence" that binds all individuals and classes within a modern community to one another. From the political economy perspective, people are primarily individual buyers and producers rather than members of classes, orders, or estates. And in its "remoter ramifications" the "chain of dependence" between buyers and producers "encircles the entire globe, the four quarters of which are often laid under contribution for the furniture of a single house, and supply the provisions of a single table." Together with Montesquieu, Ryerson envisaged the world as constituting "but a single state, of which all the particular societies are members."[56] He believed that "the oceans and seas are highways of unrestricted intercourse; and the arts of manufacture, commerce and navigation are alike the developments and instruments of universal fraternity."[57] The science that takes as its first principle the separate individuality of each person promotes in the end the complex interdependence of all classes and nations in a worldwide mercantile republic.

Ryerson, then, must be classified with those liberal thinkers of the eighteenth and nineteenth century who were inclined to be too optimistic about commerce's power to bring about world peace and co-operation. Like these thinkers he seems to have underestimated the likelihood of commercial nations being led into war out of competition for resources, markets, and colonies, war that would be all the more destructive because of the advanced technology that these nations would develop for the sake of industrial production.

But for all his belief in the commercial spirit, the division of labour, and the application of scientific principles to the methods of production, Ryerson resisted the idea of a purely economic approach to the political realm. In his view, the analyst who reduces all of politics to simply economic considerations, such as Goldwin Smith, is devoid of "largeness of views," and overlooks what might be decisive in shaping the political order:

Making the connection between England and Canada a mere question of arithmetic of mutual doing and gain is quite natural for a Lancashire manufacturer, but is rather odd for an Oxford Professor. . . . [C]annot the Oxford Regius Professor imagine some other grounds, and some other advantages in the connection of countries, the alliance of nations as of individuals, besides the Manchester one of pounds, shillings and pence? . . . Is there not something in the thinkings, feelings, associations and sympathies of an entire people to be considered? These considerations may be but a cypher in the figures of Mr. Goldwin Smith's utilitarianism, but they scarcely admit of computation in the national life, character, enjoyments, aspirations and destinies of a whole people.[58]

While being a strong believer in economic rationality, Ryerson was also a kind of political sentimentalist. The economic was one standard among others and had to be weighed in the balance against the more intangible yet equally important considerations that go to make up what today might be called "political culture." In line with his reading of Burke,[59] Ryerson sought to reconcile the practical necessities of modern economic and political life with a concern for longstanding "feelings, associations and sympathies." These things, which are the product of the people's shared historical experience, form part of the public mind and must form part of political leaders' calculations when they are deliberating policy. In the specifically Canadian context Ryerson was a Burke-style defender of such "irrational" traditional institutions as the monarchy, which, with its symbolism and history, could elevate the citizens' gaze, at least momentarily, beyond the taste for physical gratification and the single-minded pursuit of wealth. Such institutions, while in no way compromising the progressive, commercial, and egalitarian principles of the wider society, serve to temper and moderate those pernicious tendencies to which these very principles give rise.

Ryerson's reservations concerning the purely economic mode of thought do not in any way remove him from the political economy tradition. Rather, they serve to show the extent to which he was a thorough exponent of this tradition. This is because all the best theorists involved in developing the political economy perspective gave expression to various fears and doubts concerning the fate of the new form of society that would be guided by this new science. Ryerson, to be sure, was cautiously hopeful that the new regime of the solid, practically- and commercially-minded middle ranks would not prove self-destructive. But like Montesquieu, Hume, Smith, Tocqueville, and the whig reviewers, he harboured certain serious reservations about the impact and prospects of the commercial society. He certainly did not believe in the possibility of human perfectibility as did some believers in progress. "There must be moderation and reasonableness in our expectations. . . . [P]erfect happiness appertains not to a state of imperfection, danger, affliction and mortality, and must not, therefore, be expected in this life."[60]

Ryerson was no Tom Paine. The "cause of mind may go backward as well as forward."[61] With many of the Edinburgh Reviewers, Ryerson was apprehensive that "while material conditions may continue to improve no comparable amelioration—in fact rather the reverse—is to be expected in the spiritual or moral realms."[62] He feared that the new economy might lead to boredom, selfishness, and "materialism," and incline people away from the "sterner duties of life."

193

It is possible that [the necessary accumulation of wealth] may come upon us, and lead to the indulgence of appetites and passions which will curse rather than elevate our social as well as moral well-being in connection with the social fabric. Large wealth does not beget large views. We often see in the possession of the greatest wealth the smallest and most contemptible mind.[63]

The commercial society, then, was part of Ryerson's solution and part of his problem. To state the matter succinctly, while believing in the liberal commercial project, Ryerson was not persuaded that the reform of the laws, the expansion of the economy, the evolution of sophisticated institutional arrangements, and the spread of general enlightenment could substitute entirely for moral virtue and individual character. For a society to hope for enduring freedom and progress, it must go beyond the sciences of economics and government and focus on the moral, which is ultimately to say the religious, dimension of human existence.

I have often revolved in my mind . . . the theories of those political economists, who maintain that the essential well-being of man consists in health of body, sufficiency of food, and personal liberty,—and who propose to remedy the existing ills of society and bring about the universal reign of millenial happiness, by altered forms of government, improved balances of power, other distributions of property, new constitutions and laws of the latest invention, from the exhaustless manufactories of human ingenuity and speculation. I have also endeavoured to examine the dogmas of those professed philosophers, who, independent of any Divine Agency, and leaving Christianity altogether out of the question, are about to create all things new by the power of science and education. In both these plausible and too widely spread theories there appears to me this radical defect, an irrational as well as anti-Scriptural omission; Man, as a moral being is entirely overlooked.[64]

Ryerson's claim is that political economy and philosophy are necessarily incomplete to the extent that they do not confront the moral-religious dimension of human existence. It follows from this very claim that Ryerson himself sought to make such a confrontation. This means that his views on religion must be considered before the full shape of his political thought can come to light.

RYERSON'S RELIGION

Ryerson's views on church and state give further evidence of the thoroughly liberal basis of his thought. In line with John Locke's *Letter Concerning Toleration* and *The Reasonableness of Christianity*, he argued that "although religion is essential to the welfare and even the existence of civil government, the state is not the Divinely appointed instructor of the people."[65] According to Ryerson, religion's true power rests in the fact that it "operates on the consciences of men" and depends on belief in "invisible realities." It "can derive no weight or solemnity from human sanctions."[66] Only an unenlightened and irrational Christianity would seek to make the state an instrument for the direct inculcation of its doctrines. Reasonable Christians should not insist that their faith entitles them to special claims, which, given the diversity of religious opinion in modern society, must lead to conflict. Such Christians should know how to live in peace in a society where there are no official teachings about God, but where they are free to follow the dictates of their conscience in the private realm. Such is the basis of "enlightened views of Christian relations." Modern nations should look to the political experiment in the United States, which, as a direct result of its having "no national or state establishment of religion," has "succeeded beyond all precedent of either ancient or modern history."[67]

But it did not follow for Ryerson that because he accepted the liberal arguments for church-state separation that he must also acquiesce in those elements of modern thought that sought to lay the axe to the root of traditional religious belief once and for all. Such thought aimed to promote theological liberalism by showing how the miracles on which orthodoxy was based were incompatible with what had been discovered about the laws of nature. Modern science had uncovered enough knowledge about the world to at least be sure that God did not indulge in miracle making. For men like Tom Paine this meant that the "absurd" and "ridiculous" teachings of Christianity should be dispensed with and the Scriptures replaced with the "book of Creation."[68] The opinions of men like Paine were, naturally enough, associated with the enormities of the French Revolution, an experience that engendered doubt as to whether a religion in accordance with natural reason alone was compatible with the good order society. Revealed religion once again looked attractive for its effect on the moral life of the people. Certain elements of religion, it was argued, should be protected from withering criticism, for the sake of popular morality and public safety. These considerations alone would serve to explain why Ryerson dismissed Hume's objections to miracles as both "unreasonable and absurd," and repeated only by "superficial and thoughtless persons."[69]

Given the various social and political forces that modern civilization had unleashed, Ryerson was inclined to the view that "the common Biblical inheritance of Christendom" was more crucial to the moral health of civil society than at any time previously. If the knowledge of Biblical religion were to atrophy, "there would be comparatively no instruction in duties and virtue," and this would have grave consequences for "the happiness of society."[70] Ryerson gave a very high profile to "Scriptural Christianity," defined as "what Christians of every form of worship hold in common without reference to the peculiarities of any," because he was persuaded that the moral foundations for a viable liberal society could not be derived from the "degrading systems of Hobbes and Mandeville."[71] And he was not averse to criticizing other adherents of the "liberal party" for being insufficiently attentive to this fact of political philosophy. Thus, early in his career he attacked the British whigs for having "no peculiar tendency . . . to improve the religious and moral character of the nation."[72] And in Canada he criticized those who "have gone to the extreme of viewing all religious persuasions as evils to be dreaded, and, as far as possible proscribed," instead of as beneficial "agencies" that propagate in common "the great principles of virtue and morality."[73]

But is this all there was to it in Ryerson's case? Did he simply believe that the liberal society was dependent on the moral capital of "the common Biblical inheritance of Christendom" and therefore resolve to defend this capital solely on the grounds of its "advantages to society"? Or was Ryerson a true believer in the revealed faith, albeit a thoughtful and rational one? A final answer to this question cannot be given with any certainty. In the case of someone as sensitive to the requirements of the political health of the community as was Ryerson it is not easy to distinguish between that which is said for the sake of this health and that which might have been his fundamental view.[74] Furthermore, Ryerson's mentor, "the immortal Locke," that "great light of his day and benefactor of the

Christian world," had argued that "true and saving religion consists in the inward persuasion of the mind,"[75] and the extent of such "inward persuasion" is not externally ascertainable.

Be this as it may, it almost goes without saying that Ryerson's liberalism and his Protestant Scriptural Christianity were deeply interrelated. To show this it is only necessary to notice his argument that the way to the "improvements in philosophy in modern times" that are associated with names like Bacon, Locke, and Newton was paved by the theology associated with Luther, Melancthon, and Cranmer. The latter "unsealed the Scriptures and broke the spell with which human reason had been bound for ages."[76]

I do not propose in this article to enter into the enormous question of the "co-penetration of Protestantism and liberalism." Suffice it to say that the theories of Max Weber, Ernst Troeltsch, R. H. Tawney, Christopher Dawson, and George Grant[77] are of great value in approaching a figure like Ryerson, and then leave it at A. V. Dicey's observation that there was a "community of feeling" between Wesleyanism and liberal utilitarianism based on the shared principle of individualism. Ryerson, the Methodist, whiggish, utilitarian liberal was attached to both a theology and a political philosophy that regarded "men almost exclusively as separate individuals."[78]

Given the complexity of the relation between Protestant theology and liberal rationalism it is useful to bracket Ryerson with Alexis de Tocqueville. Like the French political philosopher, Ryerson was attempting to combine the "spirit of liberty" with the "spirit of religion." It was one of Tocqueville's central concerns that when at long last the people became their own masters they might cease to be "submissive to the Deity." In Tocqueville's view, the spirit of religion was crucial to the viability of the popular regime. Modern society might be destroyed if "the moral tie" were not strengthened as "the political tie" relaxed.[79] There is little doubt that similar considerations lay behind Ryerson's stipulating that although "the form and specific organization of civil government . . . may be said to emanate from the people," "the institution of government" is nevertheless "ordained of God."[80] Ryerson's entire political philosophy is encapsulated in his statement that "there can be no free state—no government of law—no security of person and property—without religious faith and morals."[81]

197

CONCLUSION

Ryerson's thought betrays many influences. The ideas of classical liberalism, whig utilitarianism, Smithian economism, American reformism, Burkean sentimentalism, Blackstonian constitutionalism, Scottish moralism, and Wesleyan Protestantism can be seen in his writings. Ryerson's manipulation of these ideas shows him to be at a certain distance from his age and capable of criticizing some of its profoundest tendencies. He can be credited, in large measure, with having foreseen and assessed some of the vital problems confronting the modern, liberal, capitalist, industrial order, problems such as materialism, self-indulgence, lack of public-spiritedness, political pettiness, and declining independence of thought. He posed the right questions to the rising tide of liberalism. What will be the substantive character of people's lives in the new order? How will they associate and co-operate? From what source will spring public spirit? How will social sympathy fare against private individualism? What will happen to religious belief? For his awareness of these questions and for posing them forthrightly in an era of unreflective optimism, Ryerson deserves to be recognized as a thoughtful critic of modernity. At the same time his firm belief in private property, the free economy, freedom of speech, religious tolerance, churchstate separation, and representative government places him squarely in the tradition of modern liberalism.

NOTES

* I would like to thank professors R. A. Manzer, H. D. Forbes, P. H. Russell, J. S. Dupré, and R. Preece for their advice and comments on the thesis from which this article is derived. I would also like to thank the anonymous reviewers of the *Canadian Journal of Political Science* for their helpful suggestions.

1. Nathaniel Burwash, *Egerton Ryerson* (Toronto: Morang, 1910) 44; S. D. Clark, Review of C. B. Sissons, "Egerton Ryerson: His Life and Letters," *Canadian Journal of Economics and Political Science* 14 (1948) 256; Goldwin S. French, "Egerton Ryerson and the Methodist Model for Upper Canada," in Neil McDonald and Alf Chaiton, eds., *Egerton Ryerson and His Times* (Toronto: Macmillan, 1978) 57; R. D. Gidney, "Egerton Ryerson," *Dictionary of Canadian Biography*, vol. 11 (Toronto: University of Toronto Press, 1982) 786;

Robin S. Harris, "Egerton Ryerson," in Robert L. MacDougall, ed., *Our Living Tradition* (Toronto: University of Toronto Press, 1959) 257; William Kilbourn, *The Firebrand* (Toronto: Clark, Irwin, 1956) 102; Alison Prentice, *The School Promoters* (Toronto: McClelland and Stewart, 1977) 139; and Clara Thomas, *Ryerson of Upper Canada* (Toronto: Ryerson Press, 1969) 68.

2. French, "Egerton Ryerson and the Methodist Model for Upper Canada" 47; Albert F. Fiorino, "The Moral Foundation of Egerton Ryerson's Idea of Education," in McDonald and Chaiton, eds., *Egerton Ryerson and His Times* 78.

3. Harris, "Egerton Ryerson" 258.

4. Fiorino, "The Moral Foundation of Egerton Ryerson's Idea of Education" 78.

5. Gidney, "Egerton Ryerson" 786.

6. French, "Egerton Ryerson and the Methodist Model for Upper Canada" 51.

7. Harris, "Egerton Ryerson" 258.

8. Peter J. Smith, "The Ideological Origins of Canadian Confederation," *Canadian Journal of Political Science* 20 (1987) 5.

9. Biancamaria Fontana, *Rethinking the Politics of Commercial Society* (Cambridge: Cambridge University Press, 1985) 6. See also Stefan Collini, Donald Winch, and John Burrow, eds., *That Noble Science of Politics* (Cambridge: Cambridge University Press, 1983); Duncan Forbes, "Sceptical Whiggism, Commerce and Liberty," in Andrew Skinner and Thomas Wilson, eds., *Essays on Adam Smith* (Oxford: Clarendon Press, 1975): 179-201; John Clive, *The Scotch Reviewers* (London: Faber and Faber, 1957); Leslie Stephen, "The First Edinburgh Reviewers," *The Eclectic* (1878): 666-77; Walter Bagehot, "The First Edinburgh Reviewers," in Richard Hutton, ed., *Literary Studies* (London: Longman, Green, 1882) 1: 144-87; and Maurice Cross, *Selections From the Edinburgh Review with a Preliminary Dissertation* (London: Longmans, 1833) 1: ix-cxxvii.

10. Henry Lord Brougham, "A Discourse on Natural Theology," *Works* (Edinburgh: Adam and Charles Black, 1872) 6: 1-174. See also Chester W. New, *The Life of Henry Lord Brougham* (Oxford: Clarendon Press, 1961) 358.

11. Egerton Ryerson, *The New Canadian Dominion: Dangers and Duties of the People in Regard to Their Government* (Toronto: Lovell and Gibson, 1867) 5.

12. Henry Lord Brougham, *Political Philosophy*, 3 vols. (London: Charles Knight, 1844).

13. Ronald Hamowy, "Jefferson and the Scottish Enlightenment," *William and Mary Quarterly* 36 (1979) 505.

14. A partial exception here is A. B. McKillop whose studies of Canadian intellectual history consider the influence of Scottish thought. McKillop notes: "Baconian science, with Scottish 'Common Sense' philosophy and Paleyite natural theology, completed the triumvirate of intellectual orthodoxy that dominated many Anglo-Canadian minds for the first three-quarters of the

nineteenth century" (*Contours of Canadian Thought* [Toronto: University of Toronto Press, 1987] 44). See also A. B. McKillop, *A Disciplined Intelligence* (Montreal: McGill-Queen's University Press, 1979) 95.

15. Henry D. Aiken, ed., *Hume's Moral and Political Philosophy* (New York: Hafner, 1972) 189; M. L. Clarke, *Paley: Evidences for the Man* (Toronto: University of Toronto Press, 1974) 74; Douglas G. Long, *Bentham on Liberty* (Toronto: University of Toronto Press, 1977) 36-37, 217; Brougham, *Political Philosophy* 1: 34-35. The classic account of the turn in liberal thought away from natural rights and toward utility is Élie Halévy, *The Growth of Philosophical Radicalism* (Boston: Beacon Press, 1955). More recent contributions in this large area are Jeremy Waldron, ed., *Nonsense Upon Stilts* (London: Methuen, 1987) and Edward Andrew, *Shylock's Rights* (Toronto: University of Toronto Press, 1988). See also Marc F. Plattner, ed., *Human Rights in Our Time* (Boulder: Westview Press, 1984) esp. 1-22.

16. Egerton Ryerson, *Civil Government: The Late Conspiracy* (Toronto: Joseph H. Lawrence, 1838) 3.

17. Ryerson, *Civil Government* 3. Compare Brougham, *Political Philosophy* 1: 40.

18. Egerton Ryerson, "Obligations of Educated Men," *Journal of Education for Upper Canada* 1 (1848) 162. Ryerson's thinking on women and the family would appear to be problematic. Needless to say it would be unacceptable to modern feminism. Although Ryerson defended the education of women, he nevertheless believed they should be homemakers. "Let her be intellectually educated as highly as possible . . . [but] let the domestic virtues find ample place" (*First Lessons in Agriculture* [Toronto: Buntin Brother, 1871] 173). Ryerson's difficulty was that while defending the "nuclear" family he was also a promoter of liberal individualism in politics. He might not have recognized that this political individualism would sooner or later exercise a dissolving effect on the family sphere and thereby effect a transformation in the role of women.

19. Egerton Ryerson, "A Lecture on the Social Advancement of Canada," *Journal of Education for Upper Canada* 2 (1849) 181.

20. Ryerson, "Obligations of Educated Men" 162. Compare Edmund Burke, *Reflections on the Revolution in France* (Harmondsworth: Penguin, 1969) 135.

21. Egerton Ryerson, "The Education of Mechanics," in J. George Hodgins, ed., *Documentary History of Education in Upper Canada* (Toronto: Warwick Brothers and Rutter, 1987) 9: 42.

22. Ryerson, "A Lecture on the Social Advancement of Canada" 162.

23. ———, "Social Advancement" 177; emphasis added.

24. ———, *Civil Government* 19.

25. ———, *Civil Government* 19.

26. Ryerson, *Civil Government* 3. "By a principle of right, deeply implanted in the moral constitution of man, and recognized in almost all forms of human society, each labourer claims and is assured the fruits of his own industry. This is the basis of all property—the right of each man to appropriate and enjoy the fruits of his labour—and is the great stimulant of human industry" (Egerton Ryerson, "Political Economy: A Branch of Public Education," *Journal of Education for Upper Canada* 5 [1852] 131).

27. Ryerson's distance from Locke himself would be another question. See Nathan Tarcov, "A 'Non-Lockean' Locke and the Character of Liberalism," in Douglas MacLean and Claudia Mills, eds., *Liberalism Reconsidered* (Totowa, NJ: Rowman and Allanheld, 1983) 131-40; and Nathan Tarcov, *Locke's Education for Liberty* (Chicago: University of Chicago Press, 1985).

28. Egerton Ryerson, *Claims of the Churchmen and Dissenters of Upper Canada Brought to the Test* (Kingston: The Herald Office, 1828) 94.

29. Ryerson, *First Lessons in Agriculture* 173.

30. Egerton Ryerson, "The Importance of Education to a Manufacturing and a Free People," *Journal of Education for Upper Canada* 1 (1848) 294. Lord Brougham argues that it is essential that the people develop "the habit of justly estimating the character and conduct of men who guide the affairs of nations" (*Political Philosophy* 1: 29). Compare also Montesquieu, *The Spirit of the Laws* 11: 6: "For though few men can tell the exact degree of men's capacities, yet there are none but are capable of knowing in general whether the person they choose is better qualified (plus éclairé) than most of his neighbours."

31. *The Federalist* No. 63.

32. Smith, "The Ideological Origins of Canadian Confederation" 4. Ryerson was a "monarchical republican" in that he always argued that constitutional monarchy was the best form of republican government. In modern times the monarchy had evolved from being "the absolute disposer of the people's religion, liberties, property and lives" into the "impartial guardian of public rights and freedom" and the "keystone in the arch of equal law and liberty" (Egerton Ryerson, *Remarks on the Historical Mis-statements and Fallacies of Mr. Goldwin Smith* [Toronto: Leader Steam Press, 1866] 11). It should be noted here that all serious discussion of the "republicanism question" will henceforward have to begin from the new starting point provided by Thomas L. Pangle in his recent *The Spirit of Modern Republicanism* (Chicago: University of Chicago Press, 1988).

33. Egerton Ryerson, "Canada, Land of Our Birth," in Ontario, Council of Public Instruction, *The Fifth Book of Reading Lessons* (Montreal: John Lovell, 1880) 388.

34. Ryerson, "The Importance of Education to a Manufacturing and a Free People" 301.

35. Ryerson, *Claims of the Churchmen and Dissenters* 187.

36. Ryerson, "Obligations of Educated Men" 198.

37. Egerton Ryerson, *Christians on Earth and in Heaven* (Toronto: Wesleyan Methodist Bookroom, 1848) 18.

38. Ryerson, "Obligations of Educated Men" 198. According to Lord Brougham the representative principle is "the greatest of all improvements which have ever been made in the science of government and legislation" (*Political Philosophy* 3: 37). Compare also Sir James Mackintosh, *Dissertation on the Progress of Ethical Philosophy* (Edinburgh: Adam and Charles Black, 1835) 308; and *The Federalist* No. 9, by Alexander Hamilton.

39. Ryerson, "Obligations of Educated Men" 198. On this point see the famous exchange between Dr. Johnson and Sir Adam Ferguson in James Boswell, *The Life of Dr. Samuel Johnson* (London: George Routledge, 1867) 171.

40. Ryerson, "Obligations of Educated Men" 198.

41. Egerton Ryerson, "Inaugural Address at Victoria College," in Nathaniel Burwash, *The History of Victoria College* (Toronto: Victoria College Press, 1927) 499.

42. The case of Ryerson poses problems for Peter J. Smith's thesis that nineteenth-century Canadian political thought involved not so much variations on the theme of Lockean liberalism as a debate between enlightenment commercialism and classical republicanism. If, as Smith says, "Montesquieu was an authority on all sides" ("Ideological Origins of Canadian Confederation" 9), then there could have been no defenders of the idea of man as *homo politicus*. Anybody who followed Montesquieu, or any of the followers of Montesquieu, had by this fact alone opted for Lockean liberal republicanism over the classical republicanism of Plato, Aristotle, Xenophon, and Cicero. Ryerson was one of these and so were his more radical opponents such as William Lyon Mackenzie. It is arguable that there never have been any simple defenders of the older republican tradition in the modern world, and certainly none in Canada (or the United States for that matter). See Thomas L. Pangle, *Montesquieu's Philosophy of Liberalism* (Chicago: University of Chicago Press, 1973) 48-160. For a discussion of the relationship of Montesquieu to the Canadian political tradition see the following articles from the *Canadian Journal of Political Science*: Philip Resnick, "Montesquieu Revisited, or the Mixed Constitution and the Separation of Powers," 20 (1987): 97-115; Janet Ajzenstat, "Comment: The Separation of Powers in 1867," 20 (1987): 117-20; Rod Preece, "Comment: Montesquieuan Principles of Canadian Politics?" 20 (1987): 121-24; and Philip Resnick, "Reply to Comments on 'The Mixed Constitution and the Separation of Powers in Canada,'" 20 (1987): 125-29.

43. Ryerson, "A Lecture on the Social Advancement of Canada" 177.

44. Egerton Ryerson, "The Importance of Education to an Agricultural People," in Hodgins, *Documentary History* 7: 142. Clara Thomas calls this particular lecture Ryerson's "keynote speech" (*Ryerson of Upper Canada* 107). Compare Brougham, *Works* 8: 108-14.

45. Ryerson, "A Lecture on the Social Advancement of Canada" 177.

46. Ryerson, "The Importance of Education to an Agricultural People" 141.

47. Ryerson, "The Education of Mechanics" 49. Compare Brougham, *Political Philosophy* 2: 25 and 1: 30: "They [the people] have lavished upon tyrants and conquerors, and intriguers, who were their worst enemies, their loudest applause; for those pests of the world securing the fame that should have been kept sacred to virtuous and beneficent deeds."

48. Egerton Ryerson, *The Story of My Life* (Toronto: William Briggs, 1883) 73. It is perhaps worth noting here that Franklin is a central figure in Max Weber's exposition of the psychological interconnections between Protestantism and capitalism (*The Protestant Ethic and the Spirit of Capitalism* [New York: Charles Scribner's Sons, 1959] 48-54). Significantly enough, however, both for Weber's thesis and for Ryerson's alleged traditionalism, Franklin was not a Protestant Christian but an Enlightenment Deist. Clara Thomas states that Ryerson's admiration for Franklin is surprising because his "Methodism would seem to be worlds apart from Benjamin's general ease of spirit" (*Ryerson of Upper Canada* 110). However, this is surprising only if one has overestimated the traditionalism of Ryerson's thought in the first place.

49. Ryerson, "The Education of Mechanics" 49.

50. Bernard Bailyn, *The Ideological Origins of the American Revolution* (Cambridge: Harvard University Press, 1967) 26.

51. Egerton Ryerson, *Report on a System of Public Elementary Instruction for Upper Canada* (Montreal: Lovell and Gibson, 1847) 10.

52. "Letter from Ryerson to Lord Sydenham, October 5, 1840," in C. B. Sissons, *Egerton Ryerson: His Life and Letters* (Toronto: Clark, Irwin, 1937) 1: 562.

53. Egerton Ryerson, *Elements of Political Economy, Or, How Individuals and a Nation Become Rich* (Toronto: Copp Clark, 1877). Ryerson was in some sense following in a tradition of clergymen-economists. Archbishop Whately was the first Professor of Political Economy at Oxford and Ryerson made use of his work. And the Scot, Thomas Chalmers (1780-1847), while being "one of the most prominent pulpit orators of his time," was also an "ardent economist" who wrote copiously on the subject. See Gary F. Langer, *The Coming of Age of Political Economy* 1815-1825 (New York: Greenwood Press, 1987) 14; and Stewart J. Brown, *Thomas Chalmers* (Oxford: Oxford University Press, 1982).

54. Ryerson, "Political Economy: A Branch of Public Education" 131.

55. ———, "Political Economy" 131.

56. *The Spirit of the Laws* 20: 23.

57. Ryerson, "Obligations of Educated Men" 162-63.

58. ———, *Remarks on Goldwin Smith* 14-15.

59. Ryerson identified himself explicitly with Burke in the controversy over the policies of Governor Metcalfe in 1844. See *Sir Charles Metcalfe Defended Against the Attacks of His Late Counsellors* (Toronto: The British Colonist Office, 1844) 132. It should be noted that while Ryerson was a defender of Burkean political sentimentalism he was a staunch opponent of "Rousseauian" private sentimentalism. He argued that "the maudlin sentiment of the novelist is alien to true love, true benevolence and compassion." Moreover, the "most extensive readers of fiction" are often "the least disposed to the real duties of life" ("A Lecture on the Social Advancement of Canada" 182. Compare Étienne Parent, "On the Study of Political Economy," in H. D. Forbes, ed., *Canadian Political Thought* [Toronto: Oxford University Press, 1985] 45. Ryerson had much in common with the great French-Canadian liberal despite their "national" and religious differences.) Ryerson was prone to insist that Canadians put down their novels and read about the "great subjects and great characters" of classical and Biblical literature. Unlike novelistic sentimentalism, which draws the individual more tightly into the private world, sentimental admiration of political and national heroes pulls in the direction of the public realm and the life of citizenship. Ryerson himself was the object of this kind of sentimentalism shortly after his death. See J. Antisell Allen, *Dr. Ryerson: A Review and a Study* (Toronto: The Week, 1884); and J. G. Hodgins, "Sketch of the Reverend Doctor Ryerson," *The Methodist Magazine* (1894): 5-15.

60. Egerton Ryerson, *First Lessons in Christian Morals* (Toronto: Copp Clark, 1871) 91.

61. Ryerson, "Obligations of Educated Men" 195.

62. Clive, *The Scotch Reviewers* 175.

63. Egerton Ryerson, "Elements of Social Progress," *Journal of Education for Upper Canada* 13 (1860) 50.

64. ———, *Wesleyan Methodism in Upper Canada* (Toronto: The Conference Office, 1837) 1. See Prentice, *The School Promoters* 30-31; and Fiorino, "The Moral Foundation of Egerton Ryerson's Idea of Education" 69.

65. ———, "The Chief Superintendent's Report for 1857," in Hodgins, *Documentary History* 13: 210.

66. Ryerson, *Claims of the Churchmen and Dissenters* 35.

CANADIAN LIBERALISM

67. Ryerson, "The Importance of Education to a Manufacturing and a Free People" 296. Ryerson was very open to American liberal and reforming ideas, particularly as they were articulated by such writers and educationalists as Horace Mann, Jared Sparks, Henry Barnard, Francis Wayland, Joseph Story, and Fennimore Cooper.

68. Ryerson was a firm opponent of the Paine-Jefferson political tradition. He described Paine as "a blasphemous infidel and beastly drunkard" (*The Loyalists of America and Their Times* [Toronto: William Briggs, 1880] 2: 66). The tradition to which Paine and Jefferson belonged turned from the Providential God of Biblical Revelation to "Nature and Nature's God." In a word, Ryerson was unwilling to drop the Biblical God completely. But it would be a mistake to conclude from this that he was genuinely orthodox. Like the "infidel" Paine he was profoundly influenced by the natural theology tradition that is at the foundation of modern liberal thought. His writings are strewn with natural theology arguments taken mainly from the work of William Paley. Thus, in line with the "Free-thinking" tradition most commonly associated with names like Spinoza, Shaftesbury, and Bolingbroke, Ryerson was willing to allow that the "God of Grace is the God of Nature." But unlike the radical Enlightenment, he was inclined to split the difference between narrow orthodoxy and Deistic enthusiasm. Modern rationalist thought may well have shown that the "footsteps" of God are evident in "the laws of the material universe," but these "footsteps" nevertheless continue to be evident in "the pages of Revelation." Thus, whatever Ryerson's private thoughts on the relation of the God of Revelation to the God of Nature, he sought to follow in the Swift, Warburton, Johnson, Burke "reaction" to the excesses of modern rationalism by insisting that natural theology was by itself insufficient as a basis for popular religion. For a religion to "render the men professing it perceptibly better," he argued, it must call their attention to God's "holiness, justice, truth and mercy," and above all to "a state of future retribution." In these particulars the teaching of the Bible is "superior to that of natural religion." The Bible teaches religion through "the express declarations of Jehovah, plain to the understanding of a child." Natural theology, by contrast, depends on "speculations and inferences of reasoning beyond the habits and capacity of the masses of mankind" (*First Lessons in Christian Morals* 65). "Men of science" who study the laws of nature may, by progress of the intellect, become well enough acquainted with the "works of God" so as to be less in need of the "express declarations of Jehovah" for the maintenance of a moral life. But this can never be the case for "the masses of mankind." Natural theology may constitute a crucial element in a reasoned approach to religious faith but it cannot be substituted for revealed

205

faith on the political or social level. It will not do as a basis for social morality. "Deny the divine origin of Scripture and nevertheless you must keep the volume as a kind of textbook of morality" (*First Lessons in Christian Morals* iv). Compare "Washington's Farewell Address," in Henry Steele Commager, ed., *Documents of American History* (New York: Crofts, 1946) 173.

69. Ryerson, *First Lessons in Christian Morals* 71.

70. ———, *First Lessons* iv.

71. ———, *First Lessons* 58.

72. Egerton Ryerson, "Impressions of England," in Sissons, *Egerton Ryerson: His Life and Letters* 1: 196. More recently, Professor Joseph Hamburger has followed Ryerson in arguing that the skepticism or antipathy on the part of the whigs toward religion constituted a fundamental defect in their political theory. According to Hamburger, it "made it difficult for a whig to express those moral impulses and principles that can never be driven out of the political arena" ("The Whig Conscience," in Peter Marsh, ed., *The Conscience of the Victorian State* [Syracuse: Syracuse University Press, 1979] 23). About the Philosophical Radicals or Utilitarians in the Britain of the 1830s Ryerson had little good to say. In the end they were a group of "Infidels, Unitarians and Socinians" whose association with the cause of political and ecclesiastical reform resulted in the driving away of "the truly religious portion of the nation" (Sissons, *Egerton Ryerson: His Life and Letters* 1: 197).

73. Egerton Ryerson, "The Question of Religious Instruction in Schools," in Hodgins, *Documentary History*, 11: 226. In 1851 Ryerson attacked certain "newspaper-writers" who sought the "abolition of all religious corporations" regardless of their missionary, charitable, or educational purposes. According to Ryerson such people were exhibiting "the intolerant and proscriptive spirit of Canadian socialism" as contrasted with "the tolerant and enlightened spirit of our American neighbours" (*A Few Remarks on Religious Corporations and American Examples of Them* [Toronto: Thomas H. Bentley, 1851] 3).

74. This point can be readily illustrated by a few observations on Ryerson's approach to the theory of the "moral sense." Ryerson was familiar with the moral sense argument as it descended from Shaftesbury, Hutcheson, Reid, Stewart, and others. But he was clearly dubious about the very idea of the moral sense, having early been trained in the thought of Locke and Paley, who dispensed with the idea. In 1828 he argued that the "approbation of one's own conscience" proved only one's sincerity, and "can be no criterion of moral rectitude" (Egerton Ryerson, *Letters from the Reverend Egerton Ryerson to the Honourable Reverend Doctor Strachan* [Kingston: The Herald Office, 1828] 6). And even when he allowed for the moral sense being an "original faculty of the mind," he insisted that "it may be darkened and debased by ignorance and vice,

as well as enlightened by moral and religious culture" (*First Lessons in Christian Morals* 56). But whatever his doubts about the philosophical plausibility of the moral sense arguments, Ryerson clearly thought them politically salutary. He liked the teaching of the Scottish school because it described individuals as at bottom "moral beings." This meant it was an indirect boost to "religious culture," because "the cultivation of [man's moral powers and feelings] is the province of Christianity" (*Report on a System of Public Elementary Instruction* 34). Thus, although Ryerson was more intellectually inclined toward Locke and Paley, than to the Scots on this question, he could say, in a book of "lessons" on Christianity, that "whatever may be the diversity of the terms of exposition, all agree as to the existence and office of conscience" (*First Lessons on Christian Morals* 52). It is to be preferred that "Canadian families and schools" believe in the existence of conscience or the moral sense, regardless of the doubts that Locke, Paley, and others have raised about the idea.

75. John Locke, *A Letter Concerning Toleration* (Indianapolis: Bobbs-Merrill, 1955) 18.

76. Egerton Ryerson, "The Advantages of Religion to Society," *Christian Guardian* 16 July 1834. Compare Mackintosh, *Progress of Ethical Philosophy* 308.

77. See especially George Grant, *English-Speaking Justice* (Sackville, New Brunswick: Mount Allison University, 1974) 62-73.

78. A. V. Dicey, *Lectures on the Relationship Between Law and Public Opinion in England During the Nineteenth Century* (London: Macmillan, 1962) 403. See also William Westfall, "Order and Experience: Patterns of Religious Metaphor in Early Nineteenth Century Upper Canada," *Journal of Canadian Studies* 20 (1985): 5-25; and Richard G. Brantley, *Locke, Wesley and the Method of English Romanticism* (Gainesville: University of Florida Press, 1984) 16-19. This point about political and religious individualism is worthy of emphasis, because of the ongoing debate as to whether "English Canada's 'essence' is both liberal and non-liberal" and has been shaped in some sense by "corporate-organic-collectivist ideas." See H. D. Forbes, "Hartz-Horowitz at Twenty," *Canadian Journal of Political Science* 20 (1987): 287-315. Ryerson's Methodism definitely "touches" his liberalism, but Methodist theology was far from being "corporate-organic-collectivist" in character. "Christianity recognizes in each and every man, a moral agent—a personal accountability to God" (Ryerson, *Letters from the Reverend Egerton Ryerson to the Honourable Reverend Doctor Strachan* 170). Thus, it might be possible to allow Frank Underhill's assertion of a half-century ago that "there is nothing more distinctively and essentially Canadian than [the] combination . . . of pioneer loyalism and

pioneer Methodism" (*In Search of Canadian Liberalism* [Toronto: Macmillan, 1960] 149). But this would not involve the suggestion that "corporate-organic-collectivist ideas" are at the base of English-Canadian political culture. See also Ryerson, *The Loyalists of America* 1: iii; and Burwash, *The History of Victoria College* xv, 1, 5.

79. Alexis de Tocqueville, *Democracy in America* (New York: Vintage Books, 1945) 1: 318. For an excellent discussion of this aspect of Tocqueville's thought with a Canadian focus, see Janet Ajzenstat, *The Political Thought of Lord Durham* (Montreal: McGill-Queen's University Press, 1988) 35-41. See also Judith N. Shklar, *After Utopia: The Decline of Political Faith* (Princeton, NJ: Princeton University Press, 1957) 226.

80. Ryerson, *Civil Government* 4.

81. ——, "Obligations of Educated Men" 205.

CHAPTER NINE

THE CONSTITUTIONALISM
OF ÉTIENNE PARENT AND JOSEPH HOWE

Janet Ajzenstat

I

Two sharply different political ideologies—two visions of good
government—shaped colonial politics in the British North America of the 1830s. Proponents of the first argued that the constitutional tradition inherited from Britain had subjected the inhabitants
of British North America to the rule of intolerant and unjust élites.
The constitution of 1791 had to be overturned, by force if necessary. When power had been seized from the imperial party in the
colonies, it would be possible to establish a true democracy,
government by "the people."

The second ideology rejected the idea that colonial grievances
could be remedied by the introduction of a more democratic form of
government. Its proponents argued that although the attempt in 1791
to introduce the principles of the British constitution had not been
successful, it was still the case that the colonists' best hope for freedom and prosperity depended on establishing in British North America a form of government closely modelled on the British. The great

merit of the British constitution, according to this line of thought, was that it held in check all tendencies toward extremism, including the extremism that went by the name of democracy.

In this paper the first ideology will be called "democratic," and the second, "constitutionalist." Papineau and Mackenzie exemplify the democratic vision; Étienne Parent and Joseph Howe, the constitutionalist.

The drama of Canadian events in the 1830s tends to obscure our perception of these ideologies. The contest between reformers and the local élites in each province overshadows the story of the ideological differences in the reform camp. Parent and Howe were closely associated with the popular party and the popular cause, on occasion allies of Papineau and Mackenzie, in opposition to British officialdom and the oligarchic cliques entrenched in the legislative and executive councils.[1] When they list the injustices of life in British North America, Parent and Howe echo arguments of the democrats.

The fact that in the 1830s Parent and Howe recommended the introduction in the colonies of the constitutional principle we now call responsible government is another factor contributing to the idea that constitutionalists and democrats pursued similar political goals. Responsible government requires the cabinet, or political executive—in the colonies of this period, the executive council—to secure the support of the majority of the representatives in the popular house. It is the central feature of the parliamentary system today. Their endorsement of responsible government suggests that Parent and Howe were forward-looking reformers who deserve as much as Papineau and Mackenzie to be called democrats. It is true that the democrats usually argued for an elective executive council, preferring the idea that the executive should answer to the people directly. But in the usual interpretation, this suggests merely that Papineau and Mackenzie favoured the Jacksonian democracy of the United States while Parent and Howe supported supported democracy in its parliamentary form.[2]

Papineau for one argued that the constitutionalists and democrats worked for the same objectives. In the grand scheme of things, he said, the "liberals, radicals [and] constitutionals" were enlisted in the democratic cause, against an opposition comprising "serviles, royalists and tories."[3] Commentators on this period of Canadian history seldom fail to mention that there were ideological differences of interest among the reformers during the 1830s. But the substance of those differences remains obscure.

In this chapter I suggest that the debate within the reform camp between constitutionalists and democrats was more important for the future of Canada, and teaches us more today, than the contest between reformers and the official parties. The two nineteenth-century British North American ideologies represent two important trends of political thought in the modern era. I believe indeed that they represent the most important trends.

The democratic vision in the nineteenth-century colonies, like any political ideology, is a constellation of not always compatible ideas. It includes the dream of a simple life, and the idea of political "virtue."[4] It owes much to Rousseau, and at times looks like a forerunner of today's communitarianism.[5] It has a high idea of the importance of politics, regarding it as the vehicle for the realization of a way of life. Papineau's political vision in these crucial years was both progressive and particularist. As a democrat he could represent himself as spokesman for the aspirations of all men everywhere. As leader of the *Parti patriote*, he was the voice of a particular nationality and way of life.

Central to democracy in both its nineteenth-century form and later manifestations is the idea that political power belongs to "the people."[6] "The people" in the language of nineteenth-century democracy does not denote the shifting and continually changing aggregation of groups and interests that Canadians have in mind today when they think of a popular majority. "The people" is a homogeneous and permanent body of citizens—a permanent class. Papineau pinned much of his case on the fact that the majority of the populace in Lower Canada indeed comprised a more or less homogeneous group defined by language, history, and way of life, a group that had been excluded from politics by the minority "official" party. The history and politics of Lower Canada lent veracity to his claim to represent a single body of people, a class that had suffered real grievances, and known real injustice. When Papineau looked to the future he envisaged the rise of the *Parti patriote* to power, and justified *patriote* capture of power on the grounds that it was the people's party. Conspicuously lacking in his arguments from the 1830s is evidence that he was prepared to entertain the idea of the alternation of parties in office.

Parent and Howe utterly rejected the idea of democracy represented by Papineau. They were friends of the popular cause in the sense that they hoped to benefit the inhabitants of British North America. But they were not "democrats." I suggest that "constitutionalist" is an appropriate name for their vision of good government, because it was used in their period, but also, and more importantly, because Parent and Howe adhered to principles and ideas that are still today regarded as central to constitutionalism. In the first place, they were advocates of party government. They recommended responsible government because they regarded it as the constitutional principle that best ensures the alternation of political parties in office. Moreover, they assumed, as constitutionalists do today, that government should not determine all aspects of life in a polity. In other words, they were proponents of what we now call limited government.

Above all Parent and Howe opposed absolutism. They are famous in Canadian history for their opposition to the absolutism of the colonial oligarchs. What is less well known is that with equal energy they opposed the absolutism that surfaced in the reform camp during this decade. They feared Papineau's democracy because they believed that it would lead to rule by one party in the name of the people. What they called democracy we would describe as democratic absolutism, that form of total government so familiar today because until recently it characterized the regimes of Eastern Europe and the Soviet Union.[7]

The clue to their doctrine lies in the fact that they took as their model of good government the institutions of eighteenth-century England. "Let us 'keep the old paths,'" wrote Howe in one effusive passage. "Let us adopt the good old practices of our ancestors." He explicitly dissociated himself from the "new experiments" in government prescribed by men like Papineau and Mackenzie.[8]

I do not mean to suggest that Parent and Howe regarded reform of the British constitution as impossible or undesirable. Both admired the spirit of political change evident in the Britain of the Reform Bill years. Nevertheless, they believed that there was an essential guarantee of political freedom in the British constitution that had been present from 1688 or early in the eighteenth century, and was beautifully evident in the mother country in their own time. "The principles of our constitution ought to be those of the constitution of the Mother Country," said Parent.[9] They depicted even responsible government as a long-established constitutional principle. Neither suggested that it was a recent innovation in Britain, or a measure that had only recently recommended itself to the colonists.

Commentators have had difficulty with this backward-looking aspect of their argument. In the usual description the British constitution of the eighteenth century is not particularly admirable: it is said to have bolstered the privileges of the aristocracy and ignored the welfare of the mass of the people.[10] The Constitutional Act of 1791 is similarly depicted as a set of political institutions enshrining the autocratic notions of the British upper classes—a regressive document for the period, not to be compared with the American Constitution, or the Declaration of the Rights of Man and Citizen.[11] Commentators who adhere to this picture of British institutions in the eighteenth and early nineteenth centuries find it difficult to entertain the idea that Parent and Howe, known above all as advocates of responsible government, could ever regard them as a model.

In defending the principles of the British Constitution during a period of social disorder and rebellion, Parent and Howe followed a difficult and sometimes dangerous course. They opposed the democrats while working with them to expose the injustice of government by the official parties. They set themselves against British officialdom while insisting that the British institutions were the best possible guarantor of political freedom. It is remarkable, and I would argue very fortunate for this country, that their views triumphed. In the end they persuaded British administrators of the justice of their cause. They humbled the local élites, and converted the democrats. It is the constitutionalists' vision that shapes Canadian politics in the ensuing decades, and until well into our own time.

II

The heart of liberal constitutionalism is the idea that for all politically relevant purposes human beings are equal. No individual, class, hierarchy, or political interest has a natural title to rule. Priests, the wealthy, the high born, are not privileged in political debate. In the British tradition this idea, often termed equality of right, stems from the teaching of Hobbes and Locke. It is the ground of the argument against the absolute monarchs of the seventeenth century. It shapes the politics of eighteenth-century Britain—no doubt it was sometimes forgotten in the press of day-to-day politics, but it was always the standard—and it is crucial for Parent and Howe.[12]

Their adherence to equality of right fuelled their argument against the colonial élites; they regarded the oligarchs' claim that wealth and family connection gave them title to rule as an absurd attempt to ape the absolutism of the seventeenth century. Equality of right led Howe to oppose Colonial Office meddling in the affairs of Nova Scotia. He saw no reason why the discretionary opinion of a British official should automatically compel attention in the colony. Equality of right led Parent to reject the argument, a favourite one with the "English" party in Lower Canada, that those of British stock could naturally claim positions of power. He rejected as well, although he was deeply patriotic, demands for a privileged status for the French Canadian way of life. In the constitutionalist view, the threat of absolutism hovers around nationalist claims. Neither "race" nor nationality should be elevated above the law.[13]

What is important for the argument in this paper is the assumption by Parent and Howe that constitutionalism is as hostile to an assertion of constitutional privilege by political leaders professing to speak for "the people" as it is to any other assertion of privilege. Parent writes, "The idea that some have sought to spread that the Chamber (the legislative assembly of Lower Canada) alone is capable of leading the country, and that the body . . . and the reputations of the members who compose it are little sacred, inviolable idols . . . is monstrous."[14]

He depicts attempts by the Third Estate in France to usurp the powers of the executive branch of government "on the pretext that the voice of the people was the voice of God" as instrumental in bringing about the excesses of Robespierre and Marat. Parent was certainly not alone in suggesting that the Terror was the consequence of an unchecked concentration of power in the hands of popular leaders in revolutionary France. The argument was a favourite one with British whigs and tories at this time. Moreover, it was certainly the case that writers in French Canada had many prudent reasons to dissociate themselves from those French revolutionaries. But in these passages Parent is not aping others, and is not simply taking the expedient course. He has appropriated as his own the idea that the voice of the people cannot be accorded privileged status in the good constitution. The "people" and the people's leaders have no more title to privilege than a priestly caste that claims to speak for God.

In the articles he wrote in 1820s Parent describes the British Constitution as a form of "mixed" or "balanced" government. He does not make an outright argument for the constitutional principle we now call responsible government until the 1830s. But whether he is using the language of mixed government or of responsible government, he argues against the unconstitutional aggrandizement of the "popular branch of the legislature."

He begins from the assumption that the legislators of 1791 wished to give the Canadas a version of the British parliamentary system. Parliament in Parent's description comprises three branches: the monarchic branch (in Britain the ministers of the Crown; in the colonies the executive council); the aristocratic branch (the House of Lords, and legislative council) and the democratic branch (the House of Commons, and legislative assembly). Each branch should be "independent," with distinctive constitutional powers. At the same time no branch should function alone; the three together are said to "balance" or "harmonize."[15]

He maintained that the problems of Lower Canada did not stem from supposed flaws in British institutions but from a failure to put British principles into practice. In particular the principle of the "independence" of the three parliamentary branches had been allowed to lapse. The colonial monarchic and aristocratic branches were both nominated by the Governor, and, far from being "independent," took up the same causes and had the same goals.[16] A single oligarchic élite was ensconced in the executive and legislative Councils, furthering their own interest and thwarting efforts by the majority party in the assembly to initiate measures on behalf of the populace.

The Ninety-two Resolutions, a statement on colonial grievances published in 1834, lists the sins of the oligarchy. The colonial executive had used provincial revenues to provide salaries for "sinecure offices" and to support "other objects" for which the House after deliberation had denied funds.[17] The Receiver General of the Province had paid away large sums of money from the public purse "without any regard to the obedience which is always due to the law."[18] The executive had created new and wholly unauthorized revenues through the sale of Crown lands when existing revenue proved insuffcent to satisfy offical party greed.[19] That Parent argued against such practices hardly needs to be said. He was a staunch and unflagging opponent of the oligarchic party. It is his remedy that needs careful examination.

He did not accept the democratic argument that the transgressions of the executive and legislative Councils made it necessary to reduce the powers of these bodies. The *patriote* formula called for the legislative assembly to assume the powers of government from the councils. Parent disagrees: "The Assembly forms only one branch of the legislative body, and can do nothing with respect to the passage of laws without the agreement of the two other branches." Were the assembly of Lower Canada to take on itself the powers of government, confusion and disorder would result: "The idea that the Assembly forms a legislative body separate from the other branches is false and dangerous."[20]

Nor did he endorse that other favourite remedy of the democrats, an elective legislative council. He agreed with the radicals that the machinations of the legislative council were contributing to the colony's problems, but maintained that what was required was an appointed and "independent" upper house: "We must have an independent aristocratic branch, which owes nothing for its existence to another branch, a body that finds its interest in the general prosperity of the country and not in exhorbitant salaries."[21] Parent's remedy, in short, was "independence" for the three parliamentary bodies. All would be well when the principles of the British Constitution were at last fully realized in Lower Canada.

By the 1830s Parent's language has changed.[22] Gone are the references to the monarchic, aristocratic, and democratic branches of the legislature. He now espouses the principle we call responsible government. But it is still his assumption that the colonial constitution should be modelled on the British: "Under pain of renouncing their portfolios, the Ministers in England must command the confidence and the majority in the Chambers, and above all that of the Commons, in all great measures, which almost always in England emanate from the government." In the colonies the introduction of this practice would mean that the King would nominate the executive councillors. "They would be his councillors as today, but with the great difference that they could be held accountable for all acts of government by the Chambers."[23]

The standard view of mixed government holds that the doctrine flourished in the age of aristocracy, and died out in the early- to mid-nineteenth century with the introduction of responsible government. The notion of three "independent" branches of parliament was abandoned, to be succeeded by the "fusion" of political executive and popular house that characterizes the modern parliamentary system. It is not a view that will help us with Parent.

We have already noted that he writes about responsible government as a doctrine that had long been a feature of the British system. He maintains indeed that it had been familiar to constitutional thinkers in the colonies from 1812.[24] How did Parent think of responsible government in relation to his earlier understanding of the British constitution as a mixed regime? Did he believe he had been mistaken in describing the British constitution as balanced government?

His most comprehensive discussion of responsible government includes this picture of the tribulations of assembly members under the colonial practice: "One has generally so little time to give to public affairs that the sessions pass in demanding one piece of information after another, document after document, testimony after testimony, and years pass before a committee is able to unravel the chaos that is before it. The session ends, everyone returns to his particular affairs, and one returns at the next session as innocent as one was at the beginning of the last. And if in response to popular demand, one passes a law, it is nothing but an outline that has to be retouched at each subsequent session."[25]

He continues: if legislation were prepared by ministers (from either chamber) who headed administrative departments, it would reach the assembly "already digested," and one would have someone to call on for an explanation of the bill. In short, a "provincial ministry" is need, modelled on the "imperial ministry." In short, responsible government for Parent is ministerial government, and ministerial government yields more coherent legislation, more efficient adminstration, and better accountability.[26]

Notice that his analysis of grievances is not very different from the one he advanced in the 1820s. His argument is still that the oligarchy entrenched in the executive and legislative councils had the will and power to impede the legislators in the popular house. Moreover, he is no more ready in the 1830s than in the 1820s to accept the idea that the assembly should bypass the obstructive party in the upper houses and assume executive powers. On the contrary, his depiction of ministerial government suggests that what is required is an executive council with strong powers. In keeping with the principle we know as responsible government, they will be chosen from among those who have the sympathy of the lower house, but they will not be ordinary members of the lower house. They will wield the powers of the Crown, and have responsibility for the departments of government. Parent points out that in Britain legislation is initiated by the executive branch. He recommends the same practice for Lower Canada. The executive branch of government is to initiate legislation, and account for it in the assembly. The doctrine of responsible government in Parent's description requires a political executive that wields concentrated powers of government.

To enable the lower house to perform its function of calling for explanations and holding the executive accountable, the assembly is the guardian of the public purse.[27] It is the constitutional right of the lower house to vote on spending legislation introduced by the executive branch.[28] Parent depicts the power of the purse as a counterweight to "the kind of tyranny that the Executive is able to exercise over its subjects."[29] The assembly must act as a check on the executive. At the same time he opposes the idea, so often endorsed in these years by Papineau, that the popular house should disburse public funds according to its own program. In the 1820s he argued that a popular house raising and spending public funds could be led to imitate the excesses of Third Estate.[30] He is of the same view in the 1830s. The dispersal of public moneys must remain a prerogative of the executive. Just as the assembly checks the executive, so the executive must check the assembly.

In other words, Parent's espousal of responsible government did not require him to abandon the idea that the cabinet and popular house are two "branches of the legislature," and in an important sense, independent. The two constitutional bodies are inseparable, but distinguishable.[31] Each has its proper constitutional powers.

In the passage in which he says that responsible government was known to the men of 1812, Parent points out that their successors "have made progress in constitutional knowledge and can formulate the demand more precisely." When he adopted the language of responsible government he found new ways to formulate old demands. He was not describing a startling new development. The constitution he described in the 1820s as a mixed regime, he can now write about in terms of a plea for responsible government. What is supremely excellent about this constitution, whether responsible government or mixed government, what enables Parent to describe it as the best possible guarantee of political freedom, has yet to be seen.

III

Like Parent, Joseph Howe confronted a governing clique bent on frustrating proposals for reform of the economy and the constitution. The executive and legislative councils of Nova Scotia were dominated by a "small knot of individuals" who owed their seats to the influence and intrigues of their friends and relatives.[32] United by their common interest in "promoting extravagance, resisting economy, and keeping up the system exactly as it stands," they remained in power whatever the outcome of elections and whatever the composition of the legislative assembly. They enjoyed the best salaries in the country, and distributed "nearly all the patronage."[33]

Responsible government, the "cornerstone of the British Constitution," is Howe's remedy.[34] In 1839 he wrote four open letters to Lord John Russell arguing that colonial grievances would cease only with the implementation of the British constitution in the colonies.[35] In England, he writes, "the government is invariably trusted to men whose principles and policy the mass of those who possess the elective franchise approve and who are sustained by a majority in the House of Commons."[36] They govern until they find their "representative majority diminished" and some "rival combination of able and influential men" are in a position to "displace" them. This is the principle that should obtain in the colonies.

Howe defines responsible government as requiring the political executive to "answer" to the majority in the popular house. It would "place" the government of the colony, "as it always is in England, in a majority in the Commons, watched, controlled and yet aided by a constitutional opposition."[37] He means, as Parent did, that the government is sustained by the majority in the lower house. Responsible government concentrates the power of government in the cabinet. The cabinet must take the lead in public affairs, with "energy and ability."[38] No more than Parent is Howe thinking of the cabinet as a subordinate institution, docilely carrying out the assembly's instructions.

Howe's idea of the prerogatives proper to the executive branch of Parliament are illuminated by his discussion of patronage. The official party in Nova Scotia appointed some nine hundred administrative officers.[39] Howe's objection to these appointments is not made on the ground that patronage is wrong or distasteful. What was intolerable about the situation was that the nine hundred appointments were made by an executive council that did not have the support of the people of the province.[40] The distribution of patronage took no account of the wishes of the populace.

Responsible government, in Howe's analysis, would place patronage and spending powers in the hands of a party that was required to maintain the support of the assembly and the electorate. He regarded the patronage prerogative as an aspect of what is sometimes called the executive spending power, or "royal recommendation," the constitutional principle requiring that a minister of the Crown introduce spending legislation in the lower house.[41] The important consequence of this principle is that the popular house does not raise and spend public funds on its own initiative. The patronage prerogative, concentrating the power to govern in the cabinet, enables the executive to present the assembly, and the public, with a coherent program to accept or reject. The executive branch of the legislature governs, while the popular branch—and the public—scrutinize, criticize, and approve or disapprove. Howe regards the fact that the cabinet, not the assembly, wields the patronage power as a necessary condition of governmental accountability.[42]

The old language of mixed government surfaces occasionally in Howe's argument.[43] At one point, for example, he speaks of the Governor's power of dissolution as his means to "adjust the balance of power"—harking back to the idea that the political executive, upper house, and lower house must "balance." From the context it is evident that he is thinking of a situation where an executive council that has lost the confidence of the house refuses to leave office. The executive has attempted to override the constitutional powers of the assembly, upsetting the "balance." Howe suggests that in such a situation the Governor would exercise his power to call an election, presumably freeing him and the country of the offending party, in this way redressing the balance.[44] But whether he uses the new terminology or the old, it is clear that, like Parent,

Howe holds to that central tenet of the mixed constitution as it was expounded in the early eighteenth century: the political executive and lower house are connected, but nevertheless distinct branches of the legislative power, each with its constitutional powers.

IV

As long as Parent and Howe inveighed against the injustices of the official party, their arguments had a simple appeal. Whether they were addressing their home constituency or British officialdom, they had a sound case and a wealth of undisputed grievances to cite. They were the friends of freedom and the foes of oligarchy. But consider their difficulties when they began to set out the case for the assumption of power by colonial parties. Both, as we shall see, felt it necessary to disguise the fact that colonial élites might be as ambitious as the imperial ones. Both take care when they are describing the perhaps unsavoury constitutionalist teaching about the nature of politicians.

Parent must explain to his readers that once the "official" clique has been voted out, the leaders of the popular party will take up salaried offices in the executive council, spending the public revenue, and dispensing patronage. He knows very well that many of those readers, especially, as he says, the ones "who take pleasure in calumniating the free and honest motives of the liberal press," will conclude that the advocates of responsible government are advancing the measure for no other reason than to obtain positions for themselves and their friends.[45]

If we were merely interested in promoting our friends' interests, he says, we would recommend careers in commerce for those attracted by the glamour of money, or in the liberal professions for those who desire honour and distinction. Politics offers only a false glamour and uncertain prospects. The reason for recommending responsible government, he continues, is that it will put representatives of the people in a position where they are able to render the services that the people need. Parent's difficulty is that, as he knows very well, the argument for responsible government does not presuppose disinterested, high-minded politicians. It assumes rather that politicians are eager for the rewards of office, and is intended precisely to accommodate and contain ambition. Parent knew that political leaders of all parties want the glamour of public office as much as or more than the chance to serve the public interest, but he could not be entirely forthright with a population still unfamiliar with the political game of ins and outs. The passage glosses over, and yet reveals, Parent's understanding that one of the secrets of good government is the utilization of low human motives.

Howe's reasons for not being forthright with readers arose from the fact that the popular parties in the Canadas had endorsed armed rebellion against the British government. Howe cannot deny that under responsible government the leaders of the popular party of the day occupy places in the cabinet. But it will do him no good with his readers in Britain, or with his own moderate reform constituency in Nova Scotia, to speak favourably about the "Canadian demogogues," leaders of the "maddest rebellions on record."[46] Sir Francis Head apparently considered it a sufficient argument against responsible government to say that if it had been in operation, demagogues like Papineau and Mackenzie would have been ministers in their respective provinces.[47]

Howe first suggests that Papineau and Mackenzie would never have grown to importance under responsible government, because they lacked "sound sense" and "prudence." Agitators like them arise only under conditions of injustice: "who dreams that, but for the wretched system upheld in all the Colonies, and the entire absence of responsibility, by which faction or intrigue were made the only roads to power, either of the Canadian demogogues would ever have had an inducement or been placed in a position to disturb the public peace?"[48]

The argument is not entirely convincing. Indeed, Howe soon abandons it, going on to say that if responsible government had been introduced Papineau and Mackenzie might after all have become "conspicious and influential." He then admits outright that it is not improbable that they would have been executive councillors, guiding the internal policy of the colony and dispensing the local patronage. Remember that Howe's four letters have made the case for concentration of governing power in the cabinet. Now he is involved in arguing that responsible government could put that concentrated power in the hands of demogogues and rebels.

As he continues his careful presentation in these passages, it becomes apparent that Howe regards it as an advantage, not a disadvantage, that the British constitution concentrates power in the hands of men of the type to become demogogues and rebels. Such men exist in every society. They will always make a bid for power. The remarkable thing about the British constitution is that men of this character wield power under conditions that require them to act in statesmanlike fashion. Howe asks, "If the sovereigns had continued, as of old, alone responsible; if hundreds of able men all running the same course of honourable ambition had not been encouraged to watch and control each other . . . who, I ask, will assure us that Chatham and Fox, instead of being able ministers and loyal men might not have been sturdy rebels?"[49]

Papineau and Mackenzie are now compared to Chatham and Fox! The argument that began with the suggestion that under a good constitution demagogues will never be admitted to power now says that if ambitious men are not allowed into power they will become demagogues.

Howe's argument at bottom is that the incomparable British Constitution encourages demagogues to act like the great statesmen of British history because it rewards their ambition under institutions that curtail it. They find that they can gratify their ambitions only by maintaining the support of a party that has the support of the country. Their use of the power of the Crown is subject to the scrutiny of the opposition and the public. Rebels "have become exceedingly scarce at home [in England]," he says, "yet they were as plentiful as blackberries in the good old times when the sovereigns contended." He goes on, "Turn back and you will find that they began to disappear altogether in England about 1688."[50]

Given this account of the salutary clash of élites under a good constitution, we can see why Parent and Howe cling to the idea that the cabinet is a separate branch of the legislature, and why they regard this feature of the British constitution as one of the great guarantees of freedom, a guarantee especially against democratic absolutism. It is above all a way of denying to the ambitious men in the branch of the legislature that can fairly claim to represent "the people," the right to wield the power of the Crown. The political executive, the executive council, represents the majority in the lower house, and speaks for many, perhaps a majority, in the electorate, the majority of the moment. But it cannot claim to speak for "the people." There is always that vocal and ambitious minority in the legislative assembly ready to oppose and criticize the party in power, a constant reminder that the title to govern can be revoked.

The lower house has a much better claim to represent "the people" because it contains members from every constituency. But in the British Constitution this representative house is denied the power to govern. The constitution thus ensures that no political leader may govern in the name of all. It provides government in the interest of the majority of the moment, while guaranteeing freedom from democratic tyranny.

That political leaders must compete for their rewards under rules that force them to seek the approval of the public is what gives England government in the public interest. What does the ambitious man do when he loses office? asks Howe. He does not mourn his loss as if it were "an irreparable stroke of fortune." Nor need he start a rebellion. He "rallies his friends," and connects himself "with some great interest in the state whose accumulating strength may bear him into the counsels of his sovereign."[51] "Under English government," Parent argues, "public opinion is everything; the authorities challenge its power in vain; they are obliged to submit to it."[52] Government in the public interest with security against popular absolutism: the parliamentary system that Parent and Howe describe is a better formula for pleasing the people than the democracy favoured by Papineau and Mackenzie.

Parent's conviction that the British Constitution was the best possible form of government for Lower Canada tells us that he regarded it as a universal prescription. The fact that the constitution originated in England in the eighteenth century did not mean that it was suitable only for Englishmen. French Canadians were as capable as the British of appreciating the benefits of good political institutions, and as capable of using them to their own advantage. Howe compares the British constitution to the "unerring principles of science." Like the principles of science, he says, it is as applicable to "one side of the Atlantic as to the other."[53]

V

Howe sums up his case for responsible government in this passage: "Until it can be shown that there are forms of government, combining stronger executive power with more of individual liberty; offering nobler inducement of individual ambition, and more security to unaspiring ease and humble industry," it cannot be assumed that the inhabitants of the provinces of North America are "panting for new experiments."[54] What he means by individual ambition and the necessity for strong executive power we have seen. By the phrase "security to unaspiring ease," I suggest, he indicates that there is, and should be, a sphere of social and economic activity beyond politics. In other words he is an advocate of limited government. J. Murray Beck describes him as "a vigorous advocate of freedom from the unwarranted restriction of individual activity."[55]

Could Beck's description be as easily applied to Parent? H. D. Forbes argues that Parent was willing to see governments use their power to equalize political opportunities. "Parent believed ... it was not sufficient that [government] enforce contracts, prohibit the use of violence and undertake a few public works; it also had to adopt policies respecting education and taxation that would give the poor man's sons some real help in competing with the rich man's son for the leading positions in society."[56] But if Parent was more tolerant of government activity than Howe, he would never have countenanced its extension into all spheres of society.[57] Neither Parent nor Howe accepted the idea of politics as an all-encompassing human activity, a panacea for all social ills.

In the constitutional regime, the alternation of parties in office is the condition of political freedom. Limited government is the condition of individual freedom. Both features protect citizens from their political leaders, the first by pitting élites against each other for the approval of the electorate, and the second by curtailing government intrusion. They are the guarantee against the absolutism of leaders who claim title to govern on the basis of birth, wealth, or "race," and the absolutism of those who would argue that they govern in the people's name. For the democrats of the 1830s, flushed by revolutionary excitement, these principles of liberal constitutionalism must have seemed antiquated indeed. When the people's representatives had at last attained the positions in government office to which they were entitled, when the *demos* had triumphed, constitutional provisions that might unseat "the people's party," or limit the scope of government, would be unnecessary.

In the 1830s it was apparent to all that the colonies could not continue under the practices that had grown up in the decade succeeding 1791. It was a period of founding, or re-founding. To participants in the debates of this crucial decade it must have seemed as if two very different futures stretched ahead. But with the introduction of responsible government the democrats' arguments went down to defeat. Constitutionalism triumphed. The form of government established in 1867 had already been determined by the ideological debates of the 1830s. This is not to say that the democratic vision was entirely forgotten. In the late nineteenth century the argument for "balance" and the mixed regime lost credence. Mixed government came to be depicted as an outmoded notion of the eighteenth century, irrelevant in a liberal democratic society like Canada.[58] The idea that the democratic and the liberal (or constitutionalist) elements in liberal democracy are in tension was no longer in the forefront of political debate. The result was that although liberal constitutionalist practices continued, and appeared to be as well entrenched as ever, the way was opened for a revival of the democratic ideology. Peter J. Smith, describing Papineau's political vision, says, "The political ideology of agrarian democracy was not to be extinguished in Canada. It emerged as powerful as ever on the prairies in the twentieth century, giving sustenance to radical movements of both the left and the right."[59]

Proof that the democratic vision lingers in Canada's political subconscious might be found in today's constitutional debate. Among the arguments made on behalf of constitution-making by means of a constituent assembly is the suggestion that the representative character of such an assembly would be enough to ensure its responsiveness to Canadian interests. No further formula for accountability (like responsible government) is required. The democratic thrust in the argument for a constituent assembly does not support agrarian democracy, or the simple life; it is not the nineteenth-century vision in all its purity. But it rings with echoes of the nineteenth century.

When Canadians today speak of "the people," and appeal to the idea of a national general will, they are using the accents of the democrats of the 1830s. Today's populists and democrats, I would argue, are most like the democrats of the nineteenth century when they become impatient with constitutional forms, like the parliamentary system and the principle of limited government, because forms are seen as impeding progress toward worthy political goals.

Constitutionalism and democracy are the two poles of modern political thought; in the British North American debates of the 1830s we see one swing of the pendulum. At the democratic pole cluster the demand for political virtue, equality of condition, the sense of nationality, hopes for community, and the idea that government should be of "the people." Constitutionalism may well appear less attractive: it does not ask for high-minded leadership, expects little from the populace in the way of citizenly virtue, and, if we are to believe its critics, fails to respect the human need for community.[60] It demands equality of right, but tolerates inequality of condition. It stands on solid ground when it opposes the absolutism of the few, but its opposition to the absolutism of the many can easily appear like a betrayal of popular interests.

What we find in Parent and Howe is an argument that illuminates the constitutionalist pole. They explain and defend the nineteenth-century doctrine, especially its anti-democratic thrust. And they usefully remind us today that democracy may not be a sufficient formula for government in the popular interest.

NOTES

*The author is grateful for the support of the Social Sciences and Humanities Research Council of Canada, grant no. 410-89-02431.

1. In the 1830s Howe was a member of the legislative assembly in Nova Scotia and editor of the *Novascotian*. Parent, associated with the *Parti patriote*, was editor of the influential journal *le Canadien*. J. Murray Beck calls Howe "the greatest Nova Scotian" (*Joseph Howe, Conservative Reformer 1804-1848* [Kingston 1982] vii). Jean-Charles Falardeau argues that Parent exemplified in the highest degree the virtues of the intellectual and political class of that period (*Étienne Parent 1801-1874: Biographie, textes et bibliographie* [Montréal 1975] 12). And see Jean-Charles Falardeau, "Étienne Parent," *Dictionary of Canadian Biography*, Volume X, 1871-1880 (Toronto 1971). Both Howe and Parent played a significant role in the politics of their respective provinces in later decades. Parent's admiration for British institutions and political traditions is especially impressive when we remember that he was imprisoned for three months by the British administration for cataloguing the injustices of the "English" party in the provincial councils.

2. The United States was often held up by the colonial radicals as an instance of the democracy they favoured. It was the Jacksonian ideal they admired, not the system of checks and balances described by men like Hamilton and Madison. For an argument suggesting that the U.S. founders express the kind of reservations about democracy that I find in Parent and Howe, see Thomas L. Pangle, "The Federalist Papers' Vision of Civic Health and the Tradition Out of Which that Vision Emerges," *Western Political Quarterly* 39.4 (December 1986).

3. See the Ninety-two Resolutions, reprinted in W. P. M. Kennedy, *Statutes, Treaties and Documents of the Canadian Constitution, 1713-1929* (Toronto 1930) 277, the 37th Resolution.

4. For an exploration of the idea of public "virtue" in Canadian political thought in this period, see Peter J. Smith, "The Ideological Origins of Canadian Confederation," *Canadian Journal of Political Science* 20.1 (March 1987), and Gordon T. Stewart, *The Origins of Canadian Politics: A Comparative Approach* (Vancouver 1986). Compare C. B. Macpherson on "non-liberal democracy" in *The Real World of Democracy* (Canadian Broadcasting Corporation 1965).

5. See Michael Sandel on the connection between civic virtue in the nineteenth century and today's communitarianism ("The Political Theory of the Procedural Republic," in Allan C. Hutchinson and Patrick Monahan, eds., *The Rule of Law: Ideal or Ideology* [Toronto 1987]). Ouellet draws our attention to Rousseau's influence on Papineau ("Louis-Joseph Papineau," *Dictionary of Canadian Biography*, vol. X [Toronto 1972]).

6. Fernand Ouellet finds a contradiction between Papineau's progressive political ideas and his social thought. He argues that Papineau's idea of a simple agrarian society was highly conservative ("Louis-Joseph Papineau," *Dictionary of Canadian Biography*). No doubt Ouellet is right to argue that in the Lower Canada of the period seigneurial tenure bolstered hierarchy, not equality. But on the theoretical level there is no contradiction in Papineau. Rousseau would have applauded Papineau's dream of a nation of small farmers, living in the simplicity of poverty, and would have had no difficulty with the idea that such a society could be governed by the democratic general will.

7. See the excellent description of democratic absolutism in Douglas V. Verney, *The Analysis of Political Systems* (Glencoe 1959). Verney's term for this form of absolutism is "convention government," and he traces its history from "the notorious Convention of 1792-5" to the modern communist period.

8. Howe to Lord John Russell, September 1839 (Kennedy, *Statutes, Treaties and Documents* 410).

9. *Le Canadien* 8 September 1824 (my translation). The articles of Parent's from *Le Canadien* cited in this paper can all be found in Falardeau, *Étienne Parent, 1801-1874*.

10. See, for example, H. T. Dickinson, *Liberty and Property: Political Ideology in Eighteenth-Century Britain* (London 1977) and A. H. Birch, *Representative and Responsible Government* (Toronto 1964). Contrast the better view in a standard text in political science, Mark O. Dickerson and Thomas Flanagan, *An Introduction to Government and Politics* (Scarborough 1988). For Dickerson and Flanagan 1688 marks the introduction of constitutionalism in

England. It is fair to say that most but not all historians regard eighteenth-century Britain as an aristocracy, while most but not all political scientists see it as a modern polity grounded on the principle of equality under the law.

11. Jean-Pierre Wallot, *Un Québec qui Bougeait: trame socio-politique du Québec au tournant du XIXe siècle* (Québec 1973); Pierre Tousignant, "Problématique pour une nouvelle approche de la Constitution de 1791," *Revue d'Histoire de l'Amérique Française* 27.2 (September 1973).

12. Hobbes, *Leviathan* Chapter XIII; Locke, *A Letter Concerning Toleration*. We find a perfect expression of this central tenet in Section 15 (1) of the Canadian Charter of Rights and Freedoms: "Every individual is equal before and under the law and has the right to the equal protection and equal benefit of the law." I explore the importance of the equality tenet for the colonies in *The Political Thought of Lord Durham* (Kingston 1988); Rainer Knopff describes its implications for a later liberal in "The Triumph of Liberalism in Canada: Laurier on Representation and Party Government," *Journal of Canadian Studies* Special Issue on Canadian Political Thought (Summer 1991).

13. *Le Canadien* 17 October 1838, 7 October 1839, 23 October 1839, 21 October 1842. David J. Bercuson and Barry Cooper explore the idea that privileged demands made in the name of ethnicity and nationality cannot be tolerated in liberal democracies (*Deconfederation: Canada without Quebec* [Toronto 1991]).

14. *Le Canadien* 18 February 1824.

15. *Le Canadien* 18 February 1824, 8 September 1824. This view of the parliamentary system was standard among liberals in Britain and the colonies at the time.

16. *Le Canadien* 8 September 1824.

17. Resolution 65 (Kennedy, *Statutes* 283). A number of the Resolutions derived from *le Canadien* and bear Parent's stamp. But as Kennedy notes, the publication of the Resolutions marked the parting of the ways among the reformers: "They illustrate better than any other document the matured attitude of Papineau and his followers, and distinguish them from the moderate and constitutional radicals" (*Statutes* 270n). And see the description of the Resolutions, probably by John Neilson, cited in W. P. M. Kennedy, *The Constitution of Canada: An Introduction to Its Development and Law* (London 1922) 108: "Eleven stood true; six contained both truth and falsehood; sixteen stood wholly false; seventeen stood doubtful; twelve were ridiculous; seven were repetitions; fourteen consisted only of abuse; four were false and seditious and five were good or indifferent." Neilson disagreed with at least two-thirds of the resolutions. We could make the same claim for Parent.

18. Resolution 34.

19. Resolution 66.

20. *Le Canadien* 18 February 1824.

21. *Le Canadien* 8 September 1824.

22. In March 1825 *le Canadien* went out of circulation, resuming in May 1831.

23. *Le Canadien* 19 June 1833. Falardeau's title for this article is "Nécessité d'un gouvernement responsable." The phrase "responsible government" does not come into common use until after the publication of the Durham Report, and Parent does not use it in this article. "Nécessité" was reprinted as a preface to Marcel-Pierre Hamel's edition of the Durham Report ("Retrospective d'Étienne Parent," *Le Rapport de Durham* [Québec 1948]).

24. *Le Canadien* 19 June 1833.

25. *Le Canadien* 19 June 1833.

26. *Le Canadien* 19 June 1833.

27. Parent tells the story of the legislative assembly's long struggle to exercise this right in "Pierre Bédard et ses deux fils" (Falardeau, *Étienne Parent* 1801-1874 37-38). And see *Le Canadien* 7 October 1839.

28. *Le Canadien* 18 February 1824, 7 October 1839.

29. *Le Canadien* 18 February 1824.

30. *Le Canadien* 18 February 1824.

31. Compare Verney, *The Analysis of Political Systems* 57, where it is argued that in both presidential and parliamentary government, the executive and legislative functions are "separated" "to a greater or lesser degree."

32. Howe to Lord John Russell (Kennedy, *Statutes* 405-06, 409).

33. Kennedy, *Statutes* 387-88, 406. Howe makes a distinction between "political" parties, defined as parties that are "pledged to approve certain principles of . . . policy which the people for a time approve," and "official" parties, that is, parties "pledged to keep themselves and their friends in office and to keep all others out." See page 406. Political parties were characteristic of England; an official party dominated the politics of Nova Scotia.

34. Kennedy, *Statutes* 384-87. Howe uses the term responsible government, by now accepted usage. Parent was familar with Howe's arguments. See *le Canadien* 23 October 1839.

35. Russell's speech on the union bill, 3 June 1839, was the immediate occasion for the four letters; Russell argued that responsible government was inappropriate in colonial dependencies. Howe draws on the arguments of the Durham Report, pitting Durham against Russell. The four letters were widely read in the period, and highly regarded. Howe never wrote anything better. For Russell's address, see Kennedy, *Statutes* 383-93.

36. Kennedy, *Statutes* 386. And see 389-90, 405-06. Beck writes, "Howe's acceptance of the Durham Report represented a fundamental change in attitude on his part . . . . A single reading of the Report had made him an instant convert." *Joseph Howe, Conservative Reformer, 1804-1848*, 2 vols. (Kingston 1982)

2: 199. It might be more accurate to say that in Durham Howe found arguments to lend his position focus.

37. Kennedy, *Statutes* 407.

38. Kennedy, *Statutes* 408.

39. Kennedy, *Statutes* 408.

40. Howe assures his readers that there would not be a constant turnover in the public service. A new party in office would not necessarily dismiss all previous appointments (Kennedy, *Statutes* 408).

41. Howe found the following formula in the Durham Report: "No money-votes should be allowed to originate without the previous consent of the Crown" (C. P. Lucas, ed., *Lord Durham's Report on the Affair of British North America*, 3 vols. [Oxford 1912] 2: 328).

42. Kennedy, *Statutes* 406.

43. See also Kennedy, *Statutes* 407, where in arguing against an elective upper legislative chamber—that favoured measure of the democrats—he says that an appointed upper chamber is useful to review measures and check undue haste or corruption in the popular branch. If legislative councillors held their seats for life, he goes on, "their independence of the Executive and of the people would be secured."

44. Kennedy, *Statutes* 390. Howe in fact thinks that parties would seldom or never cling to office after losing the confidence of the lower house.

45. *Le Canadien* 19 June 1833.

46. Kennedy, *Statutes* 410. See Howe's praise of the brave and able men who crushed Mackenzie's rebellion, 396.

47. ———, *Statutes* 410.

48. ———, *Statutes* 410.

49. ———, *Statutes* 411.

50. ———, *Statutes* 411.

51. ———, *Statutes* 386.

52. *Le Canadien* 7 May 1831.

53. Kennedy, *Statutes* 386.

54. ———, *Statutes* 385.

55. J. Murray Beck, "Joseph Howe, A Liberal, But With Qualifications," in Wayne A. Hunt, ed., *The Proceedings of the Joseph Howe Symposium* (Halifax 1984) 5.

56. H. D. Forbes, "Étienne Parent: Nationalist and Liberal," manuscript, 1983.

57. In public lectures given in the 1840s he argued for the expansion of commerce and industry in Lower Canada. See expecially those reprinted in Falardeau, *Étienne Parent 1802-1874* 113-99.

58. See Walter Bagehot, *The English Constitution*, first published in 1867. J. W. Burrow provides a brief account of Bagehot's rejection of "balance" in *Whigs*

and Liberals: Continuity and Change in English Political Thought (Oxford 1988). See also R. C. B. Risk, "Common Law Thought in Late Nineteenth-Century Canada: On Burying One's Grandfather," manuscript, 1988.

59. Smith, "The Ideological Origins of Canadian Confederation" 29.
60. Michael Sandel, *Liberalism and the Limits of Justice* (Cambridge 1982); Will Kymlicka, *Liberalism, Community and Culture* (Cambridge 1989).

CHAPTER TEN

THE PROVINCIAL RIGHTS MOVEMENT:
TENSIONS BETWEEN LIBERTY AND
COMMUNITY IN LEGAL LIBERALISM

Robert C. Vipond

Editors' introduction: "Tensions Between Liberty and Community in Legal
Liberalism" is an abbreviated version of Chapter 5 of Robert C. Vipond's
*Liberty and Community: Canadian Federalism and the Failure of the Consti-
tution* (Albany NY: State University of New York 1991). Earlier in the original
chapter Vipond sets out in more detail the objections of the provincial rights
movement to Sir John A. Macdonald's disallowance in 1881 of the Ontario
Rivers and Streams Act. The provincial autonomists argued that the prime
minister's action was intolerable not only because it transgressed the division
of legislative powers in the British North America Act, but because it violated
the principle of self-government associated with parliamentary responsible
government, and, more than this, threatened the very rule of law. The
subsequent sections of the chapter are given here in their entirety.

I

During the first decade of Confederation there was no serious partisan disagreement about the general rules governing the federal

government's exercise of disallowance. The opposition, whether Liberal or Conservative, sometimes quibbled with the government's use of the power in particular cases, but there was no disagreement about the general principle that the disallowance of provincial legislation was legitimate as long as, but only as long as, it was confined to jurisdictional questions. That consensus was shattered in the 1880s. As the nation-building pretensions of the Macdonald government grew, so did its use of disallowance. And as disallowance came to be used more broadly, so its legitimacy became more questionable and the debate surrounding it more partisan.

The growing controversy over the use of disallowance came to a head in 1881 when the Macdonald government struck down Ontario's Rivers and Streams Act, an act that declared that all persons have the right to float logs down Ontario waterways. In addition it stipulated how those who had invested time and money in improving these waterways were to be compensated for their efforts by those who made use of the improvements. The law had been passed in part to resolve a dispute between Peter McLaren, who had widened a tributary of the Ottawa River, and Boyd Caldwell, a logger whose attempts to use the widened river had been thwarted by McLaren. McLaren complained that the Ontario law deprived him of his property rights. Having at considerable expense transformed a stream that was un-navigable "in a state of nature"[1] into a small river, McLaren maintained that he had certain proprietary rights, among them the absolute right to decide who could use the river and at what price. He therefore petitioned the federal government to have the law disallowed.

It is a sign both of the depth of partisan feeling and the constitutional moment that when it came time to explain the reasons for the disallowance, John A. Macdonald himself took responsibility for writing the official report. Macdonald concentrated in the report, as McLaren had in his petition, on the effect of the Rivers and Streams Act on property rights. "The effect of the Act," Macdonald asserted, "seems to be to take away the use of his property from one person and give it to another, forcing the owner, practically, to become a toll-keeper against his will, if he wishes to get any compensation for being deprived of his rights."[2]

Macdonald's defence of his disallowance of the Rivers and Streams Act was a turning point in the development of the provincial rights movement in Ontario in that it provoked the first concerted attack on the veto power itself. The Mowat government's protest was joined by Liberal Members of Parliament and the Liberal press. Edward Blake argued that Macdonald's action "would impair the Federal principle, and injuriously affect the autonomy of the institutions of our several Provinces were this power to be exercised on subjects which are within the exclusive competence of the Local Legislatures, on the ground that in the opinion of His Excellency's advisors, or of that of Parliament, any such legislation is wrong."[3] The Toronto *Globe* put it more pithily:

Never once for fifteen years has the Dominion interfered, never at all has there been any cause for interference. And now for the first time in the history of Confederation, the Dominion has asserted a right to interfere in matters within our own concern under the Constitution, within our own province. An Act dealing with our rivers and streams has been flung back in our face and the whole force of the Union used to prevent its becoming law.[4]

The Rivers and Streams case thus fundamentally recast the debate over disallowance. The provincial autonomists had argued for the first fifteen years of Confederation that the disallowance power, when used as a jurisdictional veto "to guard [the federal government] against encroachments by the Provinces,"[5] was consistent with the federal principle and the fundamental conventions of responsible, parliamentary self-government. Macdonald's tortured defence of the Rivers and Streams veto forced the autonomists to reconsider this compromise. It demonstrated that as long as disallowance could be used legitimately and routinely to strike down provincial legislation on the pretext that a provincial act offended against "the general interests of the Dominion," it could be used against provincial legislation that clearly was *intra vires* the provincial government. The autonomists began to understand, in other words, that the great flaw in the power of disallowance was that it granted discretion to the federal government to determine whether legislation was jurisdictionally sound and consistent with the national interest. And they began to realize, equally, that as long as disallowance were controlled by someone like Macdonald, the definition of what was in the national interest was almost infinitely expandable. If a question as parochial as the one at issue in the Rivers and Streams case could be construed as a matter of national importance, almost anything could; and as Macdonald came in the 1880s to disallow provincial laws more frequently on the shadowy grounds that they were inconsistent with the "national interest," the autonomists tumbled to the conclusion that the power of disallowance had become a dangerous weapon in the prime minister's larger plan of centralization.[6]

What was at stake in the Rivers and Streams case, argued the London *Advertiser,* "was not simply a matter of rivers and streams," nor even a matter of private rights or the compensation to be given therefor." What was at issue, rather, was "something above and beyond both," namely "the right of the Province to enjoy the inestimable privilege of local self-government" on matters "within [its] own sphere."[7] The autonomists had believed that their sphere of jurisdiction was protected by "a barrier of a superior law."[8] The Rivers and Streams episode demonstrated, to the contrary, that the federal government was prepared to "trample under foot the barriers which the principles of the Constitution impose."[9] The charge, in short, was not simply that Macdonald had applied the rules inconsistently, but that the rules were themselves flawed. Macdonald's policy of disallowance was "a death blow" aimed "at the Federal system, and the responsibility of the Provincial Ministry to the Local Legislature and electorate."[10] That is why the Rivers and Streams case elicited such a fierce response.

II

The autonomists insisted on making the Rivers and Streams disallowance a major constitutional issue, because it illustrated rather graphically that, however defined, a federal veto threatened provincial power and the larger idea of federalism on which provincial power rested. But this summary still fails to capture the deepest strain of the autonomists' objection to Macdonald's use of disallowance. For if the Rivers and Streams episode was a turning point in the understanding and practice of disallowance in Canada, it is still more significant for the light it sheds on the broader intellectual context in which the provincial autonomists positioned themselves. As the foregoing passages suggest, the autonomists took issue with the Macdonald government's use of disallowance not merely because it deviated from the established rules that were meant to govern and limit the use of the veto power, nor simply because they came to believe that the veto power could not be reconciled with the federal principle under any circumstances. The more general and ultimately more serious claim, rather, was that disallowance was incompatible with the ideal of the rule of law and with the larger "transatlantic project" of liberal reform being carried on in the name of the rule of law.

In one respect, of course, there is nothing surprising about the autonomists' emphasis on the rule of law. Most of them, after all, were lawyers turned politicians who, if nothing else, had a solid professional interest in asserting the importance of law. Most were committed to the view that politics was best studied and understood through the lens of constitutional politics and legal forms. Moreover, the ideology of the rule of law was a crucial component of their imperialism. One of the basic claims for the superiority of the empire and, indeed, British civilization more generally, was its ancient and honourable tradition that arbitrary power must be curbed and that the rule of law is especially important in protecting liberty against tyranny. By the mid-nineteenth century this view had been reduced to a common political slogan and had become a test of conventional legitimacy. Certainly in Canada no mainstream politician would have dissented from it.

In the late-nineteenth century, however, the ideal of the rule of law came to be associated more precisely with a powerful intellectual movement of Anglo-American legal reform that attempted to show how a scientific understanding of the law could be put in the service of liberal ends. The spiritual home of this "legal liberalism" (as it has been called) was in the universities, and while it "began to appear as early as 1850" it "became most conspicuously abundant in Anglo-American academic circles during the 1870s and 1880s,"[11] that is, at precisely the moment the provincial rights movement was hitting its stride. In England the movement was centred at Oxford, where it came to be associated with the likes of Dicey, Pollock, Anson, Holland, and Bryce; in the United States, it was most closely associated with Harvard and the efforts of Langdell, Holmes, Ames, and Williston. In either case, it profited from an extraordinary transatlantic collaboration among legal scholars who were also friends. There were, of course, many important differences among such scholars, some of which reflected different national styles and problems, others of which are more idiosyncratic and difficult to categorize. Still, it is possible to describe relatively easily, at least at the level of intellectual caricature, what united these various minds and what forms the core of legal liberalism.[12]

The movement of legal liberalism was concerned to place the law, and more specifically courts guided by scientific principles, in the service of individual liberty. As David Sugarman has pointed out,[13] legal scholars like Dicey were much taken with John Stuart Mill's celebration of creative individualism, and they took no less seriously than did Mill the problem of protecting individual autonomy either from other individuals or from the state, or both. Given the apparently natural predilection for individuals and political bodies to want to expand their power at the expense of others, the crucial political problem for late-nineteenth-century liberalism was to set clear limits or boundaries within which each actor is sovereign, that is, free to will without interference from others. The task for liberalism was to distinguish public from private, state from society, other-regarding from self-regarding behaviour. In short, the irreducible liberal aim was to maximize liberty by keeping each actor within appropriate and assigned limits.

The distinctive contribution of legal scholarship in the late nineteenth century was to suggest that the law contained objective principles that could be used to enforce the boundaries or limits of individual or state behaviour. Rather than entrusting the protection of liberty to the discretion of political officials whose judgment could be distorted by self-interest in one of its many forms; rather than making the protection of rights a matter of statesmanlike balancing of individual and public considerations, the view of legal liberalism was that the boundaries should be settled, inferred scientifically from a number of general principles, and applied objectively by the courts.

Perhaps the greatest champion of this vision of the rule of law was A. V. Dicey, whose *Law of the Constitution*[14] furnished an extraordinarily influential interpretation of the systematic, purposeful development of the rule of law in England. Dicey's story of the triumph of the rule of law in England was unapologetically nationalistic; the British story thus stood in stark contrast to the baleful decline of the rule of law in France. Yet for all his anglophilia, even Dicey seems to have been willing to admit that the rule of law (and from that, the rule of courts) was most deeply entrenched not in Britain, but in the United States, where the common law was supplemented by judicial review and by a legalistic conception of federalism.[15] The European "americomania" that Dicey described as a

238

correspondent for *The Nation*, and which he seems to have shared, was an entirely apt manifestation of legal liberalism.[16]

To the legal liberal, the beauty of the American conception of the rule of law was its versatility in describing and explaining a whole universe of legal and political relationships between individuals and the state. The premise of legal liberalism, as Duncan Kennedy has noted,[17] "was that the legal system consisted of a set of institutions, each of which had the traits of a legal actor," and each of which was comparable or even convertible one to the other. "Each institution had been delegated by the sovereign people a power to carry out its will, which was absolute within but void outside its sphere." "The physical boundaries between citizens" were in this sense "like those between states," and "the non-physical division of jurisdiction over a given object between legislature and citizen was like that between state and federal governments." Moreover, each legal actor had to worry that this sphere of sovereignty would be challenged, violated, or compromised by another actor. Precisely "because all the actors held formally identical powers of absolute dominion, one could speak equally of trespass by neighbor against neighbor, by state against citizen, and by citizen against state." And precisely because the problem of setting and maintaining boundaries was the same throughout the system, the task of the judge was "identical whether the occasion of its exercise was a quarrel between neighbors, between sovereigns, or between citizen and legislature." The task of the law, be it the common law, the law of federalism, or judicial review under the Bill of Rights, was to prevent usurpation and preserve rights.

This understanding of the purpose and function of the law was developed largely in the universities, but it cannot be overstressed that it was at base a project to reform the way in which the law was actually applied by lawyers and courts. The historical importance of this conception of legal liberalism consists in its influence in shaping political and legal practice in the 1880s, the 1890s, and beyond. In England, for example, Dicey's understanding of the rule of law was a crucial element in the political debate over the legitimacy of administrative tribunals and the regulatory state. In the United States, this conception clearly had great appeal to the Supreme Court in what has been called the *laissez-faire* era, that is, roughly 1880 to 1930. In Canada, the least studied or known of the three, this vision of the rule of law was adapted for practice in a rather pure, albeit inchoate, form by the provincial rights movement.

The Canadian legal community contributed little to the general or theoretical elaboration of legal liberalism in England and the United States, but it followed developments in both places closely. In a few important cases the external influence in shaping the Canadian legal mind was quite direct and explicit. David Mills, whose elaborate defence of provincial autonomy is arguably unparalleled in English Canada, learned his law at the University of Michigan under one of the great mid-century systematizers of American law, Thomas Cooley. Through Cooley and others, Mills was introduced quite directly to a vision of law that anticipated many of the core concepts of legal liberalism, and he kept abreast of American legal developments thereafter.[18] In most of the other cases, the foreign influence was less direct but scarcely less important. American cases were frequently cited in Ontario courts well before Confederation,[19] and the names of Story, Kent, and others cropped up not infrequently in the provincialists' defence of provincial autonomy.[20] More typically, however, especially from the 1880s on,[21] Canadians looked to English law for guidance and to English lawyers for authority. The autonomists had read Dicey,[22] admired Bryce,[23] and generally attempted to keep astride of developments in English law.

The provincial autonomists were quick to realize that the doctrine of legal liberalism provided a congenial framework for understanding their own experiences with and hopes for federalism. The BNA Act was a "superior law," a "constitution" that divided legislative jurisdiction into two independent "spheres" of power that "are mutually exclusive."[24] Within each sphere, therefore, each government was "sovereign or supreme," subject only to the will of its electorate. If the federal government attempted to act on a matter within provincial jurisdiction, it was in effect "trespassing" on another government's property. "So far as the Provinces continue their autonomy as Provinces," the *Advertiser* concluded, "the Federal Government has no more authority than it has over the affairs of the state of New York."[25] "The Provinces for Provincial purposes are not in the Union. For all these exclusive purposes, they are as much out of the Union as if no Union existed."[26]

The object of federalism was thus to preserve the "freedom," "autonomy," "independence," indeed the "rights" of the individual provinces from other governments in much the same way as the object of the liberal state was to protect the rights of individuals from overbearing governmental power. The autonomists were quite aware of the rhetorical possibilities of describing provincial autonomy as a form of liberalism, and they therefore drew out the analogy between provincial and individual rights enthusiastically. Thus Mills, in a particularly expressive editorial written for the *Advertiser* in March 1883, explained to his readers that, within the sphere of their jurisdiction, the provinces had the right to do what they pleased so long as it did not encroach "upon the rights of others."[27] That qualification understood (and it is an exception that again reflects Mills's liberalism), the provincial legislatures were free to act as they pleased. They were as free, that is, as any rights-bearing individual in a liberal state.

Mills drew out the implications of the analogy explicitly. The federal government, he argued, had no more right to second-guess the wisdom of an act that was within provincial jurisdiction than the state had a right to tell citizens what religious beliefs they must hold, what foods they must eat, what colour clothes they must wear, or what crops they must plant:

We go to the farmer, and we find him cultivating his fields in a way which we think a system of scientific agriculture does not warrant. We tell him that the prosperity of the country depends upon the prosperity of each individual, and that the wrongheadedness of himself and hundreds of others are interfering with the general well-being of the country. We call in some one else of our own way of thinking who expresses similar opinions. He replies, "I am cultivating my own lands; upon them I am master of my own actions; in their cultivation my judgment and not yours must prevail, because I, and not you, have exclusive jurisdiction here. It is possible I may err, but I don't think you are infallible, and since the judgment of somebody must prevail, the law which gives me exclusive control here says that it is my judgment and not yours which shall be preferred. It is your privilege to give me advice, but it is not your right to give me commands."[28]

The idea that the state had a right to tell individuals how to act or behave within that sphere of individual autonomy was, from this perspective, simply indefensible. "The most absolute Government that the world has ever known never ventured to carry out in minute detail any such political theory,"[29] and nothing could justify it if it tried. "It may be wrong to invest money in a steamboat instead of a farm," he argued in another version, "but these are wrongs based upon the rights of a man to do what he pleases with his own—the right of preferring his own discretion to the discretion of his neighbor."[30] These illustrations all occurred in the context of Mills's attempts to explain why Macdonald's use of the disallowance power was wrong. As individuals have rights to do as they please consistent with the rights of others, so too the "Local Legislature has the power to do as it chooses, so long as it does not interfere with the corresponding rights of others."[31] And just as the state has no right to tell the farmer how to plant his crops, so "neither Sir John Macdonald nor any other outside party has any right to substitute their judgment for the judgment of those to whom the constitution has entrusted the matter."[32]

The analogy between federalism and liberalism was useful, in other words, in explaining the autonomists' growing discontent with the Macdonald administration. The protection of rights turned on the strict maintenance of the boundaries that separated individual from individual, state from individual, and, in federalism, state from state. For the provinces to enjoy their rights, each government, federal and provincial, had to "keep within the boundaries drawn by the constitution,"[33] just as the state had to recognize the boundaries of legitimate public power if individual rights were to be maintained. The difficulty in federal Canada, according to the autonomists, was that the Macdonald government had shown scant regard for these jurisdictional boundaries and for the provincial rights they protected. Nowhere was this clearer to the autonomists than in the controversy over disallowance, and that is why it became a rallying point. The Rivers and Streams case was interpreted as a grave threat to provincial rights because it signalled the federal government's intention to "interfere" with, "violate," "trespass" upon, "invade," "plunder," and "usurp" provincial rights. As long as the exercise of disallowance was considered acceptable, it was subject to the "treachery," "vindictiveness," and "intrigue" of a prime minister trying to "impose his will upon" unwilling provinces.[34]

As the autonomists viewed the problem of disallowance within the context of the rule of law, so they looked to the rule of law to provide a solution. If the federal government had taken to using the veto power to impose its political will upon the provinces, then the remedy was to have "a clear, explicit amendment to our Constitution, which [would] put an end to the vetoing power of the

Dominion Administration,"[35] and would leave the resolution of jurisdictional disputes "as in the neighboring republic, entirely to the courts."[36] Only this would "relieve the Local Legislature from all possible intrigue between the leader of the [provincial] Opposition and his confederates in the Dominion Administration."[37]

Of course this was not the first time an amendment to do away with disallowance had been suggested; Mills had objected to the veto power as early as 1869.[38] But it was only in the 1880s, with the theory of the rule of law and the practice of the Macdonald administration fresh in their minds, that it became fashionable to advocate the abolition of disallowance. David Mills used the editorial columns of the London *Advertiser* to advance the idea of abolishing disallowance formally;[39] the Toronto *Globe* supported the idea of a constitutional amendment to jettison the veto;[40] and Oliver Mowat made it the first item on the agenda of the first Interprovincial Conference of provincial premiers, in 1887.[41] The federal government was obviously opposed to any change, but this did not deter the autonomists from trying to convince the Imperial Parliament that the disallowance power should be expunged from the BNA Act, even if that had to be done without the federal government's consent. Even here the convertible categories of constitutional law and private law, federalism and contracts, proved a useful guide. The BNA Act, the autonomists urged, should be understood as a "contract" among the several provinces, which collectively had agreed to delegate a specified set of legislative powers upon a federal government that, by the terms of the contract, they had created. As the federal government was a creation of the contract, not one of the contractees, it was perfectly legitimate to alter the terms of the contract without its consent.[42]

In the end, the autonomists' demands fell on deaf ears. Neither the federal government nor the imperial authorities took the provincial "compact theory" particularly seriously. Indeed, the imperial authorities did not even pay the provincial premiers the courtesy of replying officially to the request.[43] This failure, however, only served to redouble the autonomists' efforts. If they could not read disallowance out of the BNA Act altogether, they could at least render it expendable. To that end, Edward Blake proposed an amendment to the Supreme Court Act, the object of which was to make judicial review a more attractive alternative to disallowance than it previously had been.[44]

Blake's argument followed directly from the premise of legal liberalism. The idea of the federal principle, he argued, was to create two mutually exclusive compartments of legislative power in which "the sphere of the jurisdiction of the one is limited by the sphere of the jurisdiction of the other."[45] To allow the federal government to strike down provincial legislation was in effect to allow "one of these two limited Governments ... [to] decide the extent of the limits, of what in a sense, is its rival government."[46] Disallowance thus permitted a "political executive" to discharge "a legal and a judicial function."[47] Understood as such, it violated one of the fundamental principles of Anglo-Saxon law, for it allowed the federal government to judge cases in whose outcome it had an interest. There was a sense, Blake argued, in which the act of disallowance therefore "is the decision of a party in his own cause."[48] It would be far better to enlist "neutral, dignified and judicial aid"[49] in the enforcement of jurisdictional boundaries. It would be far preferable to leave the interpretation of the constitutional division of powers to those who are trained to see federal and provincial jurisdiction, in Mills's memorable phrase, "as if they were separated by land marks visible to the eye."[50]

On the surface, this concerted attack on disallowance triumphed impressively. The view that policing the boundaries between federal and provincial jurisdiction is a "legal and judicial function" became dogma, and as dogma changed so practice was gradually altered. To be sure, the practice of disallowing provincial legislation did not disappear overnight, but by the early decades of this century the disallowance power had almost completely been replaced by judicial review.[51] In light of the historical record, it seems plausible to suppose that the power of disallowance became unusable by the early decades of this century because the crucial audiences—provincial premiers, federal cabinet ministers, and certain portions of the electorate—came to view the veto power as the autonomists wanted them to view it: as a violation of constitutional principle to which political costs were attached and for which there was a principled, that is, judicial, alternative. This certainly seems to have been the attitude of Ernest Lapointe, Mackenzie King's veteran minister of justice, who rose before the House of Commons in 1937 to explain that as long as "the provincial legislatures feel that they are still supreme and sovereign within the sphere of their jurisdiction"[52] it would be difficult for Ottawa to veto provincial acts. The very fact that disallowance has essentially passed into desuetude suggests that the autonomists' view of disallowance has carried the day.[53]

III

Yet, at a deeper level, the Millsian attack upon disallowance did not end the debate over disallowance so much as it brought it back full circle to its point of origin; and in doing so, it paradoxically brought to the surface the problem of protecting individual and minority rights that had been largely submerged in the 1880s and 1890s. To recall, a number of the leading Confederationists had assumed that disallowance would and should be used to protect individuals and minorities from tyrannical provincial legislation. As we have seen in detail, this view of disallowance was quickly repudiated both by Conservative and Liberal administrations, who preferred to use disallowance as a jurisdictional veto when they used it at all. As we have also seen, the debate over disallowance therefore quite quickly resolved itself into a debate about federalism and the integrity of provincial communities and their legislatures.

Mills's original contribution to this debate in the 1880s and early 1890s inadvertently challenged the terms of the debate, for his contention that disallowance violated the rule of law, and his analogy between individual and provincial rights, re-introduced the theme of individual rights and the problem for which disallowance had once been seen as the solution. Mills had meant to use the analogy between individual and provincial rights to strengthen the case for the complete and utter autonomy of local decision-making. But the analogy was only as strong as the object of the comparison was deep. In Mills's view, the rights of the provinces were worthy of protection in the same way or to the extent that the rights of individuals were worthy of protection. To Mills the idea of rights protected by law was not simply a neat linguistic analogy that helped him to illustrate the dangers of federal disallowance; it was, more fundamentally, a valuable and intrinsically worthwhile model of political organization. Mills found the rights analogy persuasive, in other words, because he believed not merely that provincial rights could be compared to individual rights, but because, as a liberal, he believed that individuals have rights.

The difficulty with the analogy between provincial and individual rights, therefore, is that it cut both ways. On the one hand, it reinforced the argument for provincial autonomy by providing a well-nigh unassailable foundation for the integrity of provincial legislation. But the same association that strengthened the claim for provincial autonomy could be used just as easily to undercut it. For if the basis of the claim for provincial autonomy was its likeness or comparability to individual autonomy, could the consistent provincialist really sit idly by as a provincial legislature violated the rights of its citizens? If the provincial autonomists were really committed to the rule of law as the bulwark of liberty, could they simply ignore it when a provincial legislature abridged the liberty of some of its citizens? And if they could not, did not disallowance provide one means by which to thwart vicious provincial legislation, even (or perhaps especially) that provincial legislation that was clearly within provincial jurisdiction?

One answer to these questions was supplied by Mills himself when, as minister of justice in the Laurier cabinet between 1897 and 1902, he discharged the responsibility of vetting provincial legislation with a view to its disallowance. Considering Mills's firmly held and frequently expressed view that disallowance ought to be abolished, it is curious that as minister of justice he considered the use of disallowance at all. Yet use it he did. In all, Mills was responsible for recommending the disallowance of thirteen provincial and territorial acts in his tenure as minister of justice, which is to say that he disallowed as many acts in his five years as minister of justice as his predecessors in the post had vetoed in the previous ten.[54]

The way Mills used the veto power is still more remarkable than the sheer number of laws disallowed, however. Mills's patience was tested most sorely by the government of British Columbia, which passed a series of bills at the turn of the century that attempted to prohibit Asians from either immigrating to or working in British Columbia. In most cases, Mills seems to have proceeded on the traditional assumption that the federal government could legitimately invalidate only those laws that were *ultra vires* the British Columbia legislature or were inconsistent with some more general federal policy. Thus when Mills was called upon to judge a British Columbia law that effectively prohibited the immigration into the province of any person who could not write out an application "in the characters of some European language,"[55] he did not hesitate to exercise the veto. Such educational requirements, he wrote, were simply "inconsistent with the general policy of the law"[56] of the federal government. When, on the other hand, the British Columbia legislature acted in a way that was clearly within its exclusive jurisdiction, Mills usually stayed his hand. Having explained that the aforementioned immigration bill was repugnant to the federal government's policy, Mills turned around in the same memorandum to explain that he could do nothing to blunt the effect of a similarly discriminatory law that disenfranchised Chinese, Japanese, and Indian voters in Vancouver municipal elections. "Such enactments," he explained dryly, "are entirely local and domestic in their nature, and sufficiently justified, so far as the powers to be exercised by the government of Canada are concerned, by the fact that the local legislature has considered their provisions expedient or desirable."[57]

In fact, however, Mills was neither able nor, it seems, disposed, to contrive such a neat jurisdictional rationale for every one of the British Columbia acts that came to his attention. Mills's duty as minister of justice in these cases was complicated by the fact that British Columbia's legislation had elicited a formal diplomatic protest from the Japanese government. Mills was clearly under significant pressure from the Foreign Office to prevent these provincial acts from jeopardizing Britain's relations with Japan. In the course of disallowing two acts that sought to disqualify those of Japanese and Chinese extraction from being employed by provincial corporations, he essentially suggested to the government of British Columbia that the disallowance of these acts was a small price to pay for "a friendly sentiment on the part of Japan in matters of commerce and otherwise."[58] The British Columbia laws might well have been *ultra vires* anyway as legislation the pith and substance of which dealt with matters—immigration and the rights of aliens—on which the federal government has paramount authority. From Mills's point of view, however, the existence of clear imperial interests obviated any need for a detailed jurisdictional analysis along these lines. For the purposes of disallowance, it was sufficient that the British Columbia legislation conflicted with larger, imperial interests.

Yet by shifting the discussion over the British Columbia laws from jurisdiction strictly speaking to the larger, political interests at stake, Mills also made it easier to inject into the review of these laws the very considerations of justice that he had earlier argued were incompatible with the exercise of disallowance. For at the root of the Foreign Office's fears that the British Columbia legislation could poison British-Japanese relations, was the serious, and from Mills's perspective legitimate, complaint that the British Columbia laws discriminated gratuitously and unjustly against the rights of Japanese workers in the province. In his explanatory report to the British Columbia government, Mills could easily have confined himself to a description of the *realpolitik* of the situation, concluded that the British Columbia legislation had to be sacrificed for the larger good of the empire, and left it at that. He did not. He considered the premier of British Columbia to be an "unscrupulous and dangerous" character;[59] he seems personally to have disliked the British Columbia policy; and as a result he apparently could not resist the temptation to read the British Columbia government a lesson in liberalism. The problem with the legislation, he argued, was not merely that it threatened to become an irritant in British-Japanese relations; the problem was that the legislation was "*justly* regarded as offensive by a friendly power."[60] In the end, Mills's decision to disallow some but not all of the acts on jurisdictional grounds clearly reflected the dilemma that he faced in attempting to find a balance between provincial sovereignty, the larger interests of the empire, and what he called quite explicitly "the justice of the case."[61]

Admittedly, it is easy to overstate the importance of such considerations of justice, of the rights of a minority subjected to systematic discrimination, in Mills's calculations. These considerations were probably no more than an undercurrent in his discussion of the British Columbia legislation, and Mills was himself ambivalent on the question of equal rights for Asian immigrants. Still, given the very powerful pressure to exclude such considerations altogether from the discussion of disallowance, even such an undercurrent is noteworthy. Moreover, when the issue was one that Mills considered to be morally unambiguous, protecting the rights of property, for instance, the question of rights came to the fore.

The most striking example in this latter category concerns Mills's threat to strike down an Ontario law that required companies not incorporated in Ontario to apply and pay for a licence to do business in the province. Again, Mills could well have disposed of the Ontario law simply on jurisdictional grounds. As he put it in his official report to the attorney general of Ontario, the Licensing Act arguably trenched both on the federal government's authority to legislate for the "peace, order and good government of the country" and on its exclusive power to regulate trade and commerce; it flew in the face of several judicial precedents; and the Ontario act was similar to several others that had already been disallowed.[62]

What is curious, then, is that when the premier of Ontario, George Ross, responded to Mills's report with a promise to amend the sections that were jurisdictionally questionable, Mills rejoined by saying in effect that Mr. Ross had misunderstood the federal government's objections. "The question is not," Mills wrote, "whether you have the power to tax Dominion corporations more than you do those of the local legislature, created for a similar purpose, but whether we ought to permit the policy of the Dominion to be frustrated by such unjust provincial legislation."[63] The real objection to the Ontario law, therefore, was not that it exceeded Provincial jurisdiction, although Mills was certainly suspicious of it on those grounds. The more basic problem, rather, was that it imposed a burden on companies incorporated under federal law that it did not impose on Ontario companies; it discriminated against federal corporations as if these were somehow "foreign corporations."[64] Were the shoe on the other foot, were Ottawa to pass a similar licensing law that disadvantaged Ontario corporations, Mills was quite sure that Ontario "would at once cry out against our legislation, not because it was *ultra vires*, but because it would be unjust."[65] All the federal government was asking was that Ontario "recognize the principle of equality."[66] He concluded: "I think you see what my position is. The question of *ultra vires* in this matter is quite subordinate to the general question of public policy."[67]

These opinions cannot easily be reconciled with the purely jurisdictional use of disallowance that was current in the 1870s, much less with Mills's unconditional denunciation of disallow-ance that he made quite routinely in the 1880s. But it would be a mistake to conclude that Mills's position was, on this evidence, either inexplicably contradictory or expediently self-serving. Mills did not abandon his principles in these cases so much as he began to face up to the enormous, if frequently hidden, tension within them— the tension, that is, between his devotion to provincial autonomy on the one hand and the liberal protection of rights on the other. The tension did not manifest itself as long as Mills could assume that provincial autonomy and liberal rights were mutually reinforcing, in effect, as long as Liberals controlled most provincial legislatures and Tories the federal Parliament. The possibility, post-1896, that provincial legislatures would act unjustly and that he would be in a position to stop injustice in its tracks before and in preference to a legal challenge, forced him to consider violating the rule of law (in the form of provincial autonomy) in order to protect the rule of law (in the form of equal individual rights). That is the deep tension, not to say incoherence, in Mills's Canadian application of the late-nineteenth-century understanding of the rule of law.

IV

The tension in Mills's thought between federalism and liberalism helps to explain the curious evolution of the power of disallow-ance; it also sheds light on the contemporary debate over the implications of the Charter of Rights for the preservation of community and liberty. One of the most subtle and provocative analyses of the Charter's meaning in this regard is Charles Taylor's recent contribution to the series of research reports published in conjunction with the McDonald Commission, an essay entitled "Alternative Futures: Legitimacy, Identity and Alienation in Late Twentieth Century Canada."[68] Taylor is concerned to understand, in the Canadian context, the "malaise of modernity," which in one form or another and to one degree or another seems to afflict all modern societies. By modern, Taylor means societies centrally dedicated to the maximization of freedom as understood in two distinct, and not perfectly compatible, ways. The first meaning of freedom, associated especially with the classical liberalism expounded by philosophers like John Locke, focuses on individuals as rational, independent agents "who discover their purposes in themselves" rather than seeing themselves as "part of some cosmic order, where their nature was to be understood by their relation to that order."[69] What follows from this definition of freedom as self-definition is that "as a free subject, one is owed respect for one's rights and has certain guaranteed freedoms." The condition of freedom thus understood is that one "must be able to choose and act, within limits, free from arbitrary interference of others." The "modern subject," in short, "is an equal bearer of rights. This status is part of what sustains his identity."[70]

But if freedom has often been defined as bearing rights and has centred on the individual, there is another sense of modern freedom that is better defined as self-governance, and that has historically focused on the community. "The fact that we govern ourselves

is an important part of our dignity as free subjects." But this definition of freedom as self-governance leads in quite a different direction than the first definition, for it suggests that "the modern subject . . . is far from being an independent, atomic agent." On the
contrary, "an individual is sustained . . . by the culture which elab-
orates and maintains the vocabulary of his or her self-understanding."[71] The full realization of freedom so understood can only be
achieved through identification with the community and by
participation as a citizen.

These two definitions of freedom—as individual rights and as
citizen participation—have co-existed in some form of dynamic balance since they were first expounded during the Enlightenment;
there is nothing new in this. What is distinctive about the situation
that we face in the late twentieth century, according to Taylor, is that
the individualistic, atomistic, rights-based dimension of modern liberalism has begun to crowd out or threaten the "community" dimension.[72] This threat can be illustrated in a number of ways. The
demand for greater individual freedom, defined especially in terms
of material well-being, requires, among other things: a population
that is mobile; a government that can provide a wide range of services efficiently and operate a welfare system to mitigate the effects
of economic dislocation and historical patterns of discrimination;
the concentration of public and private energies to distribute goods
and opportunities efficiently; and a system of courts that will protect
rights "even against the process of collective decision-making of the
society, against the majority will, or the prevailing consensus."[73] Yet,
as Taylor points out, these conditions of individual freedom serve
to undermine community. Mobility destroys the fabric of stable,
traditional communities; the need to provide services creates bureau-
cratized, largely unaccountable, government; the "culture of rights"
effectively "circumvent[s] majority decision making through court
judgments," and so "further entrenches taking a [position of] distance from community decision making";[74] and concentration creates
the sort of centralization that makes citizenship remote and participation difficult and unrewarding. The result, perhaps most plainly
evident in the United States, is governmental overload, ungovern-
ability, litigiousness, and a decline in even the most routine forms
of citizen participation. "Looked at in the light of the full demands
of the modern identity," Taylor concludes, "the atrophy of citizen
power negates an important dimension of our dignity as free agents,

251

and hence poses a potential long-term threat to the legitimacy of a modern society."[75]

The alternative to these modern strains and tensions, Taylor argues, is not to abandon modernity, which is probably impossible anyway, but to revitalize the other side of the modern project—what he calls the "participatory model"—which stresses decentralization, political participation, attachment to community, and the democratic protection of liberty. Taylor clearly endorses the participatory model as a matter of principle. More importantly, he argues that it is particularly well suited to Canada, where, he says, "the sense of citizen dignity" has tended historically "to take the participatory rather than the rights forms,"[76] and where there is a long history of regional resistance to centralization.

It is here that Taylor allies himself most closely with what Richard Simeon and others have called the provincialist understanding of Canada. For like the provincialists who opposed the entrenchment of a Charter of Rights on the grounds that it would undermine the integrity of local decision-making, Taylor is careful to tie the preference for greater decentralization to democratic or participatory aspirations. Decentralization is desirable because it offers the best opportunity to counter "the malaise of modernity. " "The fate of the participatory model in Canada," he argues, "of the continued health of our practices of self-rule, depends on our continuing resistance to centralization":

If our aim is to combat, rather than adjust to, the trends to growth, concentration and mobility, and the attendant bureaucratic opacity and rigidity of representative democracy, then some measures of decentralization are indispensable, with the consequent strengthening of more localized, smaller-scale units of self-rule.[77]

In the end, Taylor sketches this choice for Canada:

In a sense, to oversimplify and dramatize, we can see two package solutions emerging out of the mists to the problem of sustaining a viable modern polity in the late twentieth century. One is the route of political centralization, at the cost of some citizen alienation but compensated for by an increasing incorporation of the American model in which dignity finds political expression in the defense of rights. The other is the route of continued decentralization, and a continued attempt to maintain and extend our historic participatory model, at the cost of putting a greater and greater strain on political vision and inventiveness through mechanisms of political coordination.[78]

Taylor's preference is clear: "If we look at Canada's future . . . in terms of the way this country can best face the strains of modernity and the dangers of political breakdown implicit in them—then there seems no doubt that the centralizing solution would be an immensely regressive step."[79] Apart from everything else, the decentralizing, participatory model "is more in line with our traditional political culture."[80] Indeed, "the strength of our historic regional societies makes it virtually mandatory for us to practise a more decentralized style of government than other comparable federations."[81]

Taylor's defence of the participatory model of politics is extremely attractive, but it succeeds, I believe, only at the cost of distorting the historical tradition that is meant to sustain it. Taylor would have us believe that one of the reasons that a participatory form of politics is accessible to Canadians in a way that it may not be to Americans is that our political tradition, rooted in regional self-government, has historically "been more identified with the participatory model," while "the habit of litigation, and the elements of atomist consciousness that go along with it, are deeply rooted in American history."[82]

Yet even with the necessary qualifications, this characterization of provincialism in Canada, much less the Canadian-American contrast, is overdrawn. For one thing, it is by no means clear that the "continuing resistance to centralization"[83] in Canada has in fact been undertaken with a view to preserving and promoting greater citizen participation, or that it serves as a historical precedent for the "participatory model" on which Taylor would have us build. For the fact is that the intellectual strategy of the provincial rights movement, the earliest and most successful example of resistance to centralization in English Canada, entailed a basic ambivalence, if not hostility, to the ideal of full democratic participation of the sort Taylor thinks desirable. The core idea that informed the legal understanding of provincial autonomy, after all, was to put jurisdiction first. What mattered was not whether the provincial or federal governments acted well or wisely, but merely whether they acted permissibly or legally, within the boundaries of their jurisdiction. This was the crucial condition of autonomy, and everything, including a broader form of political discussion, fell to it. In the autonomists' legal mind the defence of autonomy depended on treating the discussion of the most controversial issues as if they raised only jurisdictional questions that could be discussed and resolved in terms of legislative rights. The integrity of provincial communities depended, more specifically, on separating law and politics as far as possible; on separating the question of whether a measure was "wise or unwise, expedient or inexpedient," from the legal question of whether a given legislature had the jurisdictional right or capacity to act.[84]

What followed was a system of constitutional rules in which the federal government was meant to be barred not only from acting in areas of provincial jurisdiction, but in which political discussion was reduced to and centred on the determination of jurisdiction. It was a system in which jurisdictional claims themselves were not really to be discussed so much as derived from the black letter text of the constitution—and this by courts, not representative bodies. And to the extent that jurisdiction was unclear and a matter for debate, it was a system in which both levels of government soon learned that jurisdictional uncertainty provided a good pretext for refusing to address issues that divided the electorate.[85] Despite their liberal "creed that a wise decision can only be arrived at through the discussion of it from every point of view,"[86] the autonomists' scrupulous attention to the defence of provincial autonomy made them limit and narrow discussion in precisely the way that Taylor says discussion is narrowed when political questions are discussed in terms of rights. The provincial autonomists in Ontario, in sum, insisted on defending their claims in the very language that Taylor associates with the "rights model," and to that extent their conception of politics suffered from some of the very symptoms that a participatory form of decentralized power is meant to cure.[87]

Put slightly differently, it is not entirely clear that the principles on which provincialism has rested historically are as hostile to the "rights model" as Taylor's depiction of these "two packages" would imply. I have wanted to argue, rather, that beneath the important superficial differences there is actually a deep affinity between the claim for provincial autonomy mediated by the rule of law and Taylor's "rights model." At the level of political rhetoric, for instance, it is useful to remember that provincial governments still couch their claims to power in terms of rights, and they still reinforce these claims by comparing provincial rights to individual rights.[88] Indeed, it is at least arguable that one of the reasons that

Canadians accepted the idea of an entrenched Charter of Rights so readily is that the longstanding debate over provincial rights had long since inured them to the usefulness and attractiveness of the language of rights, of legal boundaries, and of courts as impartial arbiters.

Yet there is a still deeper, substantive affinity here between the historical pursuit of provincial autonomy and the "rights model" that Taylor slights. For if the provincial autonomists were successful in protecting the integrity and sovereignty of local self-government, the record suggests that they neither could nor wanted to disentangle themselves completely from the liberal regard for the protection of individual freedom that informed the vision of the rule of law. To the extent that the provincial autonomists were liberals, therefore, it is arguable that, in legitimizing a rights model of federalism, they both protected provincial power and actually laid the conceptual groundwork for the Charter of Rights that places substantive limits on provincial power. In this sense the Charter represents the fulfilment of the liberal premises that informed the movement for provincial autonomy, in a way, however, that is not necessarily congenial to provincial autonomy. In sum, the Charter follows in the tradition of, and is the better alternative to, the power of disallowance as a way of protecting individual rights.

Taylor is surely right to say that the problem of community remains the crucial, unresolved question facing Canadians. And he is probably right, as well, that as long as it remains unresolved, there is bound to be a decentralizing impulse in Canadian politics that will always distinguish it from American politics. But it is too simple, even if attractive, to picture the alternative futures of Canada as resting on a choice between "two packages," one decentralized and participatory, the other centralist and rights-oriented. The truth is that these visions cannot be so easily "packaged" or disentangled from a history in which each is implicated in the other. Like it or not, the Charter of Rights and, more recently, the Meech Lake Accord are in all of their awkwardness a fair representation of the various traditions from which they have grown. The attempt to preserve rights while allowing legislatures to override them under certain circumstances; the attempt to protect minority linguistic rights across the country while acknowledging that Quebec is a distinct society; the attempt to protect mobility while allowing provinces to prefer their own citizens if need be; the declaration that rights are fundamental but also, and explicitly, subject to reasonable limitation—all of this reflects not merely a

255

compromise between two visions of Canada, but the extent to which each vision entails or is parasitic upon the other. What we are then left with is not a choice between our history and our future, between our more participatory tradition and the modern malaise, or between 1867 and 1776. We are left, rather, with two visions of Canada produced, bound inextricably together, and held in tension by our history.

NOTES

1. Macdonald's report, dated 8 June 1868, arguing for disallowance of the Rivers and Streams Act, is reproduced in W. E. Hodgins, comp., *Correspondence: Reports of the Ministers of Justice, and Orders in Council upon the Subject of Dominion and Provincial Legislation* (Ottawa: 1896) 174.

2. Hodgins, *Correspondence* 178.

3. Canada, Parliament, House of Commons Debates, 14 April 1882, 908-09. In addition see the speech by Guthrie on the same day, 896-97.

4. Toronto *Globe* 24 January 1883.

5. London *Advertiser* 9 February 1883.

6. Gerard La Forest, *Disallowance and Reservation of Provincial Legislation* (Ottawa: Queen's Printer, 1955) 58. La Forest notes that "nearly one-half of the thirty-eight Acts disallowed during this period [i.e., 1881-1896] were vetoed on the ground that they interfered with the railway policy of Canada," even though most were within provincial jurisdiction.

7. Toronto *Globe* 24 January 1883.

8. London *Advertiser* 14 March 1883.

9. London *Advertiser* 10 December 1883.

10. Toronto *Globe* 6 June 1881.

11. Robert Gordon, "Legal Thought and Legal Practice in the Age of American Enterprise," in Gerald L. Geison, ed., *Professions and Professional Ideologies in America* (Chapel Hill: University of North Carolina Press, 1983) 69.

12. My brief description of legal liberalism draws heavily on the work of Robert Gordon, especially his article "Legal Thought and Legal Practice in the Age of American Enterprise," cited in the previous note. I should note, however, that where Gordon (and others) refer to the phenomenon as "liberal legalism," I prefer to emphasize the political roots and call it "legal liberalism." For a critical analysis of this method and its relation to the Critical Legal Studies movement, see Rogers M. Smith, "After Criticism: An Analysis of the Critical Legal Studies Movement," in Michael W. McCann and Gerald L. Houseman, eds., *Judging the Constitution: Critical Essays on Judicial Lawmaking* (Glenview, Illinois: Scott, Foresman and Co., 1989) 92-124.

13. See David Sugarman, "The Legal Boundaries of Liberty: Dicey, Liberalism, and Legal Science," *Modern Law Review* 46 (1983): 102-11.

14. *Introduction to the Study of the Law of the Constitution*, 10th ed. (London: Macmillan, 1959).

15. On this point see Sugarman, "Legal Boundaries" 109-10; and H. A. Tulloch, "Changing British Attitudes Towards the United States in the 1880s," *The Historical Journal* 20.4 (1977): 825-40. Indeed, in the final page of the *Law of the Constitution*, Dicey argues that "the 'rule of law' is a conception which in the United States has received a development beyond that which it has reached in England"(*Law of the Constitution* 472).

16. Tulloch's description of the phenomenon of "americomania" is especially suggestive in this regard. See Tulloch, "Changing Attitudes" 833-39.

17. The quotations in this paragraph are all taken from Duncan Kennedy, "Toward an Historical Understanding of Legal Consciousness: The Case of Classical Legal Thought in America, 1850-1940," *Research in Law and Sociology* 3 (1980): 3-24, at 7.

18. Writing in 1898, Mills noted, "I do not think that there is any [American] constitutional case reported before 1885, which I have not read more than once." *Mills Papers*, Mills to Fitzpatrick 3 September 1898.

19. See Blaine Baker, "The Reconstitution of Upper Canadian Legal Thought in the Late-Victorian Empire," *Law and History Review* 3 (1985): 219-63.

20. When Mills, who taught law at the University of Toronto from 1888 to 1896, was asked by a correspondent to furnish a set of readings on various legal subjects, he replied, "On Federal Constitutional law, my lectures have never been written out, and so I will not be able to place them at your disposal; but as a substitute therefor, I would recommend you to take the first volume of Kent's 'Commentaries' and examine the students upon these lectures relating to United States jurisprudence, and the little volume by Cooley, and Mr. Clement's book on the 'Constitution of Canada.'" *Mills Papers*, Mills to Perry 6 January 1899.

21. Baker, "Upper Canadian Legal Thought" 263-92.

22. Mills seems to have considered Dicey an authority on parliamentary government. When he was asked about the constitutional propriety of prolonging the life of the legislature, Mills referred his correspondent to "Professor Dicey's book on the British Constitution," in which would be found "a very excellent discussion of this subject." *Mills Papers*, Mills to Cameron 4 May 1901.

23. Next to Gladstone, Bryce was arguably the English Liberal with whom the provincial autonomists most clearly identified. Mills wrote glowingly of Bryce's eulogy of Gladstone, for example (Mills to Clarke 25 May 1898), and Bryce appears to have encouraged Edward Blake to make the most of the

Canada-Irish "home rule" analogy.

24. The idea that the provincial governments are supreme within the "sphere" allotted to them by the constitution; that this is the basis of their "autonomy," "independence," and "rights"; and that the federal government's exercise of disallowance therefore amounted to "usurpation" or "trespassing," suffused the autonomists' discussions of federalism. For representative samples, see London *Advertiser* 28 April 1882, 13 October 1882, 18 October 1882, 2 December 1882, 10 January 1883, 24 January 1883, 7 February 1883, 9 February 1883, 12 February 1883, 14 March 1883. Also see Toronto *Globe* 6 June 1881, 9 September 1881, 5 January 1883, 8 January 1883, 24 January 1883, 24 February 1883.

25. London *Advertiser* 7 February 1883.

26. London *Advertiser* 13 October 1882.

27. London *Advertiser* 26 March 1883.

28. London *Advertiser* 26 March 1883.

29. London *Advertiser* 26 March 1883.

30. London *Advertiser* 9 February 1883.

31. London *Advertiser* 12 February 1883. For another example of the inter-state/individual-state analogy, see Mills's speech on Irish home rule, Canada, Parliament, *House of Commons Debates* 26 April 1887, 115.

32. London *Advertiser* 26 March 1883.

33. London *Advertiser* 14 March 1883.

34. Toronto *Globe* 24 February 1883.

35. London *Advertiser* 10 December 1883.

36. Canada, Parliament, *House of Commons Debates* 28 March 1889, 876.

37. London *Advertiser* 10 December 1883.

38. Canada, Parliament, *House of Commons Debates*, 28 April 1869, at 97.

39. London *Advertiser* 26 February 1883, 6 July 1883, 15 July 1883, 10 December 1883.

40. Toronto *Globe* 6 June 1881.

41. For a thorough account of the Interprovincial Conference of 1887, see J. C. Morrison, "Oliver Mowat and the Development of Provincial Rights in Ontario: A Study in Dominion-Provincial Relations, 1867-1896," in *Three History Theses* (Toronto: Ontario Department of Public Records and Archives, 1961) ch. 5.

42. For a more detailed analysis of the compact theory see Ramsay Cook, *Provincial Autonomy, Minority Rights and the Compact Theory, 1867-1921* (Ottawa: Queen's Printer, 1969) ch. 4.

43. See Paul Gérin-Lajoie, *Constitutional Amendment in Canada* (Toronto: University of Toronto Press, 1950) 142-43.

44. Blake's successful amendment strengthened the reference case procedure. The reference case provided a judicial alternative to disallowance that combined the expeditiousness associated with disallowance with the appearance of neutrality associated with judicial proceedings. In fact, Blake presented the reference case procedure less as an alternative to disallowance than as a supplement to it. But most seem to have realized that with a more satisfactory reference procedure in place, there would be no need for disallowance. See the comments of the Conservative minister of justice, Sir John Thompson, who was responsible for administering the new procedure: "If the court pronounced [an act] to be unconstitutional it would be most absurd, and practically impossible, for the Minister of Justice to advise that it should be disallowed, after the highest tribunal had decided that the Act was within the powers of the Provincial Legislature." *House of Commons Debates* 7 August 1891, 3587. Reference cases have since become an important feature of Canadian constitutional law whereas disallowance has passed into virtual disuse. Under the circumstances, it is not too much to connect the waxing of one with the waning of the other. Certainly there can be no question that, at a more general level, judicial review has replaced disallowance as a form of federal boundary management. On reference cases in this early context, see Gerald Rubin, "The Nature, Use and Effect of Reference Cases in Canadian Constitutional Law," in W. R. Lederman, ed., *The Courts and the Canadian Constitution* (Toronto: McClelland and Stewart, 1964) 220-48.

45. Canada, Parliament, *House of Commons Debates* 29 April 1890, 4089.

46. *House of Commons Debates* 29 April 1890, 4089.

47. *House of Commons Debates* 29 April 1890, 4088.

48. *House of Commons Debates* 29 April 1890, 4089.

49. *House of Commons Debates* 29 April 1890, 4089.

50. London *Advertiser* 14 March 1883; see also *House of Commons Debates* 8 March 1875, 576: "The line which separated the powers of the Local Legislatures from those of the Parliament of Canada, was as distinct as if it was a geographical boundary marked out by the surveyor."

51. See La Forest, *Disallowance and Reservation* ch. 8-10.

52. Canada, Parliament, *House of Commons Debates* 1937, 3: 2294.

53. That does not mean that the use of disallowance would never again be considered. Lapointe reserved the right to act in extraordinary cases, and on these grounds disallowed a series of acts passed by the Social Credit government in Alberta, all of which in one way or another conflicted with federal law or, in the federal government's opinion, supplanted federal institutions. The Social Credit episode is reviewed in La Forest, *Disallowance and Reservation* 78-80, and is the subject of one of the classic studies of Canadian politics, James

Mallory's *Social Credit and the Federal Power in Canada* (Toronto: University of Toronto Press, 1954).

A few years after the Social Credit incident, in 1945, the King government was asked, in one case by the Canadian Pacific Railway, to disallow two pieces of allegedly socialist legislation passed by the CCF government in Saskatchewan headed by T. C. (Tommy) Douglas. Douglas responded in good provincial rights fashion that this would be an entirely "arbitrary action." His attorney general argued in an official brief that any question of the constitutionality of provincial legislation ought to come before the courts, not the federal government. And the federal government rejected the petitions, arguing, according to Douglas's friend M. J. Coldwell, "that disallowance is conceivable only if provincial legislation interfered with the rights of the Dominion or placed the whole of Canada in a bad light." See Thomas H. McLeod and Ian McLeod, *Tommy Douglas: The Road to Jerusalem* (Edmonton: Hurtig, 1987) 138-39.

Disallowance has not been used since. According to La Forest's calculation, a total of 112 statutes have thus been disallowed since 1867. See La Forest, *Disallowance and Reservation* 82.

54. Tabulated from the tables in Hodgins, *Dominion and Provincial Legislation* vol. 1 (1867-1896) and 2 (1896-1920). Between 1887 and 1897, the federal government disallowed thirteen provincial acts, most of them from Manitoba.

55. Hodgins, *Legislation* 2: 594.

56. ———, *Legislation* 2: 595.

57. ———, *Legislation* 2: 597.

58. ———, *Legislation* 2: 556.

59. *Mills Papers*, Mills to Laurier 18 May 1900.

60. Hodgins, *Legislation* 2: 556; emphasis added.

61. ———, *Legislation* 2: 557.

62. ———, *Legislation* 2: 17-18.

63. ———, *Legislation* 2: 26.

64. ———, *Legislation* 2: 26.

65. ———, *Legislation* 2: 26.

66. ———, *Legislation* 2: 26.

67. ———, *Legislation* 2: 27.

68. Charles Taylor, "Alternative Futures: Legitimacy, Identity and Alienation in Late Twentieth Century Canada," in Alan Cairns and Cynthia Williams, eds., *Constitutionalism, Citizenship and Society in Canada* (Toronto: University of Toronto Press, 1985) 183-229; a study commissioned as part of the research program of the Royal Commission on the Economic Union and Development Prospects for Canada, vol. 33.

69. Taylor, "Alternative Futures" 190.
70. ——, "Alternative Futures" 193.
71. ——, "Alternative Futures" 194.
72. ——, "Alternative Futures" 206.
73. ——, "Alternative Futures" 209.
74. ——, "Alternative Futures" 211.
75. ——, "Alternative Futures" 224.
76. ——, "Alternative Futures" 211.
77. ——, "Alternative Futures" 221-22.
78. ——, "Alternative Futures" 225.
79. ——, "Alternative Futures" 224.
80. ——, "Alternative Futures" 225. Unfortunately, a typographical error in the sentence immediately prior to the one quoted here makes it sound as if Taylor ultimately supports the "centralist" solution. This is clearly not what he intended.
81. Taylor, "Alternative Futures" 224.
82. ——, "Alternative Futures" 211.
83. ——, "Alternative Futures" 221.
84. London *Advertiser* 26 March 1883. See also the issue for 23 March: "But it is not the question of the wisdom or justness of the measure which we have to consider in the case. The question is as to the constitutional rights of those to whom the people have entrusted with certain powers, to be the sole judges as to the legislation required in the public interest under these exclusive powers."
85. The Ontario government's various efforts to avoid dealing with the question of prohibition . . . are a good example.
86. London *Advertiser* 19 July 1884.
87. I have elaborated on this point in "Constitutional Politics and the Legacy of the Provincial Rights Movement in Canada," *Canadian Journal of Political Science* 18 (1985): 267-94.
88. The constitutional conferences leading to the promulgation of the Constitution Act (1982) provided several good examples of the way in which the provincial governments exploited the analogy between liberalism and federalism. In arguing for greater constitutional control over the development of natural resources, both Alberta's Peter Lougheed and Saskatchewan's Allan Blakeney compared the provincial governments' position to that of (individual) property owners who simply wanted to vindicate "the rights of the owner," including the "right to receive value for the resource as a commodity" *(Proceedings of the First Ministers' Conference on the Constitution, September 1980;* Premier Lougheed, 119-20). As Premier Blakeney put it: "Ownership by a province becomes important, then, because it allows a province to do all those things

that *any* owner can do" (Saskatchewan position paper, 12; emphasis added). Premier Lougheed drew out the analogy again in stating Alberta's position on changes to the amending formula. The priority of his government, he said, was for an amending formula "that protects us against the rights of the tyranny of the majority" (*Proceedings* 124).

V

Looking Ahead

A METAL BUCKET. **CANADA IS A**
FOREIGN FILM. **CANADA IS A FOREIGN**
FILM WITH SUBTITLES. **CANADA IS**
A NEXT DOOR NEIGHBOR. **CANADA**
S A CROW ON A HIGHWAY.

CHAPTER ELEVEN

CANADA'S POLITICAL CULTURE TODAY:
LIBERAL, REPUBLICAN, OR THIRD WAVE?

Peter J. Smith and Janet Ajzenstat

J. A.

Let's think about what our new picture of Canadian political history tells us about Canada today. I'd say our interpretation calls in question some standard ideas about the Canadian political culture and national character. The old "tory touch" school maintains that the Canadian way of life is different from the American, and better, because Canada, unlike the U.S., has been shaped by a tory ideology that encourages governments to use state power for communal ends. I think Canadians would sell their soul for an academic theory that says that Canada is not like the U.S. It's no wonder that the "tory touch" model has been so popular. But we now know that there was no significant tory influence in Canada's past.

Once we're free of the "tory touch" interpretation, we can explore the idea that the political cultures of Canada and the U.S. are similar because both are heir to the liberal constitutionalism that originated with John Locke. Both countries were primarily Lockean in the nineteenth century; both are today modifying their heritage as they become involved in redistributing income and regulating private enterprise. If the use of governmental power for the projects of the positive state is a sign that a country has a sense of the common good, we have to say that pursuit of the common good is today as characteristic of the U.S. as Canada.

Social services are comparable in the two countries. The U.S pours out money in an attempt to alleviate the problems of its underclass. According to the *Globe and Mail*, Washington spends $25 billion a year on aid to poor, single-parent families.[1] It certainly can't be said that the U.S. is less ready to regulate. While it's true that Americans don't favour regulation of gun ownership, they are more likely than Canadians to endorse environmental regulations and affirmative action.

Indeed, the use of state power for communal ends is typical of all the modern liberal democracies. Big government, big deficits, a powerful conviction that legislation can remedy all human problems—these are features of all the modern nations of the West. My point is that once Canadians have gotten rid of their obsession with Canadian "distinctiveness," we will be in a position to think clearly about how the political culture of this country relates to broad trends in modernity.

P. J. S.

No doubt modern liberal democracies, including Canada and the United States, deploy state power for communal ends. The real issue, however, is not whether significant funds are spent on social welfare but how the money is deployed and what are current trends. Although Canada is frequently lumped together with the United States in terms of social spending—neither, for example, approximates the social democratic welfare regimes of Norway and Sweden—there are significant differences in social welfare spending between the two countries. For example, in terms of provision of social services such as health and education expenditure Canada ranks near the top of eighteen OECD counties and the United States near the bottom.[2] The collective provision of health services is one example where the Canadian state, unlike the American state, does provide for the common good. Both health and education are examples of universal programs where the benefits are distributed on the basis of citizenship, and this serves to underwrite their widespread, but not unquestioned, support. The use of state power for communal ends, however, is coming under attack in industrial countries, particularly in Great Britain, New Zealand, Canada, the United States, and Australia.[3] The growing strength of liberal ideas in this age of globalization, with their emphasis on the market, privatization, economic growth, individual choice, and responsibility, for example, all lead away from the use of the state to solve common social problems. We will be fortunate to hold on to the gains that have been made.

J. A.

We agree that the current political debates are about whether to maintain or cut back the positive state. What's still not clear to me is how—or that—Canadian political culture is truly distinctive. It seems to me that the differences you talk about are pretty small.

It's sometimes said that a sign of Canada's greater openness to the idea of the common good is that Canadians are more law-abiding than Americans. We're supposed to be more deferential. Of course our distinctiveness in this respect shows up only when we compare ourselves to certain areas of the U.S. And we're not more law-abiding than Japan, or Sweden. Moreover, it's the avowed objective of the U.S.—indeed it's the avowed objective of all liberal democracies—to encourage obedience to the law and to contain violence. Canadians, Americans, and the citizens of all other nations of the West adhere to the same goals and "values" in this regard. We're not different, or noticeably better.

P. J. S.

While the United States, like Canada, encourages obedience to the law, there is no doubt that it is less successful in doing so. Historically, Canadians have been aghast at the level of violence in American society compared to their own. How often have we seen Canadian cities burn as has occurred in the United States?

I would still argue that there are significant differences between Canadian and American social welfare spending, differences that are especially significant for the poor and disadvantaged. I agree with you that the United States does have a strong propensity to regulate. James Q. Wilson argues that "no democratic nation on earth has made subject to regulation so many aspects of otherwise private transactions." This can be attributed to the historical American desire to moralize,[4] a desire I would argue is part of the American civic republican tradition. Yet, there is another tradition in the

United States, one based on individual rights, one whose impulse in the contemporary period is particularly strong, and stymies collective action for the common good.[5] The defeat of health care legislation in the United States in 1994 can be partly attributed to the fear of Americans (cultivated by the health insurance industry) that it would encourage a big, intrusive state bureaucracy that would impinge on their freedom of choice.

J. A.
You say that Canada is more inclined to use state power than the U.S. when it comes to programs for the disadvantaged. Does the Canadian republican heritage play a role? Is it the civic republican influence that encourages us to legislate social programs? But, as we would both argue, republicanism has been a factor in the United States as well as in Canada. Why doesn't the republican heritage of the U.S. induce Americans to support governmental health care?

One last point about our supposed distinctiveness. Canadians like to say that they are more tolerant than Americans, that is, more likely to support the cultural traditions of minority ethnic groups. Canada is the "mosaic," the United States, the "melting pot." We respect minority traditions; they sacrifice them on the altar of national identity. But evidence for the idea that legislation in the U.S. is less sensitive to the cultural traditions of minorities erodes with every new study. This isn't the place for a full discussion of the way in which the United States offers opportunities for minority cultures to retain language and traditions. But let me note that the two arguments most often put forward to suggest that Canada is different from, and superior to, the United States tend to contradict each other. One suggests that Canada is unlike the U.S. because it has a stronger sense of the common good and the national interest. The other suggests that Canada is unlike the U.S. because it encourages the expression of particular cultural and ethnic ways of life, that is, ways of life that are not endorsed by all Canadians and that are not part of a public sense of the common good.

P. J. S.
I would argue that since the second World War the promotion of liberal ideas in the United States, particularly in defence of capitalism in the Cold War, has spawned a society in which increasingly individual rights trump everything else, including social programs. This

is not the case in Canada, where a better, but uneasy, balance between community and the rights of individuals has been maintained, and where social welfare programs find a more receptive audience.

You are certainly correct in pointing out that the Canadian record for tolerance of minority ethnic groups is a poor one.[6] No doubt Canadians have not measured up as well as they think they have against the cardinal liberal virtue of tolerance. The question of ethnic ways of life and their relationship to the common good is extremely complex and destined to become more so as Canada becomes more ethnically and racially diverse. In principle there should be no necessary conflict between ethnicity, citizenship, and the common good. Yet today Canada's multiculturalism policy is under attack for encouraging "ghettoization," balkanization, and ethnic particularism, which reduces the "degree of effective partic- ipation in the national and civil social spheres."[7] The indictment is made despite little evidence to support it.

One can make a counterargument against this unfortunate tendency. After all, the participatory politics of citizens is premised on historic identification with a community, with the feeling that we share a common past and a common destiny. That community, in Canada, can be national, provincial, or ethnic. In Canada we would not say, for example, that because I am Albertan I cannot be a Cana- dian as well. We recognize and accept that federalism can accom- modate these twin allegiances without a necessary conflict. Simi- larly, the fact that one is a member of a particular ethnic minority and identifies and works for the common good of that community does not necessarily mean one cannot work for the common good of all Canadians. One can. A key problem, however, in Canada is that French Canada in its Quebec manifestation cannot be subsumed into a single national community.

J. A.

I didn't mean to suggest that Canada's record of tolerance for ethnic minorities is a poor one. On the contrary I think it's relatively good. At any rate I can't think of a country that's done better, unless it's the U.S.

P. J. S.

The question, in my opinion, is how the different demands for recognition, including the demands by aboriginal Canadians, can be accommodated in a manner consistent with civic republicanism. One possibility, suggested by Charles Taylor, is to decentralize as far as possible to more localized, small-scale units of self-rule.[8] However attractive this prospect may seem, opinion polls indicate that English-speaking Canadians desire a strong national government and reject any substantial decentralization of powers to the provinces.[9] How this circle can be squared is anyone's guess.

J. A.

I think a real issue between us is that you sympathize with republicanism while I distrust it. We are both convinced that civic republicanism was an element in Canada's past. But I'm less inclined to think that it was as important as liberalism, and although I might admit to a sneaking admiration for civic republicanism—a more participatory, more virtuous political community? who wouldn't want that?—I nevertheless think it's impossible to put into practice in the modern world, and that attempts to put it into practice are bound to be politically oppressive, particularly for ethnic minorities.

What lies behind my plea to reconsider the question of Canadian distinctiveness is the hope that once the "tory touch" misconceptions are cleared away Canadians will be able to see the strengths of Canadian liberal constitutionalism. We shouldn't take our liberal rights and freedoms for granted. Individual freedom, equality of right, the rule of law, the right to dissent, equal opportunity to a voice in the government of ourselves through representative institutions: these principles are in danger today, in part because the prevailing interpretation of Canadian history and political culture has argued that it is toryism or socialism, and not constitutional liberalism, that lies at the heart of the Canadian way of life.

From the perspective of liberal constitutionalism the fact that there are no uniquely Canadian attitudes and beliefs is something to be grateful for. In the liberal definition, institutions are good insofar as they conform to universal standards of political justice. The important question for the liberal is not whether Canada is unique or different, but whether Canada is a free and just country. Do we enjoy political freedom, legal rights, and a reasonable degree of material wealth?

Why ask if Canada's "different"? Why should it be any skin off our nose if other countries are also good places to live? We should rejoice when we find that Sweden, the U.S., the nations of

Western Europe, Japan, are as free and prosperous as Canada—and that the citizens of these countries value their political life and system of government for exactly the reasons Canadians value theirs. There can't be too much of a good thing.

P. J. S.

The question is not so much the distinctiveness of Canadian beliefs and attitudes as the distinctiveness of Canadian history. Canadians do have their own history, their collective memory, a critical condition for the successful participatory politics of citizenship. This sense of identification with the fate of a community has been variously described as virtue or patriotism. It is because we identify with a community and care for it and want it to continue that we are willing to take on the responsibilities of citizenship that are necessary to ensure its freedom and the well-being of its members. Let us hope that the Japanese and Swedes and others feel the same way.

Your statement that "institutions are good insofar as they conform to universal standards of political justice" can certainly be disputed. Is there really such a thing as universal standards of political justice? Rather all knowledge is grounded in a particular cultural and social context. There is no archimedean point from which the critic stands outside his/her context to render independent judgment according to universal standards of justice. In brief, "standards of justice emerge from and are part of a community's history and tradition in which they are vindicated." In fact, Rawls himself rejects the idea of a transhistorical "absolutely valid" set of standards in which to ground his theory of justice.[10]

J. A.

Is there such a thing as a universal standard of justice? I'm not sure that I can answer that question convincingly. I do think that to say there is no universal idea of justice offends common sense. It certainly puts an end to academic discussion. It would put an end to our debate. If we can't hope to agree on the meaning of "justice" it doesn't make sense to go on worrying about its definition. You and I wouldn't be able to talk about whether liberal constitutionalism is more just or less, or whether community is more precious than freedom. We'd be reduced to the futile, albeit fashionable, practice of deconstructing political texts, poking fun at the political thinkers who continue to believe that justice is real.

I'm convinced, and I think you are too, that there are ways to determine whether a regime is more just or less, even though it may be difficult to mount an argument that convincingly demonstrates the conclusion. I think the point of your question "is there such a thing?" is really that you wish to emphasize the importance of community. You think that community and the kind of participation that depends on it are valuable and you're inclined to believe that it's relatively difficult to shed communal beliefs. I agree that the sense of community is a good. I do know that particular historical traditions can be very dear. But I also think that the desire for freedom and emancipation is universal, and is part of the definition of justice.

P. J. S.

To say that there is no archimedean point does not make concepts of "political freedom" or "justice" any less important. Rather it means we cannot take their meaning for granted. For example, what is meant by the expression "political freedom"? As Isaiah Berlin reminds us, "the meaning of this term is so porous that there is little interpretation that it seems able to resist."[11] In his effort to bring order to these interpretations Berlin made a distinction worth noting between "negative" and "positive" freedom that is crucial to this discussion. Negative freedom is simply the freedom of the individual to do as he/she chooses without interference from others, whether they be governments, corporations, or other persons. It is the freedom articulated by such classic liberals as John Locke and John Stuart Mill. Positive freedom essentially consists in being one's own master. It is associated with the exercise of control, the control of one's life and the collective control over the common life. This latter concept is of critical importance for our status as citizens in terms of how we collectively make political decisions. The argument by Taylor and Sandel is that the individualistic concept of negative freedom with its emphasis on the private sphere threatens to crowd out the more public, participatory concept of freedom. There are, then, critical differences for political life in how concepts such as freedom and justice are interpreted.

J. A.

Let me say something about ways in which liberal constitutionalism—despite the arguments of its critics—includes ideas of community and communal good.

Liberal theory from Locke to Rawls argues that the state must not endorse a particular way of life. No one conception of the good life, no moral, philosophical, or religious doctrine should receive state sanction. On this point the contrast between liberalism and civic republicanism is sharp. In the liberal argument it's the refusal to sanction a conception of the good life that makes democracy possible. Citizens are able to debate, support, or dissent from, the laws under which they live—they are able to support different interest groups and political parties—because, and only because, no one doctrine is entrenched. And out of free, democratic debate come ideas for legislation for the communal good.

It's the boast of liberal democracies that they respond to the wishes of the majority of the day and to new alignments of opinions and interests. It would be absurd to suggest that measures favouring the redistribution of wealth, protecting the environment, addressing the demands of historically underprivileged groups—all typical of liberal democracies—are not in some vital sense conceived for the common good.

The fact that there's no entrenched idea of the good in liberalism is also what enables citizens to develop and maintain, in the private sphere, particular communities, and ethnic associations that preserve historical traditions. It's the most common argument of liberalism's critics to say that it fails to provide for the human need to belong to a community. But it's as false to say that associations and communities don't flourish in the liberal polity as to say that the laws in the liberal regime don't reflect the public interest. In short, the liberal refusal to entrench conceptions of the good life is what preserves the political freedoms of the public sphere, and the social freedoms of the private sphere.[12]

P. J. S.

You are right to say that liberal theory consistently argues that the state must not endorse a particular way of life. I would ask, however, is this true in fact? In my estimation, liberalism does have a concept of the good life. There are, in fact, many things liberal theory is not neutral about (including liberalism). Liberalism, for example, endorses the notion that one of the aspects of a good political community is that it promotes individual choice. As Ronald Beiner puts it, "liberalism instantiates one particular vision of the good: namely, that choice itself is the highest good."[13] A good political community in this view would put minimal, if any, restrictions, on what we can read or see or do. Similarly, the liberal is not neutral about the market, growth, or productivity, for all serve to increase the options for individual choice. There is, then, a vision of a particular way of life in liberalism.

The suggestion that liberalism may foster community is contestable. Liberalism is alive and well in industrial societies yet atomistic tendencies appear to be getting stronger. Communal relationships do not seem to come about as a by-product of individual rights and the unfettered operation of the market. In fact, the opposite appears to be true. The more individualism and the power of the market increases the more stresses are placed on communities, the public sphere and citizenship. Increasingly the idea is promoted that we should not relate to the state as citizens with the right to participate in the decisions that affect us, but as consumers, customers, clients. This is just one more indication where liberalism unchecked erodes citizenship.

The liberal emphasis on the neutrality of the state also wrongly assumes, I would argue, that only the state poses a threat to the freedom or autonomy of individuals and communities. There is a plethora of other social forces besides the state that threaten our autonomy. The coercive power of large scale institutions such as multinational corporations should not be overlooked. One could argue that the state is needed to counterbalance these forces, to prevent monopolies, and thereby to increase the autonomy of the individual. As the state changes its role and even recedes in the era of global capitalism we will probably become more aware of that fact.

Should the state be neutral in regard to particular ways of life? Should the state be neutral in the ways of life of drug addicts versus non-drug addicts?[14] Rather the opposite is true. We expect the state and associated institutions such as public schools to promote certain ways of life over others. For example, neither the state nor the public school can be neutral about patriotism, which is indispensable to the maintenance of a democratic regime.[15]

J. A.
Well, using schools to promote patriotism! Sounds like the U.S. What happens to the multi-ethnic state then? You haven't been convinced by me that banishing entrenched public ideas of the good life enables private ideas of community, and I haven't been convinced

by you that teaching patriotism sits well with multiculturalism and tolerance—although something in me wishes it did.

Let me admit that you hit a nerve with the charge that liberals aren't entitled to the boast of neutrality. Of course you're saying something like this: liberal élites use the cover of neutrality to further their own interests, and it's easier for you to say it because civic republicanism-communitarianism doesn't have much confidence in the idea of neutrality. "Neutrality" gets thrown out with the idea of "universal standards of justice." Liberal constitutionalism at least tries to hang on to these notions. But let's entertain the idea that from the beginning liberalism exhibited a major contradiction, because it argued on the one hand that the liberal state should refuse to recognize any philosophical, religious, or cultural teaching as universally true, while it claimed on the other that the basic principles of liberalism like the rule of law had a universal character.

It may be that throughout our dialogue we've ignored a vital point. Perhaps we haven't said enough about the way in which the argument for cultural relativism is undermining what's best about both liberal constitutionalism and civic republicanism.

We suggest in the Introduction that the modern era—from the period of the Enlightenment—has been dominated by two political ideologies, the first liberalism, or liberal constitutionalism, and the other civic republicanism, or civic humanism. Are there only two ideologies? I'm reminded of Leo Strauss on the "three waves of modernity."[16] The first wave originates with thinkers like John Locke, and the second with Rousseau. The third is the wave of cultural relativism and historicism. In *Canada's Origins* we're concerned with the opposition between Lockean liberalism and the civic republicanism that has its roots in Rousseau. Should we be asking if there is evidence of a third "wave," a third, new, ideology in Canada today? We say in the Introduction that understanding the debate between liberalism and civic republicanism in Canada's nineteenth century will illuminate the liberal-communitarian debate today. Do we say enough to address the ways in which the twentieth-century debate differs from the nineteenth-century one?

My own view is that there is a third wave, it's evident in Canadian politics today, and it's changing the character of both liberalism and Canadian civic republicanism. In this dialogue it's the older form of liberalism, liberal constitutionalism, that I have been

275

defending. I'm almost as uneasy as you about some aspects of liberalism in its new anti-constitutionalist guise.

Nineteenth-century liberalism in Canada was allied with the notion of progress. It argued that science and technology would create material prosperity, and that citizens living in a free regime would grow in self-reliance, and would learn to value order and self-restraint. In short there would be both scientific and moral progress. Another striking feature of the nineteenth-century ideology is its confidence in the universality of liberalism's principles. Toleration, representative government, the rule of law, free political speech—the supposition was that the regime that endorsed these principles would have universal appeal. At its best liberalism argued that all races and peoples were fitted for freedom; there are no naturally subordinate races.

Today's liberalism has all but abandoned the idea of material and moral progress. And it seems to be about to jettison the idea of universality. What about civic republicanism?

P. J. S.

The critical question is not so much whether there are other ideologies, but what ideologies have been most relevant to Canada historically, and to what extent they illuminate today's liberal-communitarian debate. First, though, it is necessary to point out that in the eighteenth and nineteenth centuries the debate between liberalism and civic republicanism was part of a widespread social and political debate involving real social and political differences that spilled out beyond the intellectual classes and into the mass of society. Incidently, while Rousseau took part in this debate, it predates and goes beyond him. It is a mistake to equate civic republicanism with Rousseau. Today, the liberal-communitarian debate is still largely a debate among political theorists. The contemporary debate, however, does reflect and illuminate our political practice.

Critical to the eighteenth- and nineteenth-century debate were profound differences over the role of the state—whether the state existed primarily to provide order and promote economic development or whether the state should reflect and promote a democratic society and work for the common good. As well, civic republicans feared the development of a division of labour and centralization of power. These, they thought, would infringe on the independence and capacity for self-rule of the citizen. That the citizen amateur was capable of deliberating on serious issues was a core belief of civic republicanism. Other institutions such as banks and the credit system were also feared, for it was believed that they could also compromise the independence of the citizenry. Although much has changed today, communitarians share similar concerns, distrusting concentrations of bureaucratic and economic power, promoting decentralization of decision-making, and downplaying the role of experts.[17]

The critical difference is that communitarians have yet to strike a mass chord and move beyond the realm of political theory to that of political ideology, and to mobilize Canadians for reform. The potential is there, however. Opinion polls taken in the 1990s reveal an underlying discontent with our system of government. One poll taken in January 1992 revealed "an electorate deeply disenchanted with traditional politics and political institutions—and people eager for radical change to both."[18] A federally established commission, the Citizen's Forum on Canada's Future (the Spicer Commission), echoed the poll results and described the demands of Canadians as being "revolutionary in Canadian terms in their desire to take control of the national agenda back into the hands of citizens."[19] The Spicer Commission operated in the atmosphere of Meech Lake, which Canadians saw as illegitimate because it was drafted behind closed doors by "eleven white men in suits." The lively debate over the Charlottetown Accord in 1992, and its subsequent defeat in a nation-wide referendum, is another indication that Canadians are intent on establishing themselves as a sovereign people in charge of their constitution and political institutions. How the demand that Canadians "want in" on decision-making is accommodated is one of the most important challenges to our political system.

It is doubtful this will be done by parties, which are increasingly in decline. The increasing rejection of parties as the appropriate vehicle of political expression has parallels with eighteenth- and nineteenth-century civic republicanism, which distrusted parties, viewing them as an impediment to the citizen's autonomy and ability to relate directly to government. "Measures, not men" were what mattered. In recent years the rise of a multiplicity of social movements—women's, gay, aboriginal, environmental, disability—all reflect a desire to relate directly to government and to have one's participation valued.

The social bases of democratic change partly reflected in social movements differ radically from the social base of eighteenth- and nineteenth-century civic republicanism in Canada and the United States, which tended to be fairly homogeneous, composed of petit bourgeois farmers, craftsmen, and small town merchants. Today the social base of reform is much more heterogeneous, composed of social movements and the new urban middle class, largely in the public sector. Indeed, the very heterogeneity of these groups makes it very unlikely they will ever be crowded under one political umbrella or one political ideology.

Moreover, as with eighteenth- and nineteenth-century civic republicanism, it is not just the political superstructure that matters. There is demand for a more democratic and inclusive society as well, one that involves people in all those decisions that affect them, at home, at work, at school, and in the church. Again the sense of inclusion is broader than it was in eighteenth- and nineteenth-century civic republicanism, but both are reflective of a centuries-old demand by citizens for inclusion in decisions that affect them.

J. A.

I agree that aspects of today's debate on constitutional reform, like the distrust of political parties, and the demand for enhanced political participation, echo arguments from the civic republicanism of the eighteenth and nineteenth centuries. But I'm not nearly as sanguine as you that political participation in the absence of parties is a good thing. What is Canada headed for? One-party government? Corporatism? I hope I'm not around. And I think you are underestimating the way in which today's arguments for constitutional reform depart from civic republicanism. I believe that the process of constitutional reform is damaging civic republicanism-communitarianism. The demand for a New Canada and a brand new constitution that characterizes the constitutional process implies that everything in Canadian history, our populist traditions and republican heritage as well as constitutionalism, was fundamentally flawed. It must be flawed, it must be broke. Otherwise why are we trying so hard to fix it?[20] The constitutional process focuses Canadian hopes on a magic utopian future—and we haven't the least idea what it will look like.

I think that the best Canadian instinct today says let's put an end to constitution making. And I think the polls show that this sentiment is at least as strong as the demand for more participation in the constitutional negotiations.[21]

P. J. S.

I am not applauding the decline of political parties. They still have a vital role to play. I am only pointing out that the system of strict party discipline in Canada does not readily permit new and divergent voices to be heard. Parties remain top-down, hierarchical institutions and relate poorly to demand for bottom-up grass-roots politics.

I think Canadians made one thing very clear in the defeat of the Charlottetown Accord, and that was that when it came to constitution-making their voices had to be heard, particularly in putting their stamp of legitimacy on any potential changes via the ballot box. In other words, Canadians were saying that the constitution was not a politicians' constitution nor a government's constitution but rather a citizens' constitution. I see this as a healthy development, one that grounds the constitution in the everyday lives of citizens and potentially strengthens constitutionalism.

Both the movement away from parties and the demand of Canadians to be included in constitutional decision-making are in keeping with an increase in civic consciousness in Canada. This must be contrasted with the United States, where a rights-based liberalism is increasingly eroding the quality of public life. In Canada, I believe, the question is where the balance should be in a liberal democracy between individual rights and collective rights, between the freedom to choose as consumers of services public and private, and the freedom to participate and make decisions public and private. Indeed, the tension between these polarities has increased, not decreased, with the outcome yet uncertain.

NOTES

1. "The myths we hold about Americans," editorial, *The Globe and Mail* 4 July 1994: A10.

2. Julia O'Connor, "Welfare Expenditure and Policy Orientation in Comparative Perspective," *Canadian Review of Sociology and Anthropology* 26.1 (1989): 127-50.

3. Francis G. Castles, "Changing Course in Economic Policy: The English Speaking Nations in the 1980s," in Francis G. Castles, ed., *Families of Nations: Patterns of Public Policy in Western Democracies* (Aldershot, England:

Dartmouth Publishing Co. Ltd., 1993) 3-35.

4. James Q. Wilson, "Policy Intellectuals and Public Policy," *The Public Interest* (Summer, 1981) 35, 37.

5. Wilson, "Policy Intellectuals"; Michael J. Sandel, "The Political Theory of the Procedural Republic," in Allan C. Hutchinson and Patrick Monahan, eds., *The Rule of Law: Ideal or Ideology* (Toronto: Carswell, 1987): 85-96.

6. On this point see V. Seymour Wilson, "The Tapestry Vision of Canadian Multiculturalism," *Canadian Journal of Political Science* 36.4 (1993) 663.

7. Gilles Paquet, "Philosophy of Multiculturalism," paper prepared for the Conference, "Multiculturalims in Canada Today," Queen's University, October 3-6, 1991, as quoted in V.S. Wilson, "Tapestry Vision" 659.

8. Charles Taylor, "Alternative Futures: Legitimacy, Identity and Alienation in Late Twentieth Century Canada," in Alan Cairns and Cynthia Williams, eds., *Constitutionalism, Citizenship, and Society in Canada* (Toronto: University of Toronto Press, 1985) 222. For a critique of Taylor's arguments see Vipond in this volume.

9. Kenneth McRoberts, "Disagreeing on Fundamentals: English Canada and Quebec," in Patrick Monahan and Kenneth McRoberts, eds., *The Charlottetown Accord, the Referendum, and the Future of Canada* (Toronto: University of Toronto Press, 1993) 250.

10. Daniel Bell, *Communitarianism and its Critics* (Oxford: Clarendon Press, 1993) 67.

11. Isaiah Berlin, "Two Concepts of Liberty," in *Four Essays on Liberty* (Oxford: Oxford University Press, 1969) 118.

12. For an illuminating debate on these issues see Charles Taylor, *Multiculturalism and "The Politics of Recognition"* (Princeton NJ: Princeton University Press, 1992). The volume includes essays by Amy Gutmann, Steven C. Rockefeller, Michael Walzer, and Susan Wolf.

13. Ronald Beiner, "What's the Matter with Liberalism?" in Allan C. Hutchinson and Leslie M. Green, eds., *Law and the Community: The End of Individualism?* (Toronto: Carswell, 1989) 45.

14. Richard J. Arneson, "Liberal Democratic Community," in John W. Chapman and Ian Shapiro, *Democratic Community* (New York: New York University Press, 1993) 193.

15. Charles Taylor, "Cross-Purposes: The Liberal-Communitarian Debate," *Liberalism and the Moral Life,* ed. Nancy L. Rosenblum (Cambridge, Mass.: Harvard University Press, 1989) 159-83.

16. Leo Strauss, *Natural Right and History* (Chicago: University of Chicago Press, 1968).

17. Sandel, "Procedural Republic," Taylor, "Alternative Futures," and Susan D. Phillips, "A More Democratic Canada . . . ?" in Susan Phillips, ed., *How*

Ottawa Spends: A More Democratic Canada . . . ? (Ottawa: Carleton University Press, 1993): 1-43.

18. Glen Allen, "MacLean's Decima poll: A verdict on politics," *Maclean's* 6 January 1992: 58-60, as quoted in Susan Phillips, "More Democratic Canada" 2.

19. Citizen's Forum on Canada's Future, *Theme Report: A Working Paper* (Ottawa: Supply and Services Canada, 1991) 8. Leo Panitch, "A Different Kind of State?" in Gregory Albo, David Langille, and Leo Panitch, *A Different Kind of State?* (Toronto: Oxford University Press, 1993) 4.

20. Janet Ajzenstat, "The Campaign Against the Constitution," *Policy Options* 15.3 (April 1994).

21. Janet Ajzenstat, "Constitution Making and the Myth of the People," in Curtis Cook, ed., *Constitutional Predicament: Canada After the Referendum of 1992* (Montreal: McGill-Queen's University Press, 1992).

THE ORIGINS OF CANADIAN IDEOLOGY:
A SELECTED BIBLIOGRAPHY

Ajzenstat, Janet. (1984) Collectivity and Individual Right in 'Mainstream' Liberalism: John Arthur Roebuck and the *Patriotes*. *Journal of Canadian Studies* (hereafter *JCS*) 19.3: 99-111.

———. (1987) Comment: The Separation of Powers in 1867. *Canadian Journal of Political Science* (hereafter *CJPS*) 20.1: 117-21.

———. (1988) *The Political Thought of Lord Durham*. Kingston: McGill-Queen's University Press.

———. (1990) Durham and Robinson: Political Faction and Moderation. *JCS* 25.1: 22-38. Reprinted in this volume.

———. (1992) The Constitutionalism of Étienne Parent and Joseph Howe. In Janet Ajzenstat, ed., *Canadian Constitutionalism: 1791-1991*. Ottawa: Canadian Study of Parliament Group. 159-76. Reprinted in this volume.

Armour, Leslie. (1981) *The Idea of Canada and the Crisis of Community*. Ottawa: Steel Rail Educational Publishing.

Baker, G. Blaine. (1985) The Reconstitution of Upper Canada Legal Thought in the Late-Victorian Empire. *Law and History Review* 3.2: 219-93.

Baker, G. Blaine. (1988) So Elegant a Web: Providential Order and the Rule of Law in Early Nineteenth-Century Upper Canada. *University of Toronto Law Journal* 38.2: 184-206.

Bazowski, Raymond. (1994) Canadian Political Thought. In James P. Bickerton and Alain-G. Gagnon, eds., *Canadian Politics*, 2nd edition. Peterborough, ON: Broadview Press, 93-109.

Belanger, André-J. (1974) *L'Apolitisme des idéologies québecoises: le grand tournant de 1934-1936*. Québec: Les Presses de l'Université Laval.

Bell, David V. J. (1970) The Loyalist Tradition in Canada. *JCS* 5.1: 22-33.

———. and Lorne Tepperman. (1991) *The Roots of Disunity: A Study of Canadian Political Culture*, rev. ed. Toronto: Oxford University Press.

Bernard, Jean-Paul. (1984) Les idéologies québecoises et américaines au XIX siècle. In Claude Savary, ed., *Les rapports culturels entre le Québec et les États-
Unis.* Montréal: Institut québecois de recherche sur la culture. 45-62.

Brooks, Stephen, ed. (1984) *Political Thought in Canada.* Toronto: Irwin.

Christian, William. (1978) A Note on Rod Preece and Red Tories. *Canadian
Journal of Political and Social Theory* 2.2: 128-34.

Christian, William, and Colin Campbell. (1990) *Political Parties and Ideologies
in Canada,* 3rd ed. Toronto: McGraw-Hill Ryerson.

Condon, Ann Gorman. (1984) *The Envy of the American States: The Loyalist
Dream for New Brunswick.* Fredericton: New Ireland Press.

Cook, Terry. (1972) John Beverley Robinson and the Conservative Blueprint for
the Upper Canadian Community. *Ontario History* 64.2: 79-95.

———. (1973) The Canadian Conservative Tradition: An Historical Perspective.
JCS 8.4: 31-39.

Desserud, Donald. (1991) Nova Scotia and the American Revolution. In
Margaret Conrad, ed., *Making Adjustments: Change and Continuity in
Planter Nova Scotia, 1759-1800.* Fredericton: Acadiensis Press. 89-112.

Dion, Stephane. (1990) Tocqueville, Le Canada français et la question nationale.
Revue française de science politique 40.4: 501-20.

Duffy, Dennis. (1982) *Gardens, Covenants, Exiles: Loyalism in the Literature of
Upper Canada/Ontario.* Toronto: University of Toronto Press.

Emberley, Peter C., ed. (1990) *By Loving Our Own: George Grant and the
Legacy of Lament for a Nation.* Ottawa: Carleton University Press.

Errington, Jane. (1987) *The Lion, the Eagle, and Upper Canada: A Developing
Canadian Ideology.* Montreal: McGill-Queen's University Press.

Finbow, Robert. (1993) Ideology and Institutions in North America. *CJPS* 26.4:
699-721.

Forbes, H. D., ed. (1985) *Canadian Political Thought.* Toronto: Oxford University Press.

———. (1987) Hartz-Horowitz at Twenty: Nationalism, Toryism, and Socialism
in Canada and the United States. *CJPS* 20.2: 287-315.

———. (1988) Rejoinder to A Note on Hartz-Horowitz at Twenty: The Case of
French Canada. *CJPS* 21.4: 807-11.

———. (1991) The Political Thought of George Grant. *JCS* 26.2: 46-69.

Grant, George. (1965) *Lament for a Nation.* Toronto: McClelland and Stewart.

Greenwood, F. Murray. (1979) Les Patriotes et le gouvernement responsable
dans les années 1830. *Revue d'histoire de l'Amérique Française* (hereafter
RHAF) 33.1: 25-37.

Hare, John. (1977) *La pensée socio-politique au Québec 1784-1812: Analyse sémantique*. Ottawa: Éditions de l'Université d'Ottawa.

Harvey, Louis-Georges, (1992) The First Distinct Society: French Canada, America, and the Constitution of 1791. In Janet Ajzenstat, ed., *Canadian Constitutionalism: 1791-1991*. Ottawa: Canadian Study of Parliament Group. 125-46. Reprinted in this volume.

———. and M. V. Olsen. (1987) French Revolutionary Forms in French-Canadian Political Language 1805-1835. *Canadian Historical Review* 58.3: 374-92.

Hibbits, Bernard J. (1989) Progress and Principle: The Legal Thought of Sir John Beverley Robinson. *McGill Law Journal* 34.3: 454-53.

Horowitz, Gad. (1965) Tories, Socialists, and the Demise of Canada. *Canadian Dimension* 2.4: 12-15.

———. (1966) Conservatism, Liberalism, and Socialism in Canada: An Interpretation. *Canadian Journal of Economics and Political Science* 32.1: 143-71.

———. (1977) The "Myth" of the Red Tory. *CJPS* 10.1: 87-88.

——— (1978) Notes on Conservatism, Liberalism, and Socialism in Canada. *CJPS* 11.2: 383-99.

Howes, David. (1985) Property, God, and Nature in the Thought of Sir John Beverley Robinson. *McGill Law Journal* 30.3: 365-414.

Knopff, Rainer. (1979) Quebec's "Holy War" as "Regime" Politics: Reflections on the Guibord Case. *CJPS* 12.2: 315-31.

———. (1991) The Triumph of Liberalism in Canada: Laurier on Representation and Party Government. *JCS* 26.2: 72-86. Reprinted in this volume.

Kymlicka, Will. (1989) *Liberalism, Community, and Culture*. Oxford: Clarendon Press.

LaSelva, Samuel. (1993) Re-imagining Confederation: Moving beyond the Trudeau-Lévesque Debate. *CJPS* 26.4: 699-721.

Lipset, Seymour Martin. (1970) Revolution and Counterrevolution: The United States and Canada. In Orest M. Kruhlak, Richard Schultz, and Sidney I. Pobihushchy, eds., *The Canadian Political Process: A Reader*. Toronto: Holt, Rinehart and Winston. 13-38.

———. (1986) Historical Traditions and National Characteristics: A Comparative Analysis of Canada and the United States. *Canadian Journal of Sociology* 11.2: 113-55.

———. (1990) *Continental Divide: The Values and Institutions of the United States and Canada*. New York: Routledge, Chapman and Hall.

McKillop, A. B. (1987) *Contours of Canadian Thought*. Toronto: University of Toronto Press.

MacKinnon, Neil. (1986) *This Unfriendly Soil: The Loyalist Experience in Nova*

Scotia, 1783-1791. Montreal: McGill-Queen's University Press.

Macpherson, C. B. (1953) *Democracy in Alberta.* Toronto: University of Toronto Press.

MacRae-Buchanan, Constance. (1992) American Influence on Canadian Constitutionalism. In Janet Ajzenstat, ed., *Canadian Constitutionalism, 1791-1991.* Ottawa: Canadian Study of Parliament Group. 147-58.

McRae K.D. (1964) The Structure of Canadian History. In Louis Hartz, ed., *The Founding of New Societies.* New York: Harcourt, Brace and World. 219-74.

———. (1978) Louis Hartz's Concept of the Fragment Society and Its Applications to Canada. *Études canadiennes* 5: 17-30.

Monière, Denis. (1977) *Le développement des idéologies au Québec.* Montréal: Québec/Amérique.

Nourry, Louis. (1973) L'idée de fédération chez Étienne Parent, 1831-1852. *RHAF* 35.4: 533-57.

Pangle, Thomas L. (1988) *The Spirit of Modern Republicanism: The Moral Vision of the American Founders.* Chicago: The University of Chicago Press.

Patterson, Graeme. (1975) Whiggery, Nationality, and the Upper Canadian Reform Tradition. *Canadian Historical Review* 56.1: 25-45.

———. (1977) An Enduring Canadian Myth: Responsible Government and the Family Compact. *JCS* 12.2: 3-17.

Pearce, Colin D. (1988) Egerton Ryerson's Canadian Liberalism. *CJPS* 21.4: 771-95. Reprinted in this volume.

Preece, Rod. (1977) The Myth of the Red Tory. *Canadian Journal of Political and Social Theory* 1.2: 3-28.

———. (1978a) Liberal-Conservatism and Feudalism in Canadian Politics: A Response to Christian. *Canadian Journal of Political and Social Theory* 2.2: 135-41.

———. (1978b) Tory Myth and Conservative Reality: Horowitz Revisited. *Canadian Journal of Political and Social Theory* 2.2: 175-79.

———. (1980) The Anglo-Saxon Conservative Tradition. *CJPS* 13.1: 3-32.

———. (1984) The Political Wisdom of Sir John A. Macdonald. *CJPS* 17.3: 459-86.

———. (1987) Comment: Montesquieuan Principles of Canadian Politics? *CJPS* 20.1: 121-25.

Rayner, Jeremy. (1991) The Very Idea of Canadian Political Thought. *JCS* 26.2: 7-25.

Resnick, Philip. (1987) Montesquieu Revisited, or the Mixed Constitution and the Separation of Powers in Canada. *CJPS* 20.1: 97-117.

Romney, Paul. (1988) Very Late Loyalist Fantasies: Nostalgic Tory "History" and the Rule of Law in Upper Canada. In W. Wesley Pue and Barry Wright, eds., *Canadian Perspectives on Law and Society: Issues in Legal History.* Ottawa: Carleton University Press. 119-47.

Romney, (1988) From the Rule of Law to Responsible Government: Ontario Political Culture and the Origins of Canadian Statism. *Historical Papers.* Presented at the Annual Meeting of the Canadian Historical Association, Windsor, 1988. 86-119.

———. (1992) The Nature and Scope of Provincial Autonomy: Sir Oliver Mowat, the Quebec Resolutions, and the Construction of the British North America Act. *CJPS* 25.1: 3-29.

Smith, Jennifer. (1988) Canadian Confederation and the Influence of American Federalism. *CJPS* 21.2: 443-63.

Smith, Peter J. (1987) The Ideological Origins of Canadian Confederation. *CJPS* 20.1: 3-29. Reprinted in this volume.

———. (1990) The Dream of Political Union: Loyalism, Toryism, and the Federal Idea in Pre-Confederation Canada. In Ged Martin, ed., *The Causes of Canadian Confederation.* Fredericton: Acadiensis Press. 148-72.

———. (1991) Civic Humanism Versus Liberalism: Fitting the Loyalists In. *JCS* 26.2: 25-44. Reprinted in this volume.

Stewart, G. T. (1986) *The Origins of Canadian Politics.* Vancouver: University of British Columbia Press.

Taylor, Charles. (1993) *Reconciling the Solitudes: Essays on Canadian Federalism and Nationalism.* Ed. Guy Laforest. Montreal: McGill-Queen's University Press.

Tousignant, Pierre. (1973) Problématique pour une nouvelle approche à la Constitution de 1791. *RHAF* 27.2: 81-234.

Truman, Tom. (1971) "A Critique of Seymour M. Lipset's Article, 'Value Differences, Absolute or Relative: The English-speaking Democracies.'" *CJPS* 4.4: 497-25.

———. (1977) A Scale for Measuring a Tory Streak in Canada and the United States. *CJPS* 10.3: 592-614.

Umar, Yusaf K., ed. (1992) *George Grant and the Future of Canada.* Calgary: University of Calgary Press.

Vachet, André. (1976) L'idéologie libérale et la pensée sociale au Québec. In C. Panaccio and P.-A. Quintin, eds., *Philosophie au Québec.* Montréal: Bellarmin. 113-26.

Vipond, Robert C. (1991) *Liberty and Community: Canadian Federalism and the Failure of the Constitution.* Albany, NY: State University of New York Press.

Weber, Bryce. (1991) The Public, the Private, and the Ideological Character of the Division of Powers in Sections 91 and 92 of the Constitution Act of 1867. *JCS* 26.2: 88-104.

Whitaker, Reginald. (1977) Images of the State in Canada. In L. Panitch, ed., *The Canadian State: Political Economy and Political Power.* Toronto: University of Toronto Press. 27-71.

Wise, S. F. (1993) *God's Peculiar Peoples: Essays on Political Culture in Nineteenth Century Canada.* Ed. A. B. McKillop and Paul Romney. Ottawa: Carleton University Press.

Wiseman, Nelson. (1988) A Note on "Hartz-Horowitz at Twenty": The Case of French Canada. *CJPS* 21: 795-806.